1998

New Political Thought:
An Introduction

New Political Thought: An Introduction

Edited by
Adam Lent

Lawrence & Wishart
LONDON

Lawrence & Wishart Limited
99a Wallis Road
London E9 5LN

First published 1998
Reprinted 1999

British Library Cataloguing in Publication data.
A catalogue record for this book is available from the
British Library.

ISBN 0 85315 859 2

Photoset in North Wales by
Derek Doyle & Associates, Mold, Flintshire.
Printed and bound in Great Britain by
Redwood Books, Trowbridge.

Contents

Acknowledgements

I would like to thank the following for their help in the writing and publication of this book: Anne Coddington, Sally Davison and all at Lawrence and Wishart, Tim Jordan (for saintly patience), Mike Kenny, Mark Perryman, Laura Sukhnandan and all the contributors for their hard work and tolerance of my various editorial failings.

The contributions to this book have been written in a style designed to be as accessible as possible without diluting too much of the sophistication and subtlety present in political thought; however, readers are advised to make use of the glossary. New political thought has inevitably given rise to new political concepts and it is not always possible to define these concepts within the text of a chapter without disrupting the flow of argument and wider explanation. I have endeavoured to include in the glossary every term which may conceivably present a problem for the reader who has only limited experience of theory and political analysis.

Introduction

Those who are new to the study of political thought may be surprised to know that there has been a long-running debate within academia about the end of ideology.[1] Since the 1950s, some have argued that ideological confrontation has died out to be replaced by limited technocratic disputes over problem-solving in industrial societies,[2] or, alternatively, a triumphant and global liberal democracy.[3] As this book hopes to show, you are right to be surprised. This volume contains a wide, vibrant and original range of ideas in fierce competition for influence over our lives – not a hint of a dead ideology. Twenty years ago, perhaps, one could have rejected religious fundamentalism, green thought, communitarianism, postmodernism and feminism as the concern only of fringe groups or the academic community but today these are the ideas without which our current world of politics would be unrecognisable. Such a rapid growth in influence for such new streams of thought provides concrete, practical evidence that ideology is far from dead.

Furthermore, despite the claims of Bell and friends[4] to the contrary, these new ideological streams *do* challenge the very fundamentals of our social and political lives. Indeed the following chapters signify a considerable change in the agenda of debate for political thinkers. New political thought is not new simply in the sense of being recent, it is also new in that it deals with issues and ideas unrecognised and highly challenging to older traditions. Ironically, if any one ideology suffers most at the hands of these new ideological streams, it is liberal democracy itself. To put it simply, many of the concepts which the majority of post-Enlightenment political thought took for granted are now open to debate. Thus, not only is ideology still very much alive, but it seems to have undergone something of a radical revival, with a number of important shifts inspiring new writings and new ideas.

The most striking shift has occurred within the realm of human reason and progress. The Enlightenment launched the notion that human reason was primary and that through its application of great progress could be made in the conditions of humanity. Much political thought took up these ideas with alacrity over the following centuries. Despite consistent challenges to these notions, the most influential political theories of the nineteenth and twentieth centuries (with the possible exception of some forms of fascism) accepted the idea of progress and the primacy of reason. Even Marxism, whose proponents argued that material conditions were more significant than reason, still lauded the capacity of objective scientific analysis to perceive the role of those material conditions and thus inform political action. In fact, the Soviet system can be said to have institutionalised the notion that those most 'advanced' in their scientific understanding of the social world should run society – at least, this was the ongoing legitimation of that system.

Of course, there were disputes over the *extent* to which progress and reason could be applied to human life – conservatism maintained something of a rearguard action against the role of rationalism in social and political affairs – but the idea that beneficial technological and economic progress would occur on the back of human invention and investigation was wholeheartedly accepted. This is no longer the case. These chapters show that the primacy of human reason and the beneficent effects of technological and economic progress are under severe attack from green ideas, postmodernism, religious fundamentalism, communitarianism and feminism.

The new generation of thinkers and activists have grown up in an era shaped by the very worst effects of technological 'progress' and the belief in the all-conquering power of rationalism – the Holocaust, nuclear weapons, environmental destruction, and the genocide of the communist systems. Inevitably this has had its effect. Much of the new political thought covered here questions the faith in rationalism and undermines the role of the technocrat and expert. Instead it calls, variously, for a politics based on religion, identity, traditional values of local communities, identification with nature, and spirituality. In short, many of the things Enlightenment rationalism sought to overturn.

Another surprising shift (particularly considering that this is *political* thought) has been the decline in the centrality of the state. The prime concern of older traditions of political thought was always the role of the state and, in particular, the extent of that role. Liberalism, almost certainly the most influential of Western ideologies, was largely constructed around the assertion that the citizen had certain rights deserving of protection against the activities of the state. While for many socialists the state was a powerful agent of change. Other factors clearly weighed on the minds of political thinkers – the state of nature, the role of God and religion, the influence of economic class, etc – but these were ultimately only significant for what they told us about the state. New political thought has a much wider scope. A broad range of agents and associations now have an equal status alongside the state, both as the focus of analysis and as potential agents of change. New thinkers now cite the local community, the religious establishment, voluntary associations, corporations, supra-national bodies, consciousness-raising movements and a host of others in their theoretical calculations and disputes.

This should not be that surprising. After the horrors of totalitarianism and the lesser failings of economic planning and welfarism in the West, the state was likely to lose the mesmeric qualities it held for some ambitious theorists. In many ways the state has been tested and found wanting so severely over the twentieth century that thinkers were bound to turn elsewhere. This is only emphasised by the post-1968 new social movements, which have changed so much in society without much help from the state, and from which a fair number of the strands of thought dealt with here have emerged. Furthermore, the spread of academic subjects such as sociology and cultural studies, which emphasise the dynamism and centrality of relationships beyond the state, have undoubtedly had a significant influence on new political thought. For example, a political theorist wishing to understand the role of women would find as much, if not more, inspiration in these other social sciences than in political thought which, with the exception of a very few theorists, has traditionally had little time for such considerations.

Of course new political thought has also been influenced by the fact that the nation state has lost its unchallenged pre-eminent role in world politics since 1945, with the rise of global technologies of communication, supra-national bodies such as the European Union and the growth of enormous transnational corporations. Such changes have placed the economic power of the state under stress. Combined with the loss of Empire and the decline in the economic fortunes of the West, these factors have ensured that debate has also focused upon the issue of declining resources for distribution. This shift has occurred most significantly within the older traditions, which are more obviously responsive to the day-to-day problems of governing.

In conservative thought, the rise of New Right ideas clearly reflects the realisation that the state cannot continue to finance the resource-intensive projects that had been accepted by the one-nation conservatism of the post-war period; and on the left, too, there has been a growing recognition of the issue. Where much democratic socialist and social democratic thought was once based upon projections of considerable economic growth and buoyancy, now these strands of thought look to ways of achieving the same goals of greater equality and liberty without making such unreasonable demands of public finances. Increased emphasis is placed upon the potential of civil society associations to provide welfare, and even the market is looked to as a new means of achieving socialist ends, albeit in a socialised, democratic form.

The concerns of new political thought have also brought whole realms of human behaviour into theoretical debate, which older thinkers would have found it preposterous to discuss. The importance of issues of sexuality and domestic life for feminist thought, the spiritual well-being of the individual for much green thought, the concern with personal morality for fundamentalism, and the role of the family for communitarianism have brought these new issues to the fore. This is after a long period in which the dominance of liberal ideas about the sanctity of the division between public and private consigned such concerns to the margins; and only totalitarian strands, in their own highly authoritarian and intrusive way, took an abiding interest in so-called private matters. Of course, as feminist thought has been keen to point out, the fact that liberalism drew this distinction between public and private does not mean that very rigid values and structures were not enforced in the private sphere. Indeed, in its widened remit, new political thought has very effectively undermined the traditional liberal assertion that wherever the state did not rule, there freedom reigned. Much new political thought has shown and increasingly accepted that conflict and control occur in all spheres of life.

One further concern that this collection may serve to illuminate is the issue of the decline or otherwise of the traditional Left–Right spectrum. It has been an assertion of much journalistic analysis and political rhetoric in recent years that the strict division between Left and Right which had existed since the French Revolution has become obsolete. If anything these chapters tend to uphold such a view. Any firm distinction between Left and Right that one cares to construct is nearly always defeated by some strand of new political thought which fails to accord with such a distinction.

If the Left is seen as basically dubious about capitalism and the Right as enthusiastic, then this leaves us with some very strange bedfellows: can liberal feminism really sit easily alongside the New Right and Christian fundamentalism? Equally, where do communitarianism, market socialism, much of contemporary liberalism and postmodernism sit? – all are enthusiastic about some aspects of capitalism but not others. And where does Islamism fit into this schema – not fundamentally anti-capitalist but still built upon demands for social justice and certainly no friend of *Western* capitalism.

Alternatively if the Left-Right distinction is regarded as a construction around the opposition or support for the *status quo*, once again we find strange and uncomfortable alliances. Does this mean the New Right is left-wing? Is religious fundamentalism right- or left-wing on this model? It certainly wishes for major change in some areas but then bitterly condemns feminist assaults on the status quo as it exists for gender relations.

Even if we accept as broad a definition as one along the lines that the Left supports the powerless while the Right upholds the powerful, we are left in confusion. Green ideas sometimes seem concerned with issues which have the potential to affect both powerful and powerless equally, while fundamentalism, once again, claims to act on behalf of the powerless but then hopes for the enhancement of the power of religious leaders and men. Some postmodernists may even reject the very notion of such a firm distinction between powerless and powerful, seeing power as too complex a network of relations to be reduced to a simple dualism.

Thus Left and Right do seem inadequate labels for new political thought. However, there is one further possibility, which is that the spectrum has *always* been problematic even when used to refer to older streams. For example, the strict anti-decadence characteristic of some radical Left thought always seemed a lot closer to traditional conservatism, and even the extreme Right, than it did to the libertarianism of other brands of socialism. Maybe Tony Fitzpatrick is closest to the truth when he argues in this volume that:

> There is nothing about a Left–Right spectrum which makes it an all-or-nothing representation of the way things are; rather, it always has been, and continues to be, a convenient *and partial* way of understanding and shaping the world ... It is those who would abandon all reference to a Left–Right spectrum who may be accused of taking it too seriously.

Despite all these changes, there *is* still a common thread running through the older and the newer strands of political thought. At heart both are still about disputes over how best to achieve, and indeed what constitutes, human freedom, security and the good life. Not one of the new approaches presented here would deny that these are their prime concerns. In truth, new political thought may have rejected some of the fundamental means of the Enlightenment but it still holds dear the great ends that that influential period of history launched upon the world. As one can see in Simon Thompson's chapter, even postmodernists, the most self-conscious iconoclasts of Enlightenment values, have a hard time denying themselves such lofty aims.

In such a spirit of continuity and change, political thought has undergone something of a renaissance since the 1960s. The following chapters show how human inventiveness and diversity of ideas has been the real victor in the face of the new and unexpected problems of the late twentieth century rather than a dry technocracy or an arrogant liberal democracy. The real excitement generated by these new approaches, however, is their youth. Inspirational and thought-provoking as some of the ideas presented here are, they are still remarkably young compared to the older traditions. No one could have predicted in the late seventeenth century that the liberalism of Locke would be adopted and refined by later thinkers and by mass movements to the point where it became the most influential ideological strand of the next two centuries. Equally, one cannot know which of the strands of thought presented here will prove the liberalism of the future. Maybe an inspired green theorist will one day be held in the same esteem as Rousseau. Maybe a political thinker not yet born will see a current postmodernist as their great muse and build a radical theory so in tune with the times that it changes the world. No one can predict the future in such detail. It is this that makes the new political thought so exciting and it is this that makes life uncertain enough to ensure that we will probably always seek the guidance which ideology and political thought provides.

Adam Lent
Sheffield 1998

Notes

1. See: C.L. Waxman (ed.), *The End of Ideology Debate*, Funk and

Wagnalls,New York 1968; M. Rejai (ed.), *The Decline of Ideology*, Aldine Atherton, Chicago 1971.

2. This was the argument that famously launched the whole debate; see: D. Bell, *The End of Ideology*, Collier-Macmillan, London 1962.

3. This is the more recent expression of the end of ideology argument; see: F. Fukuyama, *The End of History and The Last Man*, Hamish Hamilton, London 1992.

4. D. Bell, 'The End of Ideology – Part One', *Government and Opposition*, 23, 1988.

Contemporary Liberalism

Matthew Festenstein

Introduction: Defining Liberalism

Like the other schools of thought examined in this book, liberalism is a quarrelsome family of ideas rather than a single doctrine. It is accordingly difficult to pin down quite what is meant by 'liberalism'. In part, as we shall see, this difficulty stems from controversies over the ownership of the term, as writers attempt to pass off their views as the only version of liberalism worthy of the name. Yet it can also be traced to the inevitable diversity of traditions of thought which have been developed by many different (indeed, often strikingly different) individuals in a variety of contexts and with a variety of concerns in mind. To get a fix on liberalism as a political ideology involves less the grasping of the central tenets of a doctrine than the picking out of the core areas of concern for liberals, about which they continue to argue.

Five key values of 'liberalism' can be identified in order to provide a background to contemporary debates. The first theme is the centrality of the individual human being: we are each born 'free and equal', capable of possessing and pursuing our own goals, interests and ideals. For some liberals, the differences which emerge among people – their individuality – is a simple psychological fact. For others, more romantically inclined, it is something to be cultivated and gloried in.[1]

The second aspect is an idea of the liberty which a person is thought to require if she is to be able to form and pursue their own goals. The precise definition of liberty has been the subject of intense controversy.

Some liberals believe that the only coherent conception is what has famously been called negative liberty: a person's liberty simply consists in the extent to which they can act without being constrained by the deliberate interference of others. The failure to ensure negative liberty opens the door to despotism allowing others, usually the state, to decide for us what form our freedom should take. However, some liberals see this as hopelessly weak. According to positive conceptions of liberty, factors such as poverty, lack of education, our relations with others and the extent to which we shape our public life through politics may affect our freedom.[2] Freedom is not then understood merely as the absence of deliberate constraint but as an effective capacity to govern one's own life. That there should be intense and deep disagreements over concepts of liberty, freedom and autonomy is not surprising when we consider what is at issue:

> Liberty is a concept which captures what is distinctive and important in human agency as such and in the untrammelled exercise of powers of individual deliberation, choice, and the intentional initiation of action [...] Human agency, will, and the initiation of action is a profoundly complicated business: it is the locus of one of the most intractable problems in metaphysics, and it is also the source of some of the deepest exultation and despair in human experience. Our sense of what it is to have and exercise freedom is bound up with our conception of ourselves as persons and of our relation to value, other people, society and the casual [sc. causal] order of things.[3]

However, liberals agree that freedom demands the recognition of certain basic rights possessed by each person, Benjamin Constant's 'liberty of the moderns': the right to basic physical security, the freedoms of speech and conscience, freedom of movement, the right to privacy, the right to private property, and the right to participate in politics.[4] Whatever our particular goals and interests, liberals argue, we require these rights to pursue them. Liberals are accordingly tolerant of diversity, which these rights enable.

Third, there is an interest in limiting the scope of the state, rendering it responsible to the interests of the governed. The state is not the vehicle of national destiny, of divine will, or of the personality of the monarch; it is a human contrivance which serves the needs and interests of its members:

> Men being, as has been said, by Nature, all free, equal and independent, no one can be put out of this Estate, and subjected to the Political Power of another, without his own Consent. The only way whereby any one devests himself of his Natural Liberty, and puts on the bonds of Civil Society is by agreeing with other Men to joyn and unite into a Community, for their comfortable, safe and peaceable living one amongst another, in a secure Enjoyment of their Properties, and a greater Security against any that are not of it.[6]

Although statements such as this have spawned a voluminous (and unsatisfying) literature concerning how citizens can be understood to have consented to the state, the general point is clear enough.[6] The limits to what the state can do are not set by the discretion of the sovereign, but derive from the rights possessed by each citizen: we could not agree to be members of a polity which denies us those rights.

The fourth feature of liberalism is a famously divided attitude toward the market, the system of private property and free exchange in economic goods. Some liberals argue for the overall social benefit of a system in which individuals can pursue their interests in this way; others argue that this system is valuable less for the benefits it provides than for the respect for individual property rights which it embodies. At least since John Stuart Mill, however, there has been a more or less uneasy sense among some liberals that the unconstrained market can render the liberal freedoms vacuous for many:

> No longer enslaved or made dependent by force of law, the great majority are so by force of poverty; they are still chained to a place, to an occupation, and to conformity with the will of an employer, and debarred by an accident of birth from the enjoyments, and from the mental and moral advantages, which others inherit without exertion and independently of desert. That this is an evil equal to almost any of those against which mankind have hitherto struggled, the poor are not wrong in believing.[7]

For this strand of liberalism, the state or other agencies are justified in curtailing the rights of private property for the sake of individual freedom. This ambivalence toward property and the market continues to characterise contemporary liberalism. The contemporary form of this dispute is dealt with in detail below.

The fifth aspect of liberalism is a conception of progress. At its most optimistic, it promised to sweep away the superstition, convention, prejudice and violence which underpinned the *ancien régime* in favour of enlightenment, toleration, individual freedom, and equality of opportunity. The extension of the market and, for some later liberals such as T.H. Green and L.T. Hobhouse, the modern state were to be the crucial agents of this progress.[8] The liberal concern with progress has also encompassed a more cautious awareness that its emphasis upon individualism may leave the public or social realm dangerously under-nourished.[9] Perhaps, some liberals worried, the sort of person fostered by industrial or 'mass' civilisation is not capable of forming and pursuing goals which could really be called her own.[10]

Given the disagreements which have marked these core liberal concerns with the individual, freedom, the state, the market, and progress, it is not surprising that the contemporary scene offers a variety of liberalisms: what follows is necessarily (but I hope not too laughably) a simplified sketch. Students of contemporary liberalism often start with John Rawls's magisterial treatise, *A Theory of Justice*.[11] On publication in 1971 it was greeted, even by those who disagreed with its conclusions, as a rehabilitation of liberal moral and political 'grand theory' after a notably fallow period. In its scope and ambition it particularly stands out against four key currents in liberal political thought which were prevalent at the time.

The first insisted that the only truly rational or scientific approach to politics was 'empirical', concentrating on describing and explaining political systems in a way that involved no particular evaluative commitment, to liberalism or to anything else, at all.[12] The second current of thinking modestly conceived of political philosophy as the analysis of the meaning of concepts: political philosophers could not argue for ideals, or criticise existing philosophy; all they could do was reflect on the language which people used to talk about politics.[13] The third trend was a reaction to the perceived onslaught of totalitarianism with the rise of fascist and communist regimes in the 1920s and 1930s. In different ways liberal philosophers such as Isaiah Berlin, Karl Popper and F.A. Hayek[14] attacked the view of the state as a collectivity organised around a common purpose.[15] Rather than merely furnishing a set of rules for the free and peaceful coexistence of citizens, the totalitarian state sees laws as instrumental in achieving common social goals, such as military success or prosperity. In doing so it inevitably coerces those of its members who may have other interests, thus using them as mere instruments for collective goals. These thinkers also held doubts about the power of human reason to evaluate and construct social and political institutions.[16]

The fourth current is one that Rawls himself clearly takes very seriously in *A Theory of Justice*, namely, the utilitarian conception of social welfare. This view claims that the best way to organise social welfare is for the state to pursue policies which maximise happiness throughout the society; its optimism about the power of human reason encourages it to believe that the state can do so. When encountering this view (as we shall see) Rawls is as sensitive as the anti-totalitarians to the risk that the state might end up using or coercing some citizens for the sake of others: perhaps the goal of maximising social welfare leads us unacceptably to sacrifice social and political liberties or the vital interests of some small part of society. However, he shares with utilitarians their optimism about reason and the belief that a commitment to social justice does not necessarily collapse into totalitarianism, being both coherent and defensible. At least part of the impact of Rawls's work came from the appreciation that this was an attempt to combine an argument for redistribution with a robust defence of civil and political liberties in a single theoretical design.

In doing so, Rawls was (as many commentators recognised) furnishing an ideological justification for welfare state liberalism which was friendly to the mixed economies of Western social democracy. It is an open question whether or not contemporary social democracy can reinvigorate his demanding vision of liberal individualism and social justice.

Foundations

Rawls's *A Theory of Justice* asks what principles for the just organisation of society may be arrived at by a group of people placed in an imaginary 'original position'. The subjects in the original position are behind a 'veil of ignorance': that is, they do not know the details of the society to which these principles will apply (whether or not it is capitalist, agrarian, multi-ethnic), nor their particular social and economic position in it (whether or not they will turn out to be serfs, factory owners, or doctors), nor what their tastes, interests and talents are in this society (whether or not they are lazy, entrepreneurial or devout). At the same time, their deliberation about the principles of co-operation are self-interested and rational: each wants the best result from this process that they can hope for. This veil of ignorance is thought to ensure the fairness of the principles which result: if I do not know which of the pieces of the cake I am cutting is to be given to me, then I will try to cut the cake as fairly as I can.

However, Rawls not only excludes facts about my wealth and talents from the decision-making process but also my 'conception of the good'; that is, any view that I may have about what makes for a valuable life for myself or others. The notion of a 'conception of the good' covers a multitude of more or less articulate beliefs: libertines have a different conception of the good from prudes, and Catholics have a different conception from atheists. While the *content* of different conceptions of the good varies, of course, Rawls thinks that we all share an interest in 'forming, revising and rationally pursuing' *some* conception of the good, irrespective of content.[17] This reveals a basic liberal premise of Rawls's theory: each of us has a life to lead, and this is a more basic fact about us than our particular projects and goals. It is important to remember that the deliberators are not constructing a perfect society which they then enter. They are cut-off from the real world by the veil of ignorance but will re-enter that world after their deliberations – they are being asked to consider which principles *ought* to be applied in the society they re-enter.

Rawls argues that people in the original position, ignorant of their status and abilities and motivated not by any particular conception of the good but by an interest in forming, pursuing and revising such conceptions, would agree on two principles of justice:

(i) Each person is to have an equal right to the most extensive system of equal basic liberties compatible with a similar system of liberty for all.

(ii) Social and economic benefits are to be arranged so that they are both (a) open to all under conditions of fair equality of opportunity, and (b) to the greatest benefit of the least advantaged. (Point (b) is referred to as the 'difference principle'.)

In addition, the order of these principles expresses their priority. Thus, the achievement of equal liberty (i) is considered more important than ensuring wide social and economic benefit (ii), and equality of opportunity (a) is considered more valuable than the benefit of the least advantaged (b).

In different ways, all these principles arise from the fact that the individuals in the original position would wish to minimise the risk that they run of doing badly when they emerge from behind the veil of ignorance into their real social position: 'since I don't know my social positions,' Rawls argues the individual deliberators would reason, 'I will seek to arrange matters so that I do as well as possible, even if I turn out to be one of the least advantaged'. This is known as the 'maximin' strategy in the theory of games: in conditions where we do not know what the outcome for us will be we maximise our minimum possible gains from the outcome, i.e. even if we are condemned to having the smallest slice of the cake, we still would want to ensure that the slice is as big as possible even if it can't be as big as all the others. Keeping this in mind we can understand how each of deliberators come to their conclusions.

(i) The principle of equal basic liberties derives from the deliberators' following thought: 'I hope that no single conception of the good is enshrined in the principles of social cooperation because the dominant conception (back in the real world) may not turn out to be mine; or, if it is mine, I may later come to doubt it. What I can safely do is to hope matters are arranged in such a way that, no matter what conception of the good I support, I am free to do so, or to change it if I wish'. The *equality* of these basic liberties expresses the apparent fact that the deliberators' desire to avoid risk would lead them to hope that the rich and the powerful are prevented from enjoying freedoms at the expense of the poor and the weak.

The priority of the achievement of equal liberties over access to social and economic benefits expresses Rawls's argument that the deliberators, when transplanted into actual situations, would not wish to sacrifice liberty in order to secure more wealth: since the liberties are necessary for each to pursue his own goals and lead his own life, they would not trade them for economic benefits.[18] This insures them against the risk that, should they have conceptions of the good which are not compatible with the drive for economic growth, or should they change their minds, they will still be able to pursue this conception of the good.

(ii) The principle of arranging social and economic benefits so that they are open to all under a system of equality of opportunity and to the greatest benefit of the least advantaged also rests on the caution of the deliberating parties. If I do not know which position in society I am going to occupy then I will pay most attention to the lot of the worst off when examining various arrangements for the distribution of social and economic benefits, in case I turn out to be in that category.

However, like the priority of liberty over economic benefits, the notion that fair equality of opportunity is considered more important than benefiting the least advantaged expresses the thought that the goal of social welfare ought not to over-ride the individual freedom of the members of society. Just as it would not make sense for the individual deliberators to sacrifice their own conception of the good life for economic well-being, so the deliberators would not want to trade the freedom of equality of opportunity for the goal of maximum social welfare if such a choice arose. Rawls states that '[a]nother way of putting this is to say that the principles of justice manifest in the basic structure of society men's desire to treat one another not as means only but as ends in themselves.[19] The priority of liberty, equality of opportunity and difference principle each then express the intuition that social welfare ought not to eclipse the personal integrity of citizens. Rawls suggests that his model extends the contractarianism of Locke, Rousseau and Kant:

> [T]he original position of equality corresponds to the state of nature in the traditional theory of the social contract. The original position is not, of course, thought of as an actual historical state of affairs, much less as a primitive condition of culture. It is understood as a purely hypothetical situation characterised so as to lead to a certain conception of justice.[20]

What does this hypothetical contract actually establish? Critics of Rawls puzzle over how an agreement entered into by the radically ignorant deliberators of the original position can possess any binding force over actual people. Imagine that I do less well in a society governed by the difference principle than I would do under an alternative regime. It seems strange to say that I ought to support the difference principle on the grounds that if I did not know that it was against my own interests I would agree to it. Similarly, it seems strange to say that the fact that you would pick a society governed by the difference principle if you were unaware of your fiercely egalitarian ideals provides grounds for your supporting that society once you become aware of those ideals.

One liberal response has been to preserve the contract device but to rework it in a more hard-nosed fashion.[21] In Rawls's construction, the subjects in the original position are egoistic in that they are interested only in their own lives and projects, but so stripped of information that the principles are impartial. An alternative (which has roots in Hume) is to understand principles of justice as the result of an agreement arrived at through bargaining among self-interested individuals who have not been deprived of information about their wealth, capacities and ideals. This approach has the benefit of offering a powerful answer to the problem of compliance by the principles facing Rawls: we ought to comply with conventions of justice because it is in our interest to do so. The principles which are arrived at on the basis of mutual advantage are characteristically more minimal than Rawls's demanding obligations. Rawls's contract was designed to arrive at principles which are not informed by the relative bargaining strength of the people involved, whereas mutual advantage contracts express these differences. In such contracts the obligations of the rich or powerful stem only from their supposed vulnerability to the consequences of the poor's withdrawal from the bargain, not from a recognition that to act otherwise would be to violate anyone's personal integrity. For critics, however, this approach appears to have the distasteful implication that the very weak or unproductive – those who cannot press their interests effectively in bargaining with their fellows – would not have their interests represented. These worries are reinforced by such statements, by theorists using the approach, that the infirm must fall 'beyond the pale' of justice[22] or that 'if personal differences are sufficiently great' then the powerful may impose 'something similar to the slave contract'.[23]

What these critics of the 'mutual advantage' perspective emphasise about *A Theory of Justice* is not the egoism of the original position but its attempt to model *impartiality* through the veil of ignorance: principles can 'be generated without any special devices at all, just by asking agents to give equal consideration to others, notwithstanding their knowledge of, and ability to promote, their own good.[24] From this perspective, the difficulty generated by the original position's status as an hypothetical contract is incidental. For the basic claim is that the principles of justice are derived from an intuitive idea of what the equal or impartial consideration of citizens requires: it involves, as we have seen, recognising their 'separateness' through the basic liberties and organising the effects of inequalities so that the worst off benefit to the highest possible degree.

Controversies

Libertarianism and Redistribution

It may appear as if something strange has happened. Liberalism, origi-nally a philosophy which claimed to endorse the free market, seems to have become a rationale for intervention in order to ensure the benefit of the least advantaged. In response, the strand of political thought known as libertarianism (which subscribes to many of the same basic principles as liberalism) objects that the liberal debate on distributive justice has a far too relaxed an approach to issues of property rights, the market and state intervention.

There are many strands of libertarianism. One argument emphasises the dangers of using state intervention to redistribute resources. The free market is held to be a broadly efficient means for the production and distribution of goods; to interfere with it in any ambitious way would be to kill the goose that lays the golden eggs. For others, the commitment to redistribution violates the liberal commitment to the limited state, and shepherds populations down the road to serfdom: the erosion of property rights will always lead to the destruction of civil and political liberties.

At the core of the libertarian position is a moral argument that the attempt to combine commitments to individual liberty and to the redistribution of wealth by the state is contradictory: rightly under-stood, 'private property is the embodiment of individual liberty',[25] while redistribution of property embodies the coercive use of some citizens' assets for the benefit of others; for example, taking one citi-zen's private income to fund another's welfare payments. Some propo-nents of this position accordingly argue that they are the true keepers of the liberal flame.[26] Robert Nozick summarises his position in *Anarchy, State and Utopia*:

> Individuals have rights, and there are things no person or group may do to them [without violating their rights]. So strong and far-reaching are these rights that they raise the question of what, if anything, the state and its officials may do.[27]

Like Rawls, Nozick holds to the core tenet that no individual may be sacrificed in order to achieve the goals of others: he too says that 'indi-viduals are ends and not merely means'.[28] If I am deprived of the capac-ity to shape my own life it is rendered less meaningful for me.

Nozick's attack on the principle of redistribution rests on the idea that private property can be acquired and transferred legitimately. If I possess some property to which I have a legitimate entitlement – that is, its acquisition does not violate others' basic rights – what can justify transferring some part of that property to the worst off? For the libertarian, the liberal does not place sufficient emphasis on the priority of liberty and, in the name of distributive justice, some of its citizens are treated as means, by viewing their wealth and capacities as part of a common social pool which can be drawn upon to benefit others. We may not remove an eye from a sighted person to give to a blind one, nor redistribute friends from the popular to the lonely.[29] However, liberal social justice seems to license the state to act in this way when it comes to a particular set of attributes, namely property entitlements. The role of the 'minimal' state is, on the other hand, restricted purely to ensuring that the entitlements of citizens are protected against force and fraud.

Liberals who insist on the legitimacy of redistribution in the face of the libertarian assault may offer several replies. They may argue that (as Nozick acknowledges) it is difficult to determine who is in fact legitimately entitled to what. Nozick allows that acquisition of property by coercion is illegitimate; but if current property holdings are based on past use of force (by one's ancestors, for example) are they now valid? Nozick's response is to suggest that 'rectification' on a vast scale would indeed be required for the consistent application of his views; but on what lines this is to proceed is unclear. In any case, the question arises of how property is originally acquired: if I admire a beautiful and unowned landscape does it become mine? If not, what else must I do to make it mine? It may also be argued that the analogy with removing body parts or affections is invalid because ownership of economic goods belongs in a morally less serious category than the former goods. Liberals may also argue (as the earlier quotation from Mill suggests) that extreme poverty may be as effective a way of depriving life of meaning as taxation, and that Nozick's conclusions drawn from his premises are not necessarily so straightforward. Finally, if taxation is coercion, how is even the minimal state to be funded? Nozick seems to have dramatically over-stated his case.

A more complex approach is Hayek's. He argues that social processes and individual activities are too complicated to be organised by any single social agency or political force, and the attempt to do so results in the coercive and usually disastrous imposition of supposedly rational or just goals on individuals who do not embrace them. A crucial feature of market relations is that they preserve the liberty of the agents involved. Liberty is understood in negative terms, as the absence of coercion by another, as not being forced to do things which otherwise one would not have been done. In broad terms, his arguments for the market operate on two levels. First, the market is endorsed as a spontaneous order or 'catallaxy' which has evolved through the free interaction of independent individuals pursuing their needs and interests. This complex system includes certain individual rights and liberties, and, although it has not arisen through anyone's singular intention, it has still proved a generally effective way of organising the activities of diverse individuals. Hayek counterposes the individual freedom which this system permits with the over-ambitious attempts of social agencies to control the system:

> [t]he case for individual freedom rests chiefly on the recognition of the inevitable ignorance of all of us concerning a great many of the factors on which the achievement of our ends and our welfare depends.[30]

Only through the possibilities for experiment allowed by the individual freedoms of the market can progress continue to be made.

The second argument echoes both Nozick and Rawls: coercion is an evil because it treats a person as a mere instrument. Like Nozick, Hayek is strict in what he allows to count as coercion: a person is coerced only when his options for action are controlled by the arbitrary will of another. 'Your money or your life!' constitutes coercion for Hayek. By contrast, although the threat of starvation may compel me to accept a job at a very low wage, my employer does not coerce me, because I have the choice, which is not of his making, to refuse his offer. The market is usually non-coercive because the options offered to an individual are not intended by one person's will. The conscripted soldier is less free than the homeless and impoverished tramp, Hayek tells us, as more of the former's options are determined by the intentions of others.

While the market is a more effective means of avoiding coercion than a directive state, it nevertheless sometimes requires regulation, when it has damaging effects which it cannot of itself correct. Unlike Nozick, Hayek acknowledges a role for the state in providing essential public goods and alleviating extreme hardship. Moreover, Hayek argues, coercion can only be eliminated by the threat of coercion: by giving one agency a monopoly of coercion the danger of many coercive agencies coming into existence is reduced. This requires then a set of constitutional arrangements which protect individual liberties and limit state coercion by ensuring that the rule of law is consistent and predictable. The state is just only to the extent that it allows as large a space as possible for each individual to act as she pleases without infringing the liberty of others. Unlike Rawls, Hayek argues that inequalities which arise in this system cannot be unjust since they are not intentionally created but arise through the unintended conse-quences of individuals' pursuit of their own goals and projects. Hayek came to believe that this conception of justice required quite radical political action, such as the denationalisation of money and the removal of the legal and political immunities enjoyed by trades unions.

Critics of Hayek ask whether or not his notions of liberty, justice and coercion are not too narrowly defined. The notion of 'injustice' is taken only to apply to the intended consequences of an action. However, this raises thorny questions about the status of omissions (if I can save an innocent from torture at no cost to myself but do not do so, have I acted unjustly?), and about the moral status of unintended but *foreseeable* consequences. If the latter are not covered by the concept of justice, then it is not clear why, say, manslaughter is a crime. If they are, then the unintended but foreseeable reduction of options for the poor in an unconstrained market system may count as coercion.

State Neutrality

A second site of debate for contemporary liberals is what has been called the 'neutrality of the state'. As Dworkin puts it:

> the doctrine of state neutrality requires that legislation be neutral on what might be called the question of the good life, or of what gives value to life. Since the citizens of a society differ in their conceptions [of the good], the government does not treat them as equals if it prefers one conception to another, either because the officials believe that one is intrinsically superior, or because one is held by the more numerous and powerful group.[31]

Legislation must not favour any particular doctrine of the good life on the grounds of its superiority to others, and different doctrines must be accorded equal respect. So, for example, a liberal state ought not to foster one particular religious view on the grounds that it is true or morally superior to other world views possessed by its citizens.

Nevertheless the doctrine of neutrality appears to have implications which may give liberals pause. For example, the idea that taxation ought to be used to support certain cultural activities would appear to be ruled out. If some citizens find (at least part) of their good life in gambling, while others enjoy the theatre, the neutral state ought not to use public funds to subsidise the latter activity and not the former; but this of course is what some states do. Heterosexual monogamy likewise belongs to a particular conception of the good which is not shared by all citizens; and the neutral state ought not to support this conception and not others, through legal recognition, tax and pension laws, and so on. Thus liberals cannot argue for the state to support a particular conception of the good life simply on the ground that it is a superior conception, even if they themselves believe this to be so.

Why should any liberal subscribe to such self-denial? One reason for doing so rests on the belief that '[t]he fundamental liberal insight is the inescapable controversiality of ideals of the good life and thus the need to find political principles that abstract from them.[32] It is only by distancing our considerations from any particular conception of the good (which will always be open to dispute) that we can arrive at principles which are acceptable to all; and it is only if I am governed by a principle which is acceptable to me that I am not coerced, i.e. used as a means for achieving the good of others.[33] In recent work, for example, Rawls claims that his theory of justice must be understood to rest on an 'overlapping consensus' among conceptions of the good in democratic societies, which converge on his principles but disagree about much else.

The difficulty for such theories lies in determining what the acceptable common moral denominator is. The need to overcome disagreement and arrive at commonly accepted rules does not in itself point in the direction of liberalism. A society composed of two conflicting and intolerant religious groups may abandon the belief that the state ought to impose one or other religion on all, and allow both to share the status of official religion. This is a neutral solution for the groups involved but not a liberal one since there is no freedom of conscience: those who would wish to belong to another religious group or to profess no religion at all are excluded.

Some liberals accordingly reject the notion that liberal rules necessarily have to be accepted or endorsed by all. Neutrality on this view is a distinctively liberal ideal, one which other outlooks cannot be expected to endorse.[34] It rests on the liberal belief that each individual has an essential interest in forming and pursuing a conception of the good. This interest is damaged if the state penalises ways of life necessary for pursuing conceptions of the good. Whatever conception we have may only be pursued in a manner which respects others' freedom to do the same, and, indeed, the possibility that we may change our minds. The apparently innocuous idea of a conception of the good, then, turns out to be shaped by a liberal understanding of the individual and her interests. Some commitments may not have this shape: if I take my conception of the good to be valid (I am persuaded of the truth of my religion, say, or of the evil of certain sexual practices), why should I step back from it in order to make it compatible with liberal rights? 'Neutrality', then, applies only to those conceptions of the good which are already compatible with liberalism, and thus also seems to be a more limited ideal than it may appear. One implication of this is that the 'liberal will have to concede that he has a great many more enemies (real enemies – people who will suffer under a liberal dispensation) than he has usually pretended to have.'[35] This abandons the notion that the principles of the liberal state must ultimately be acceptable to all those whom it governs.

Not all liberals have found the idea of neutrality attractive or coherent.[36] For these, the liberal rights express and define a particular form of good life whose central virtue is individual autonomy: 'one needs some conception of human good, of human flourishing, in a form (or range of forms) of communal life that fosters rather than hinders such flourishing.'[37] Thus the liberal state should not be neutral on the question of choosing between forms of life which value autonomy and those which do not; it ought to encourage worthwhile options and to discourage 'evil' or 'empty' ones.[38] Proponents of this form of liberalism nevertheless hold that the value given to autonomy requires the toleration of diverse and conflicting ways of life in a state of 'competitive pluralism', furnishing a rich set of meaningful options for the autonomous individual.

Challenges

Much of the rest of this volume explores views which explicitly criticise liberalism; and the writers discussed in this chapter have proven as tempting a target as their historical predecessors. Communitarians argue that liberalism is excessively individualistic and ignores the importance of wider collective affiliations. Feminists argue that issues raised by the social position and distinctive moral sensibility of women are neglected. Socialists argue that liberals are excessively fond of the free market, glossing over the coerciveness of market relations and the ill consequences of its unchecked operation. Conservatives argue that liberals are too optimistic in the belief that constitutional and political tinkering can increase freedom and justice, and display a juvenile hostility toward hierarchy and authority. It is not possible to discuss all the relevant arguments and rebuttals here, but two general caveats may be made. The first is that there is no simple liberalism to be defended or attacked: it is not just that the doctrine resists identification with any particular presentation of it but also that many liberal thinkers incorporate the attitudes of their critics into their liberalism. Hayek, for example, is susceptible to the conservative preoccupation with the fragility of civilisation; Dworkin and others would seem to license an egalitarian interference with the market which is as politically radical as forms of socialism.[39]

A second point is that liberalism's critics are often uncertain 'as to whether they have come to destroy liberalism or to fulfil it'.[40] That is, they claim that the values of liberalism are wholly repellent while simultaneously attacking liberals for endorsing a vision of a social order which fails to embody those same liberal values.[41] For example, when liberals are accused of overlooking the ways in which racial discrimination may affect individual freedom, the critic may believe that individual freedom is not important; but it is just as likely that her assumption is simply that liberals are insensitive to a factor (namely race) which affects freedom, not that the value itself is meaningless. Liberalism's critics often seem to attack from the contradictory position that liberal principles are both unacceptable *and*, simultaneously, unsatisfactorily implemented in liberal social systems and visions. Thus the critics of liberalism can often end up sounding suspiciously liberal.

Critics of any persuasion may be worried by the abstraction of contemporary liberalism. The ideals and arguments of the authors examined in this chapter have generally been put forward with little consideration (at least at the theoretical level) of the societies to which they are intended to apply. There is little discussion of how widely shared the liberal vision is or of how compatible the ideal of autonomy is with modern social and economic conditions. If the diagnosis is negative in each case, the doctrine may seem to be destined for impotence or paternalism. Those liberals who propose ambitious redistributive schemes also need to determine whether or not the growth of the economy upon which they depend is generally compatible with the principles of justice which underlie those programmes.[42] This is not to say that asking these questions in itself deflates liberalism or that in principle they cannot be answered satisfactorily; but they require a deeper integration of the philosophies of contemporary liberalism into an understanding of modern social, economic and political conditions.

In spite of such concerns, liberals have confidently expanded their remit, discussing liberal rights beyond civil liberties and distributive justice in the nation state in order to consider questions of international distributive justice,[43] the rights of cultural minorities,[44] and self-determination and secession.[45] Given the optimism about human reason which I have suggested informs much contemporary liberalism, this expansiveness should not be too surprising. I have also tried to suggest that the liberal camp is divided by internal conflict – or enriched by internal variety. It has been the intention of this chapter to draw attention to this variety and to supply some of the tools for thinking about it.

Notes

1. J.S. Mill, 'On Liberty', in J. Gray (ed.), *On Liberty, and Other Essays*, Oxford University Press, Oxford 1991.
2. D. Miller (ed.), *Liberty*, Oxford University Press, Oxford 1991.
3. J. Waldron, *Liberal Rights*, Cambridge University Press, Cambridge 1993, p.39.
4. B. Constant, 'The liberty of the Ancients compared with that of the Moderns', in his *Political Writings* (ed. by B. Fontana), Cambridge University Press, Cambridge 1988.
5. J. Locke, *Two Treatises on Government*, in P. Laslett (ed.), Cambridge University Press, Cambridge 1988, II, sec.95.
6. L. Green, *The Authority of the State*, Clarendon, Oxford 1988.
7. J.S. Mill, 'Chapters on Socialism', *Collected Works*, V, University of Toronto Press, Toronto 1967 p.710.
8. M. Freeden, *The New Liberalism: An Ideology of Social Reform*, Clarendon Press, Oxford 1978.
9. B. Constant, *Political Writings*, *op.cit*; A. Tocqueville, *The Old Regime and the French Revolution* (trans. by S.Gilbert), Anchor, New York 1955.
10. J.S. Mill, 'On Liberty', *op cit*.

11. J. Rawls, *A Theory of Justice*, Oxford University Press, Oxford 1971.
12. See, for example, S.M. Lipset, *Political Man*, Heinemann, London 1960. For a criticism of this view see: A. Arblaster, *The Rise and Decline of Western Liberalism*, Basil Blackwell, Oxford 1984.
13. R.M. Hare, *The Language of Morals*, Oxford University Press, Oxford 1952; T.D. Weldon, *The Vocabulary of Politics*, Penguin, Harmondsworth 1953.
14. I. Berlin, *Four Essays on Liberty*, Oxford University Press, Oxford 1969; K. Popper, *The Open Society and Its Enemies*, 3rd edn, Routledge & Kegan Paul, London 1957; K. Popper, *The Poverty of Historicism*, Routledge & Kegan Paul, London 1960; F.A. Hayek, *The Constitution of Liberty*, Routledge & Kegan Paul, London 1960.
15. This scepticism is shared with other writers more distantly related to liberalism. See: H. Arendt, *The Human Condition*, Chicago University Press, Chicago 1958; M. Oakeshott, *Rationalism in Politics*, Methuen, London 1962.
16. K. Popper, *Conjectures and Refutations*, Routledge & Kegan Paul, London 1976, p.6.
17. J. Rawls, *A Theory of Justice, op.cit.* pp.92-95; pp.407-416; J. Rawls, *Political Liberalism*, Colombia University Press, New York 1993, pp.19, 30, 104.
18. Rawls, *A Theory of Justice,op.cit.* pp151-2; pp.542-548.
19. *Ibid.* p.178.
20. *Ibid.* p.12.
21. J. Buchanan, *The Limits of Liberty: Between Anarchy and Leviathan*, University of Chicago Press, Chicago 1975; D. Gauthier, *Morals by Agreement*, Oxford University Press, Oxford 1986; J. Narveson, *The Libertarian Idea*, Temple University Press, Philadelphia 1988.
22. D. Gauthier, *Morals by Agreement, op.cit.* p.268.
23. J. Buchanan, *The Limits of Liberty, op.cit.* pp.59-60.
24. W. Kymlicka, *Contemporary Political Philosophy*, Oxford University Press, Oxford 1990, p.69.
25. J. Gray, *Liberalism*, Open University Press, Milton Keynes 1986, p.62.
26. D. Conway, *Classical Liberalism*, MacMillan, London 1995.
27. R. Nozick, *Anarchy, State and Utopia*, Basic Books, New York 1974, p.x.
28. *Ibid.* pp.30-31.
29. cf. *ibid.* pp.206-7.
30. F.A. Hayek, *The Constitution of Liberty, op.cit.* p.29.
31. R. Dworkin, *A Matter of Principle*, Oxford University Press, Oxford 1985, p.191.

32. C. Larmore, *Patterns of Moral Complexity*, Cambridge University Press, Cambridge 1987, pp.129-30.

33. J. Rawls, *Political Liberalism*, Columbia University Press, New York 1993; T. Nagel, 'Moral Conflict and Political Legitimacy', *Philosophy and Public Affairs*, 16, 1987; T. Nagel, *Equality and Partiality*, Oxford University Press, Oxford 1991.

34. R. Dworkin, 'Liberal Community', in S. Avineri and A. de-Shalit (eds.), *Communitarianism and Individualism*, Oxford University Press, Oxford 1992; R. Dworkin, 'The Foundations of Liberal Equality', in S. Darwall (ed.), *Equal Freedom: Selected Tanner Lectures on Human Values*, University of Michigan Press, Ann Arbor 1995; J. Waldron, *Liberal Rights*, *op.cit.*

35. Waldron, *ibid.* p.57.

36. J. Finnis, *Natural Law and Natural Right*, Clarendon Press, Oxford 1980; J. Raz, *The Morality of Freedom*, Clarendon Press, Oxford 1986; W. Galston, *Liberal Purposes*, Cambridge University Press, Cambridge 1989.

37. Finnis 1980, *op.cit.* p.220.

38. J. Raz, *The Morality of Freedom, op.cit.* p.133.

39. Cf. W. Kymlicka, *Contemporary Political Philosophy, op.cit..* pp.85-90.

41. J. Dunn, *Western Political Theory in the Face of the Future*, Cambridge University Press, Cambridge 1978, p.28.

42. Liberals, it is often argued, overlook the fact that these values must be supported by communal ties, or how sexual or racial discrimination may constitute specific ways in which freedom may be suppressed.

43. Cf. W. Connolly, 'The Dilemma of Legitimacy', in W. Connolly (ed.), *The Legitimacy of the State*, Basil Blackwell, Oxford 1984.

39. C. Beitz, *Political Theory and International Relations*, Princeton University Press, Princeton 1979; J. Rawls, 'The Law of Peoples', in S. Shute and S. Hurley (eds.), *On Human Rights: The Oxford Amnesty Lectures 1993*, Basic Books, New York 1993.

44. W. Kymlicka, *Multicultural Citizenship*, Clarendon Press, Oxford 1995.

45. A. Buchanan, *Secession: The Morality of Political Divorce from Fort Sumter to Quebec*, Westview, Boulder 1991; D. Gauthier, 'Breaking Up: An Essay on Secession', *Canadian Journal of Philosophy*, 1994; P Lehning (ed), *Theories of Secession*, Routledge, London 1997.

Democratic Socialism and Social Democracy[1]

Tony Fitzpatrick

Introduction

Many insist that the events of the last quarter of the twentieth century constitute an epitaph for left-wing political thought.[2] For some, the demise of the Left is demonstrated by the collapse of communism in the East and the increasing conservatism of social democracy in the West. The end of history has arrived and liberal democratic capitalism is the centre of gravity around which societies must orbit. Others go even further, insisting that the Left–Right political spectrum no longer reflects the reality of contemporary political attitudes. A radical politics may still exist, but not one which refers back to the project of the Left.

Are such critiques justified? Do we now live in a world where 'the Left' signifies nothing more than an historical movement whose time has passed? If so, does this mean that the future is to be dominated by varieties of right-wing thought, or is it that the world is now post-ideological? Or, alternatively, have rumours of the Left's demise been somewhat premature? This chapter will attempt to address these questions.

In the following section I shall outline the principal features of democratic socialism and social democracy, these being the dominant movements of the non-Marxist, non-revolutionary Left as it is addressed in this chapter. This term 'the Left' will therefore refer, generically, to both democratic socialism and social democracy. The chapter will also look at some of the main criticisms which have been at democratic socialism and social democracy, and at whether declarations concerning the death of the left-wing project are indeed premature. Finally I will examine some of the main responses which democratic socialists and social democrats have made to their critics.

History and Theory

It is all too easy to equate socialism with revolution and social democracy with reformism. Any such equation, however, is a betrayal of an influential political tradition: a non-revolutionary socialism which, while recognising the virtues and accepting the constraints of representative democracy, has nevertheless sought to be both more radical and utopian than social democracy. As such, no essay on the non-Marxist Left would be complete without reference to democratic socialism as well as to social democracy.

What I propose, therefore, is to characterise democratic socialism and social democracy according to their critiques of, and strategies towards, private capital. To be on the Left is to object to many, if not all, of the consequences of the system of private capital, i.e. social inequality and exploitation. Yet there has never been a consensus on the Left as to what such objections should actually prescribe.

Democratic socialism has been characterised by an oppositional stance towards private capital. While remaining sceptical about the historical materialism and economic analysis of Marxism, socialists have sought to confront and restrict the operation of private capital, e.g. through general strikes or through an advocacy of industrial democracy and workers' control. Socialists, then, have conceived of a distinct, non-capitalist socio-economic system.

Social democracy, meanwhile, has been characterised by an 'assimilationist' stance towards private capital. Social democrats have shared elements of the democratic socialist critique, but have been far more sceptical regarding the prospects for a radical alternative. As such, they have sought an accommodation with capitalism on the basis that no distinct socialist system is achievable, at least not in the short term. Social democrats, therefore, have argued for the creation of a 'socialised capitalism' through such things as the provision of workers' rights and the creation of a welfare state in a mixed economy of full employment.

So, both democratic socialists and social democrats have agreed upon the desirability and necessity of parliamentary democracy, but the former have wanted to inhibit the free movement and operation of capital in order to bring about a socialist system, while the latter have wanted to improve the mobility and rights of labour in order to socialise capitalism.

We must be wary of making too inflexible a distinction. Many democratic socialists have also been social democrats in that they have accepted the necessity of a moderate political strategy in the short-term; many social democrats have also been democratic socialists, in that they have accepted the possibility of a distinct socialist society and economy in the long term. Nevertheless, I think that we can identify the following four stages in the evolution of democratic socialism and social democracy during this century.[3]

The first stage runs from 1889 to 1917, roughly the period of the Second International – one of the historical bodies which attempted to unite socialist parties on a global basis. At that time, the terms democratic socialism and social democracy were often used interchangeably. This is because, in terms of both ideology and organisation, the Left was still in the process of formation and such terms had not yet 'settled down' and so were often used without much distinction being made between them. Eduard Bernstein, one of the most influential of socialist thinkers, regarded social democracy as the gradual dissolution of capitalism through socialist transformation.[4] With the First World War and the Bolshevik revolution, however, the Second International fell apart and democratic socialism and social democracy began to diverge in terms of both meaning and implication.

The second stage extends from the end of the first period up until the 1970s. During this time, social democracy was regarded by many as a more moderate means towards distinctively socialist ends.[5] Fabian gradualism, for instance, embodied this means-end conception and so epitomises the early part of this period. However, with the creation of the welfare state, the retreat of *laissez faire* economic orthodoxy, the creation of state ownership and the emergence of a universal suffrage, a genuinely socialised capitalism, rather than a completely new form of socialist society, at last began to seem an achievable reality.

We may therefore identify a third stage, extending from the Second World War up until the 1980s. Many came to regard socialism not so much as an *end* of social democratic reformism as its *symbolic motivation*: not an ideal to be realised, but an ideal to inspire.[6] For Tony Crosland, it had become a waste of time to look beyond the mixed economy; he believed that the Left should occupy itself with achieving equality of opportunity in a socialised capitalism where the capitalist class had ceased to dominate.[7]

As we can see, the second and third stages overlap to a considerable extent, thirty years or more, and the British Labour Party, especially, experienced a number of civil wars between those who interpreted socialism as a social and historical goal and those for whom it was merely a symbolic ideal. Without wishing to pretend that such debates and disputes have faded entirely we may now also identify a fourth stage.[8]

The period since the 1970s has been characterised not so much by an absence of ideas as a lack of confidence: the triumph of the New Right, parliamentary defeats, the perceived crisis of welfare, the retreat of Keynesian economics and the collapse of command economics, all of these factors threw the Left onto the defensive and engendered a sense of crisis even amongst those who worked hard to reconsider and reconstruct.[9] Socialism, whether as an end or as a motivation, has struggled both for a voice and for a constituency; social democracy has come to accept much of the New Right agenda.[10] What, then, is Left?

Let us consider that question in terms of the Left's basic principles, values and critiques using the following three headings.

Society and Human Nature

The misconception to be avoided here is the belief that the Left is anti-individualistic.

Society is often described in either holistic or individualistic terms and many have insisted that the Left subscribes to the former while the Right subscribes to the latter. The New Right, in particular, has been quick to accuse the Left of being politically and economically hostile to individual liberty. Indeed, given its suspicion of or downright opposition to capitalism, the history of the Left is littered with those who have accepted such a characterisation themselves and so have adopted an anti-individualist stance. Yet whereas the Left has had its share of anti-individualists, the Right has had its share of crude libertarians. In truth, though, both the Left and the Right draw upon holistic and individualistic explanations of both society and human nature.[11] The difference is in *how* they attempt to do so.

The Right tends to be either ahistorical or non-materialistic, to focus upon the imperfectability of humanity and to ignore political and economic contexts. The libertarian Right takes current forms of human nature and social interaction and interprets these forms as universal and natural, i.e. as ahistorical and not socially constructed; the conservative Right are more historical in their analysis but look to cultural rather than to material factors in order to explain social development. The Left, by contrast, believes that by changing our social environments we can improve human nature, even if that may not mean achieving a perfect ideal. Therefore, in order to do this, we need an approach which will identify and help rectify the injustices and imperfections to be found in our social environments.

Basically, then, the Left gives an historicised reading of the material interactions between human nature and its social contexts. Two points follow from this. Firstly, the Left's project is one of emancipation and liberation because the existing social environment is thought to stifle human potential, shaped as it is by capitalist forces. Secondly, this project must imply a cooperative ethos dedicated to the dismantling of all illegitimate inequalities and power relations.

Egalitarian Social Justice

The New Right usually regard liberty and equality as mutually exclusive: the more we have of one, the less we have of another. Therefore, unless equality is defined in purely formal terms, e.g. equality before the law, the New Right remain largely hostile towards it. There *are* those on the Right who make appeal to the concept of social justice, but usually in terms of social cohesion and stability rather than equality. By contrast, the Left is committed to a social egalitarianism of one form or another.[12] It is these differences which emerge when we consider what kind of environment is necessary to human well-being.

Both democratic socialists and social democrats object to the source, the form, the degree and the consequences of the inequalities which are generated by free market capitalism. The source of inequality is held to be the concentration of capital in private hands. This concentration means that most individuals are only able to enter into the labour market on terms vastly unfavourable to themselves. So, those who ultimately produce society's wealth are seen as receiving less of it in return, in the form of wages, than they deserve. Inequality takes the form of exploitation, therefore. But capitalism not only produces an unjust *form* of inequality but also undesirable *degrees* of inequality. Many have interpreted poverty and unemployment as caused by capitalism's need to maintain unemployment in order to drag wages down and thus increase the returns to capital. So, capitalist society grows wealthier by continually reproducing unacceptable amounts of inequality. And such inequality has many negative effects: poverty breeds ill-health, higher mortality rates and crime.

This account of why the Left opposes inequality is simplistic – not least because it does not distinguish poverty from inequality – but it does capture one of the Left's basic intuitions: an environment is socially just where individual liberty and social equality are mutually reinforcing.[13]

At this point, though, democratic socialists and social democrats tend to part company. The former believe that it is necessary to re-structure capitalism totally in order to eliminate the source of inequality; the latter argue that capitalism has altered in such a way as to make such an upheaval both unnecessary and counter-productive. Democratic socialists believe that exploitation is an inherent feature of capitalism, whereas social democrats have gradually dropped all reference to exploitation. Both have, in recent years, appealed to Rawls's 'difference principle' (see chapter on Contemporary Liberalism) as a way of criticising the inequality produced by free markets. But social democrats then tend to appeal simply to an equality of opportunity, i.e. a 'starting-gate' equality where competitors line up equally at the start of the social race and are subject to the same rules. Socialists, though, insist that to ignore equality of outcome, i.e. 'finishing-line' equality, is both incoherent and naive; for unless the positions of the competitors at the end of the race are equalised then the next race will fail to embody an equality of opportunity. Despite these differences, democratic socialists and social democrats have both traditionally appealed to statist solutions to social problems.

States and Markets

To be on the Left is to believe that it is naive to separate economic power from political power; for those who are able to mobilise the greatest economic resources invariably have greatest control over the political process and the political agenda. The Left therefore subscribes to what might be called an 'economic elitist' account of the capitalist state, which is seen to act largely in the interests of the economically privileged and powerful. In some respects, this resembles the Marxist insistence that the existing state is an instrument for the accumulation of capital, though the non-marxist Left draw back from identifying a 'ruling class' and from the notion that class conflict is the engine of social progress. So, the non-Marxist Left believe not only that economic elitism entails a political elitism, but that the state is somehow capable of being transformed into a properly pluralistic and democratic institution without a revolution.

Traditionally, both democratic socialists and social democrats have conceived of the working class as the agents of social progress, with progressive change coming about through the representatives of the workers gaining power within both the industrial and the political spheres. By forming trade unions and labour parties, the labour movement would thereby challenge the supremacy of capitalist elites: the state would come to guarantee the rights and interests of all, and markets would be reformed to serve properly democratic ends. So, while differing in their attitudes towards private capital, socialists and social democrats have both broadly supported statist solutions to the problems of capitalist markets; solutions such as state ownership, regulation and control, and a welfare state.[14] In short, they have interpreted the state as being, potentially, a 'countervailing force' to capitalism and the free market.

This, then, describes the basic position of the Left in terms of its critiques, values and strategies, a position which has never been under as much attack as over the last twenty years.

Criticisms

Before considering whether 'the Left' is a redundant term or not, there are three critiques of democratic socialism and social democracy which ought to be mentioned: feminist, ecological and postmodernist. New Right criticisms will not be dealt with since these are reviewed in detail elsewhere in this book.

Whilst much feminist thought has been sympathetic to the Left, or at least not overtly hostile, both democratic socialists and social democrats have been accused of intellectually preserving the sexual division of labour, of ignoring the importance of gender as a social relation and of retaining a conception of the public sphere as a sphere of male interests and activities. In short, the Left has been criticised for doing relatively little to challenge the patriarchal sources of women's oppression by focusing obsessively upon the workplace (historically dominated by men) and by defining the social rights of citizenship according to male employment patterns; for example, structuring the welfare state around unemployment benefit based upon national insurance contributed from wages. All too often, the Left's egalitarianism has overlooked the different identities and needs of women, and its notion of emancipation has equated oppression with a particular mode of ownership and control rather than gender relations. As such, male dominated trade unions and labour parties have been charged with doing little to recognise and advance the non-class-specific interests of women.

Ecological thought, also, has been critical of the Left. With few exceptions, socialists and social democrats have adopted an anthropocentric ethic which regards nature as a material resource to be manipulated according to potentially endless human needs and desires. Ecologists accuse the Left of perpetuating an understanding of the goal of an improved standard of living which is based upon industrial and economic concerns and which ignores post-materialist values, attitudes and practices. Democratic socialism has attempted to 'outbid' capitalism by proclaiming itself to be even more economically efficient and growth-friendly; social democracy has accommodated itself to capitalism by thinking of economic growth as the precondition of distributive justice. Accordingly, the Left has remained trapped within the entire discourse of liberal equality which fails to recognise that Man (*sic*) is *not* the measure of all things.

Nor are ecologists particularly happy about the statism of the Left. In many respects, they agree that the state can function as an effective instrument for achieving certain objectives; yet, in other respects, the Left's statism has helped to institute an impersonal bureaucratic and administrative society which organises itself through surveillance and benign forms of control. In short, ecological thought often shares with the Left a concern for justice and participation, but it wishes to revise fundamentally the meanings of these concepts to take account of a biocentric or ecocentric ethic.

Postmodern theory also offers various challenges to left-wing thought. According to Lyotard, the postmodern era is one characterised by incredulity towards all grand narratives, towards all attempts to describe and explain the world in terms of a single ideological system.[15] Both democratic socialism and social democracy therefore stand condemned as deluded attempts to speak for all people at all places and, perhaps, at all times.

In addition, such universal narratives have the effect of marginalising and 'terrorising' those different values or ways of life which they can neither acknowledge nor encompass. What such grand narratives do is to assume the existence of essences – God, History, Human

Nature, Reason etc. – which are identified as the basis or foundation of reality. Or rather, the postmodernists insist, such narratives *construct* those essences themselves, represent them as fundamental and then use them to impose hierarchies and divisions, of one form or another, onto the world. In the vocabulary of the Left, it has usually been labour, or rationally-motivated production, which has been defined as the essence of 'human being'. Consequently, the working class has been interpreted as the agent of social progress and justice and as the 'bearer' of a future society. This is the very kind of universalism and essentialism which postmodernists condemn as dangerous and redundant. These arguments have also been deployed against other ideologies, including feminism and ecologism, but it is the Left which has experienced the greatest challenge in this respect.[16]

Before moving on, it might be as well to ask whether it is possible and desirable to continue to organise political debate around the concept of a Left–Right spectrum. Firstly, it seems reasonable to dismiss those who insist that 'the Left' no longer signifies anything of contemporary value, with only variations of capitalism left to consider. Such arguments are themselves ideological manoeuvres, since the most effective way to blow your opponents out of the water is to persuade yourself, others, and eventually your opponents, that their ship is sinking anyway. For just as it would be naive to imagine that no challenges to democratic socialism and social democracy have been made over the last twenty years, it would be equally simplistic to pretend that the Left has been wiped from the political landscape. Democratic socialism and social democracy remain, if for no other reason than that the Right could not live without them: epitaphs for the Left are often composed in the same breath as dire warnings about the pheonix-like qualities of left-wing thought.

Secondly, however, what about the suggestion that the Left–Right spectrum *in its entirety* is no longer of value? Is that spectrum merely the relic of a former age? Does a radical politics now have to look beyond the old categories?

In many respects, announcing the demise of the Left–Right spectrum is both a highly original and a highly conservative thing to do. It is original because it recognises that new political actors and ideas have emerged which go a long way to subverting a simple Left–Right distinction, e.g. the new social movements.[17] Yet there is also a rather conservative mind-set behind the epitaph. Those who persist in referring to the spectrum are condemned as clinging to something which no longer describes present realities. In other words, the job of political concepts is to mirror or represent the world 'out there' and once the world out there changes, so must our concepts. Yet this 'model of representation' is itself highly one-sided and simplistic. There is nothing about a Left–Right spectrum which makes it an all-or-nothing representation of the way things are; rather, it always has been, and continues to be, a convenient *and partial* way of understanding and shaping the world. So, the intellectual conservatives are not those who continue to refer to the spectrum, but those who jettison it in an act of reification. It is those who would abandon all reference to a Left–Right spectrum who may be accused of taking it too seriously.

Recent Developments

The project of re-construction which the Left has been engaged in since the early 1980s may be briefly summarised under the following four headings.

Pluralist Socialism

Socialism has often embraced pluralism in practice without necessarily acknowledging it in principle. All too often, it has imagined that a desirable diversity of lifestyles and identities can only truly be achieved once capitalism has been transcended or at least radically humanised. But, according to Michael Rustin, radical left programmes

> ... must now be both universalist, in seeking a common definition of social rights and obligations, and pluralist in recognising unavoidable and indeed desirable differences in social values.[18]

The Left is therefore more receptive than it once was to the need for a 'plurality of differences' and this represents at least some accommodation to postmodernist critiques.

The Left's pluralism implies a pluralism of agency and of space. As already indicated, the working class have traditionally been thought of as the agents of progressive reform. A socialist or social democratic future was in the best interests of the workers and, therefore, recognising this, the workers would mobilise for such a future sooner or later. But it is rare these days to find those who insist that *only* the working class should be thought of as the agents of progressive reform. The Left has long since acknowledged that the interests of the middle class, of women, of ethnic minority communities, of disabled people, of gays and lesbians, and of broader social and protest movements cannot be reduced to variations of working-class interests.

The sheer complexity of such interests, however, means that no ready-made political programme suggests itself. Social democrats have increasingly looked to the middle class, both for their values and aspirations and for their votes. Democratic socialists range from those who still regard the working class as the foundation of the Left project, to those who insist that the Left must embrace a diversity of class, protest and social movements, to those who argue that it is misguided to talk of such movements as if their identities and interests were pre-given.[19] But, whatever the disagreements, the Left in general now acknowledges the existence of, and the need for, plural agencies and actors.

Similarly, it is also more pluralistic in its conception of the 'spaces' within which agents are to be found. Democratic socialists and social democrats, often for good reasons, have usually favoured statist solutions to the problems of free market capitalism. Yet, while it would be naive to abandon the notion of the state as a 'countervailing force', the last twenty years has seen a greater emphasis being given to civil society.[20]

Bobbio has identified political power as spreading outwards from individuals considered solely as citizens, to

> ... the sphere of social relations where individuals are considered in terms of the various functions they may have and the roles they may play in specific situations.[21]

Or, in other words, to a civil society of semi-public associations such as interest groups, social clubs, religious bodies etc, etc. Many, then, have come to regard civil society as a space of free association rather than as either a market-based space of contracts and consumption, as for the Right, or as a space of political consumers and clients, as for the statist Left. Many differences of emphasis and interpretation obviously exist, but a pluralistic civil society is now of central importance to left-wing thought.[22]

The unifying element here is a conception of citizenship as implying equal autonomy: citizens being those who carry with them universal rights and obligations which give an expressive force to diversity within the overlapping, complex associations of civil society.[23] This concern for citizenship also explains the greater support now found on the Left for electoral and constitutional reform – which used to be regarded as a diversion from truly radical reform.

So, whereas previously a progressive future was imagined to involve political consensus and harmony, a pluralism of agencies and spaces suggests to the Left a future worth fighting for precisely because the struggle for justice, equality and autonomy is now recognised to be an endless one. Pluralistic socialism is that which struggles towards the conflicts and the contradictions of the future in the belief that they will, in some way, be superior to the conflicts and contradictions of the past.

Ecosocialism

Many on the Left have become receptive to ecological perspectives, yet the ecological case has by no means been accepted uncritically. Ecologists, the argument goes, have been rather too quick to condemn both capitalist and socialist modes of production and rather too simplistic in representing themselves as being 'beyond Left and Right'. According to Weston, it is poverty which lies behind all environmental problems, whether they be physical or social.[24] And because poverty is the flip-side of the economics of profit and loss, it is *capitalism*, rather than industrialism *per se*, which is the root cause of environmental degradation. Weston does rather overstate the case; much left-wing thought *has* accepted capitalistic arguments regarding the virtues of unlimited growth. Nevertheless, for more than a decade now, there has been a widespread re-examination of leftist traditions in order to find non-industrial strategies and ideas. The purpose has been to develop a Red-Green *social* ecology suitable for the twenty-first century.[25]

Ecosocialism has come to imply the following social ecology.[26] Firstly, its notion of environmentalism is still a broadly humanist one, though it also involves an attempt to subvert the 'anthropocentrism versus biocentrism' debate (see the chapter on Green political thought). The modified humanism of ecosocialism is one which tries to avoid over-emphasising either the human or the natural.

Secondly, this social ecology means that we should not abandon questions concerning the ownership of capital.[27] At their worst, ecologists regard such questions as irrelevant – an attitude which leads some actively to *support* capitalism on the basis that nothing should divert us from pursuing specifically Green objectives.

But according to ecosocialists, *what* is produced cannot be separated from who owns the means of production. Capitalism cannot be painted

Green because its bottom line is always capital accumulation, which is resistant to all but the most minimal restrictions on the operation of market exchange. Indeed, when the Right do take account of Green thought they either defend supply and demand solutions to ecological problems or else highlight some of the conservative characteristics of the ecological cause.[28] According to ecosocialists, Greens must identify themselves far more with the Left than with the Right, which involves making some difficult decisions regarding ownership.

Thirdly, however, the Left must shift *its* position also and recognise that industrial and statist solutions to the problems of capitalist production are neither sustainable nor desirable. This partly means retrieving those traditions from left-wing thought that somehow became submerged, traditions of an anarchist or utopian nature.[29] Andre Gorz, for instance, draws upon the example of early socialist movements which took as their aim the abolition of waged labour, in contrast to the industrialised labour movement, which has often accepted an 'employment ethic' uncritically. For Gorz, it is the freeing of individuals from many of the necessities of work in the formal economy which the Left must re-establish at the heart of its project.[30]

In short, the ecosocialist project is the attempt to reconcile environmental sustainability and social justice.

Market Socialism

The debate concerning market socialism dates back to the 1920s when some socialists argued that the market coordination of production, allocation and distribution could be combined with the widespread common ownership of the means of production and that in this way the benefits of both markets and planning could be utilised. The debate subsided and remained dormant for over forty years. Then, with the intellectual fatigue of social democracy and the obvious failures of state planning, theories of market socialism came to prominence once again. In its most recent formulations, the state has a relatively minor role to play and greater importance is now attached to worker ownership and control. Governments would set an overall investment plan but economic activity would then proceed on the basis of competition between firms – competition both for custom and for investment funds lent by public banks at competitive rates of interest.[31] The literature on this type of latter-day market socialism is now immense.[32]

Market socialism is held to be desirable for three basic reasons. Firstly, some argue that it embodies the long-standing left-wing aim of carrying the liberal democratic project forward into the social and industrial spheres. It would guarantee individual liberty and political equality without creating objectionable levels of social inequality. Secondly, market socialism implies the common ownership of much (though not all) productive property, without the inefficient state bureaucracies of the old Soviet Union. Thirdly, with a greater role for workers' ownership and control, the market socialist system would be less likely to be characterised by exploitation and alienation.

There are several major criticisms, however. Gray has observed that workers simply do not desire a cooperative economy, for if they did then one would have been created long ago.[33] A counter-argument, however, observes that it is the free market nature of capitalism which means investment decisions are made in favour of profit-oriented firms. Cooperatives are undesired only because the workings of a capitalist economy makes them undesirable.[34]

Another objection insists that a market socialist economy would be unstable: either its public investment banks would cause it to implode back into a system of state centralisation, or, if they were truly autonomous and competitive, such banks would eventually become private bodies, meaning that market socialism would revert back into market capitalism. This argument, though, seems to depend upon the old 'black and white' logic of the Right which says that the only alternative to dwelling in the capitalist market-place is the (short) march down the road to serfdom.[35]

One final point, however, is more damaging. Very little work has been done on whether a market socialist economy would be environmentally sustainable. In one respect, market socialism is in accord with the Green demand for greater decentralisation and participation, yet is it really consistent with the non-industrial concerns of ecological thought? Perhaps, if market socialism and Green economics are to converge, we should not think of the former as an all-or-nothing, once-and-for-all reform of existing social relations and market practices. But if this is the case then can we talk of anything which is distinctively market *socialist* in the first place?

Radical Pragmatism

Associating radicalism with pragmatism may seem contradictory. Radicalism tends to be thought of in ideological terms, as an attempt to reform society according to a specific set of ideas; pragmatism tends to be thought of as the adaptation of ideas to social realities. But the term 'radical pragmatism' is intended to have two meanings.

Firstly, it means the project of making radicalism more pragmatic. For instance, some have characterised the Left as having been traditionally concerned with end states, with the designing of futuristic blueprints, whereas the need now is for a 'generative politics' which is concerned with the process of change itself.[36] The Left, in short, must embrace an anti-utopian radicalism. Secondly, 'radical pragmatism' refers to the attempt to make pragmatism more radical i.e. the attempt to redefine the political landscape according to a new set of ideological values. The New Right were radically pragmatic in this sense and many on the Left have wished to emulate their success.

Essentially, then, radical pragmatism does not so much imply a set of values, policies and ends, as a strategic vision of reform. Within this strategic vision, three 'tendencies' may be identified. Firstly, there is a liberal tendency to re-position the Left in terms of the individualist values of freedom, choice and opportunity. Liberty is claimed as an age-old left-wing virtue which, to be meaningful, must also imply a social inter-dependence rather than the kind of aggressive individualism of the New Right. This liberal tendency has been articulated both by politicians and by academics, some of the latter seeking to construct a Left-libertarian position.[37]

A communitarian tendency has also emerged. Here, both politicians and academics have wished the Left to utilise 'community' rather than 'equality' or 'society' as an inspirational concept.[38] What this implies is the attempt to distance the Left from its statist, egalitarian past without embracing a simplistic *laissez-faire* form of economics and social inter-action.[39] Amitai Etzioni has been an important influence and it has become commonplace to stress civic obligations and responsibilities as the corollary of social rights and entitlements.[40] However, a stress on community can have either a conservative or a reflexive emphasis.

A community can be defined as an homogenous, pre-given set of social relations, usually located within a particular geographical area. The politics of a community defined in this way tends to be oriented towards a defence of tradition, order and hierarchy; forces which are often hostile to left-wing thought.[41] But there is also a reflexive definition which sees communities as dynamic forms of association with no fixed identity or set of interests. Giddens, for instance, talks of contemporary society as a post-traditional order within which nothing, e.g. no authority or institution, can escape the force of dialogue, debate and critique.[42]

The third tendency might be thought of as an attempt to encompass both liberalism and this reflexive version of communitarianism. Radical democrats say that in an age of indeterminacy the one certainty we are left with is the desirability of democracy. So, radical democrats are those who would have the democratic imperative infiltrate every aspect of social organisation and political identity in order to encourage the general acceptance of conflict and pluralism, as well as what can be called an 'equality of differences'.[43] Again, the attempt here is to define the Left as a process of change, rather than according to specific social and political objectives. Therefore, radical democracy is both liberal, since it emphasises a politics of empowerment and liberation, and communitarian, since it observes that individuals' sense of self and well-being is dependent upon the relatively stable social contexts which we shape and in which we are shaped.

Conclusion

Each of the above represents some attempt to address the kinds of criticisms outlined in the third section. However, there is one omission. Whilst there has been something identifiable as a socialist *feminism*, I am less sure that a distinctive feminist *socialism* can be said to have emerged.[44] But whether this really is the case, and what significance it holds, is a discussion that cannot be pursued here.

Traditionally, the Right has discovered its utopias in the past while the Left has anticipated the formation of *its* utopias in the future. Recently, these positions have inverted somewhat: the Right has become more forward-looking and willing to construct capitalist utopias in the present, whereas the Left has been in danger either of becoming lost in a past golden age or of losing itself in the minutiae of the present. The Left's task today is finally to leave behind the vocabulary of decline and collapse in order to renew not just itself but wider society also.[45] Not just socialism for a sceptical age, but a Left which heralds an era less obsessed than ours with cynicism, disaffection, insecurity and short-termism.

Notes

1. I would like to thank Chris Pierson and Alison Assiter for their comments on earlier versions of this chapter.

2. This has been a mantra of the New Right, of course; and although he is now in a post-Thatcherite guise, John Gray insists that even new, moderate forms of social democracy are effectively redundant. See: J. Gray, *Endgames: Questions in Late Modern Political Thought*, Polity, Cambridge 1997, pp.11-50.

3. Whereas I was initially reluctant to impose too strict a chronology on these four stages, Donald Sassoon's recent encyclopaedic history of socialism provides some evidence for the periodisation presented: see, D. Sassoon, *One Hundred Years of Socialism: the West European Left in the Twentieth Century*, I.B. Taurus, London 1996.

4. E. Bernstein, *Evolutionary Socialism: a Criticism and Affirmation*, Schocken Books, New York 1961.

5. Sassoon observes that Left governments easily became fixated with this socialist future, to the extent that they were often less progressive than they could and should have been; see, Sassoon, *One Hundred Years of Socialism: the West European Left in the Twentieth Century, op.cit.*, pp.58-9.

6. *Ibid*, p.134, p.166, pp.197-99, pp.240-47.

7. A. Crosland, *The Future of Socialism*, Jonathan Cape, London 1956.

8. Sassoon, *op.cit.*, pp.733-35.

9. E.J. Hobsbawm, *The Forward March of Labour Halted?*, New Left Books, London 1981; G. Kitching, *Rethinking Socialism: a Theory for a Better Practice*, Methuen & Co, London 1983; T. Wright, *Socialisms: Theories and Practices*, Oxford University Press, Oxford 1987; R. Blackburn (ed), *After the Fall: the Failure of Communism and the Future of Socialism*, Verso, London 1991.

10. As Berki feared it would; see, R. N. Berki, *Socialism*, Dent, London 1975, p.38.

11. R. Keat, 'Liberal Rights and Socialism', in K. Graham (ed), *Contemporary Political Philosophy*, Cambridge University Press, Cambridge 1982.

12. For a dissenting view, B. Barry, *Liberty and Justice: Essays in Political Theory 2*, Clarendon Press, Oxford 1989.

13. R. Plant, *Equality, Markets and the New Right*, Fabian Tract 494, London 1984; B. Crick, *Socialism*, Open University Press, Milton Keynes 1987, pp.84-108; J. Franklin (ed), *Equality*, IPPR, London 1997.

14. C. Boggs, *The Socialist Tradition: from Crisis to Decline*, Routledge, London 1995.

15. J-F. Lyotard, *The Postmodern Condition: a Report on Knowledge*, Manchester University Press, Manchester 1984.

16. P. Beilharz, *Postmodern Socialism: Romanticism, City and the State*, Melbourne University Press, Carlton 1994.

17. Something which is readily acknowledged by those for whom the spectrum continues to have value. See T. Fitzpatrick, 'Postmodernism, Welfare and Radical Politics', *Journal of Social Policy*, vol. 25, no. 3, 1996, pp.303-30; also, N. Bobbio, *Left and Right. The Significance of a Political Distinction*, Polity, Cambridge 1996.

18. M. Rustin, *For a Pluralist Socialism*, Verso, London 1985; also, M. Walzer, *Spheres of Justice: a Defence of Pluralism and Equality*, Blackwell, Oxford 1983.

19. For a class analysis, E. Meiksins Wood, *The Retreat from Class: a New 'True' Socialism*, Verso, London 1986; for an attempt to relate class and social movements, M. Harrington, *Socialism: Past and Future*, Pluto Press, London 1993; for a post-structuralist analysis, E. Laclau & C. Mouffe, *Hegemony and Socialist Strategy*, Verso, London 1985.

20. J. Keane (ed), *Civil Society and the State: New European Perspectives*, Verso, London 1988; J. Keane, *Democracy and Civil Society*, Verso, London 1988; H. Wainwright, *Arguing for a New Left*, Blackwell, Oxford 1994; P. Hirst, *Associative Democracy*, Polity, Cambridge 1994; J. Cohen & J. Rogers, *Associations and Democracy*, Verso, London 1995.

21. N. Bobbio, *The Future of Democracy*, Polity, Cambridge 1987, p.54.

22. For a dissenting view, A. Levine, *Arguing for Socialism: Theoretical Considerations*, Routledge & Kegan Paul Ltd., London 1984.

23. See the work of David Held, for instance *Democracy and the Global Order*, Polity, Cambridge 1995.

24. J. Weston (ed), *Red and Green: the New Politics of the Environment*, Pluto Press, London 1986.

25. R. Bahro, *Socialism and Survival*, Heretic Books, London 1982; M. Ryle, *Ecology and Survival*, Radius, London 1988; T. Benton, *Natural Relations: Ecology, Animal Rights and Social Justice*, Verso, London 1993.

26. D. Pepper, *Eco-socialism: from Deep Ecology to Social Justice*, Routledge, London 1993, pp.232-35.

27. See the kind of articles published in the journal *Capitalism, Nature, Socialism*.

28. T. Fitzpatrick, 'The Implications of Ecological Thought for Social Welfare', *Critical Social Policy*, no. 54, 1998, pp.5-26.

29. See, B. Frankel, *The Post-Industrial Utopians: a Critical Assessment*, Polity, Cambridge 1987.

30. A. Gorz, *Critique of Economic Reason*, Verso, London 1989; A. Gorz, *Capitalism, Socialism, Ecology*, Verso, London 1994.

31. A. Buchanan, *Ethics, Efficiency and the Market*, Clarendon, Oxford 1985.

32. For supporters of market socialism: R.A. Dahl, *A Preface to Economic*

Democracy, Polity, Cambridge 1985; J. Le Grand & S. Estrin (eds), *Market Socialism*, Clarendon, Oxford 1989; D. Miller, *Market, State and Community: Theoretical Foundations of Market Socialism*, Clarendon, Oxford 1989; H. Breitenbach, T. Burden & D. Coates, *Features of a Viable Socialism*, Harvester Wheatsheaf, Hemel Hempstead 1990; A. Nove, *The Economics of Feasible Socialism Revisited*, 2nd edition, Allen & Unwin, London, 1991; J. Roemer, *A Future for Socialism*, Verso, London 1994.

For Left opponents:

E. Mandel, 'In Defence of Socialist Planning', *New Left Review*, no. 159, 1986, pp.5-37; E. Mandel, 'The Myth of Market Socialism', *New Left Review*, no. 169, 1988, pp.108-20; P. Devine, *Democracy and Economic Planning*, Polity, Cambridge 1988.

For Right opponents:

A. De Jasay, *Market Socialism*, IEA, London 1990; J. Gray, *The Moral Foundations of Market Institutions*, IEA, London 1992.

For some general critiques:

C. Pierson, *Socialism After Communism: the New Market Socialism*, Polity, Cambridge 1995; J. Roemer, *Equal Shares: Making Market Socialism Work* (edited by E.O. Wright), Verso, London 1996.

33. J. Gray, *The Moral Foundations of Market Institutions, op.cit.*

34. J. Elster, 'From here to there, or: If Co-operative Ownership is Desirable, why are there so few Co-operatives?', *Social Philosophy and Policy*, vol. 6, no. 2, 1989, pp.93-111.

35. Compare, R. Unger, *False Necessity*, Cambridge University Press, Cambridge 1987.

36. D. Miliband (ed), *Reinventing the Left*, Polity, Cambridge 1994, pp.5-6.

37. R. Hattersley, *Choose Freedom: the Future for Democratic Socialism*, Joseph, London 1987; M. Meacher, *Diffusing Power: the Key to Socialist Revival*, Pluto Press, London 1992; H. Steiner, *An Essay on Rights*, Blackwell, Oxford 1994; P. Van Parijs, *Real Freedom for All: What (if anything) Can Justify Capitalism?*, Oxford University Press, Oxford 1995.

38. For a theoretical consideration, D. Miller, 'In What Sense must Socialism be Communitarian?', *Social Philosophy and Policy*, vol. 6, no. 2, 1989, pp.51-73.

39. Recently, the notion of stakeholding has been influential in this respect; see: G. Kelly, D. Kelly & A. Gamble (eds), *Stakeholder Capitalism*, Macmillan, London 1997; also, W. Hutton, *The State We're In*, 2nd edition, Vintage, London 1996.

40. A. Etzioni, *The Spirit of Community*, Fontana, London 1995.

41. D. Selbourne, *The Principle of Duty*, Sinclair-Stevenson, London 1994; for

a critique of conservative communitarianism, Z. Bauman, *Postmodernity and its Discontents*, Polity, Cambridge 1997.

42. U. Beck, A. Giddens, S. Lash, *Reflexive Modernisation: Politics Traditions and Aesthetics in the Modern Social Order*, Polity, Cambridge 1994.

43. C. Mouffe (ed), *Dimensions of Radical Democracy*, Verso, London 1993; C. Mouffe, *The Return of the Political*, Verso, London 1994; E. Laclau, *Emancipation(s)*, Verso, London 1996.

44. Z. Eisenstein, *Capitalist Patriarchy and the Case for Socialist Feminism*, Monthly Review Press, New York 1979; L. Segal & H. Wainwright, *Beyond the Fragments: Feminism and the Making of Socialism*, Newcastle Socialist Centre, Newcastle 1979; L. Segal, *Is the Future Female?*, Virago, London 1987; N. Fraser, *Unruly Practices: Power, Discourse and Gender in Contemporary Social Theory*, Polity, Oxford 1989; D. Haraway, *Simians, Cyborgs and Women: the Reinvention of Nature*, Free Association Books, London 1991.

45. R. Miliband, *Socialism for a Sceptical Age*, Polity, Cambridge 1994.

The New Right

Mike Harris

The New Right represented a 'new' social and political as well as economic project. It has provoked questions on citizenship and identity in addition to those on the size of the state and the role of markets. As a result, it has developed a complex relationship to conservatism. But the term itself is contentious. It has been suggested that the New Right is neither particularly 'new' nor exclusively 'right', and that it presents too diverse and contradictory a range of political thought to be one movement. Indeed, many of those associated with New Right thought reject the term. In keeping with this diversity and contradiction, this chapter identifies four broad strands of thought within the New Right: neo-liberalism, Public Choice, neo-conservatism and libertarianism. This chapter will study each on its own terms and explore the similarities and contradictions between them.

These strands represent a modern and radical project which responded to the changed politics and economic conditions of the 1970s and after, and shared a common focus of attack on the 'crisis' of the social democratic welfare state. Thus it goes beyond simply representing old ideas in new language and applying them to new issues. As Gamble has noted: 'The New Right would like to be conservative but they are forced to be radicals'.[1] They have had to identify how the existing state can be reformed in order to permit the restoration of the rules, the institutions and the culture of the free market. It is not then merely the attempt to return to nineteenth-century liberal and conservative values. Rather, the New Right represents the attempt to *remake* contemporary society. The purpose of this radicalism - the new market order - may be described as the 'great market re-transformation'. This can help explain in what ways and for what reasons, the different strands of thought within the New Right are linked. In particular, it suggests an important link between the desire for authority and inequality. This also means that the relationship between the New Right and conservatism may be re-examined.

Historical Roots

The New Right has never been a political movement in the conventional sense, but has had from its earliest stages a reasonably clear organisational form.[2] This form dates from just before the Second World War, and a conference in Paris in 1938 designed to unite a number of academics around the arguments made in Walter Lippmann's *The Good Society*. Among those in attendence were Raymond Aron, Friedrich von Hayek and Ludwig von Mises. All were concerned with the apparent decline of liberalism in Europe and were disillusioned with the collectivist values of the time. Out of this emerged the Mont Pelerin Society (established in 1947), an international congress of neo-liberal intellectuals.

Hayek's work in the 1930s was the beginning of his case against the central planning proposed by the growing followers of Keynes. In *The Road to Serfdom*,[3] a deliberately populist book, Hayek argued that there was no conceivable 'middle way' between totalitarianism/socialism (there was no real difference for Hayek) and the liberal society. Along with Karl Popper's *The Open Society and its Enemies*,[4] which similarly pitted liberalism against totalitarianism, the intellectual foundations of the neo-liberal New Right had been laid.

Many of the ideas of the New Right developed within 'think-tanks' and meetings between individuals. In Britain, there were three main organisations. From the mid-1950s, the Institute for Economic Affairs (IEA) had a strong commitment to limited government and the technical superiority of markets. From the mid-1970s, the Centre for Policy Studies (CPS), established by Margaret Thatcher and Keith Joseph, tried to link economic liberalism with traditional conservative themes of authority, order and responsibility. And subsequently, the Adam Smith Institute (ASI) developed a Public Choice-influenced political analysis, and a comprehensive programme for government reform.

These were joined by a multitude of other bodies which included amongst many others: the Salisbury Group, Conservative Philosophy

Group, the Conservative Family Campaign, the Conservative Political Centre, the National Association for Freedom (later the Freedom Association), and the Institute for the Study of Conflict. In addition there were longer established Conservative associations such as the Monday Club and the Selsdon Group.

It is also worth noting the importance of Enoch Powell in the public dissemination of New Right thought. Though usually associated with his views on immigration, of more significance was his development of 'Powellism'. This mix of neo-liberal economics (the limited state, dena-tionalisation and anti-corporatism), opposition to universal welfare rights, populism and conservative cultural traditionalism formulated a framework for the later development of Thatcherite ideas. As he argued:

> Whatever else the Conservative Party stands for, unless it is the party of capitalism then it has no function in the contemporary world, then it has nothing to say to modern Britain.[5]

The New Right only began to make significant impact in the 1970s, helped by the particular social, political and economic conditions shared across many western democracies. Its breakthrough was based on its increasingly public argument that the problems of inflation, trade union militancy, growing welfare expenditures, state monopolies, the denial of free consumer choice in the market, and the undermining of traditional social and moral values had produced a crisis.

The political context of the New Right's breakthrough into power was the 'failure' of Heath's Government, and the subsequent effort by a minority inside and outside the Conservative Party to renew its thought and governing capacity by drawing on New Right ideas. Indeed, the CPS was created to achieve this. Further, after the publica-tion of Buchannan and Tullock's *The Calculus of Consent*,[6] Public Choice Theory began to develop and be referred to by commentators in Britain as well as the United States.

Philosophical Aspects

What then are the core ideas of the New Right? Though they may disagree on many solutions, the four strands of New Right thought mentioned in the introduction share three targets. They resist egalitarianism, collectivism, and the 'new politics' of identity such as feminism, anti-racism and gay rights. But it is worth discussing each strand in more depth before suggesting the purpose of the New Right as a whole.

Neo-liberalism

Neo-liberalism draws on the 'classical liberal' tradition of individual autonomy and property rights, and a sharp distinction between the private and public spheres with the private having priority.

Neo-liberalism has always centred on a preference for the 'free market' but the revival of liberal political economy has gone further than arguments for the efficiency of market competition. Markets are now proposed as the foundation of the social order. They induce every individual to use their unique knowledge and abilities for their self-interest, but in a way which is said to benefit society as a whole. 'Planned' economies and societies cannot utilise these dispersed resources to the same effect. Market freedoms (particularly the owner-ship of private property) are seen to be the best guarantor of political and social liberties. Planned societies therefore erode freedom. Thus this 'freedom' maximised in markets (essentially, the satisfaction of wants) is *the* arbiter of social arrangements and policies.

State provision limits the role of market processes and, since it is financed by taxation, interferes with the maximum possible accumula-tion of private property. It undermines the two 'natural' channels through which an individual's needs are properly met: the private market and the family. Markets are said to work with the grain of 'human nature', the innate need for individual responsibility and self (and family) interest, and are not dependent on the vagaries of altruism and communal responsibility. As such, an expanded state does not restrain self-interest, but merely transfers it to the political sphere where the scope for abuse is greater. Social discord and the unjust distribution of rewards follows. For the neo-liberal, the proper role of the state has been obscured in the era of big government. Only a small proportion of the products and services supplied by the state are genuine 'public goods' such as national defence and security.[7]

Instead, and somewhat paradoxically, social integration should be promoted by the pursuit of independence via markets. Mutual respect is created not by explicit mutual dependence, but mutual indepen-dence. This is why freedom (defined with reference to markets, of course), rather than 'paternalism', is the only starting-point for responsibility. Contrary to the claims of socialists, the market does not erode freedom but is the arena in which it is encouraged and exercised.

Neo-liberals particularly resent the way in which justice and individual rights have become so strongly associated with the welfare ideal. A welfare safety net may be permissible to varying degrees but the idea of 'social justice' has led the state into providing inefficient and discriminatory services, and has convinced citizens that they are entitled to a certain standard of living merely because of membership of the community. The state, rather than being the guarantor of citizenship, instead becomes its greatest threat. Thus inequality can be justified because redistribution can not. Equality of opportunity (best provided by the market society) cannot co-exist with equality of results such as parity of income.[8]

However, in addition, neo-liberals have suggested that the market has greater egalitarian potential than the political or public sphere. Because of its wealth-generating ability, it benefits all to varying degrees. It has been argued that historically capitalism has reduced inequality, rather than being the motor producing it. But further, markets allow greater opportunities for lower classes in society than do political processes, which are restricted by cultural and social barriers such as class, contacts and ideology. Enterprise and initiative are the keys to success in the marketplace. Thus the democracy of the market - a genuinely 'populist democracy' - offers ordinary citizens more than the democracy of politics. Hence the neo-liberal New Right accept only the *limited political* sovereignty of the people because they see the market as offering *unlimited* sovereignty.

Public Choice

With regards to the above view, neo-liberalism has been aided by Public Choice analysis in its critique of political processes of representation. Public Choice represents the application of economic methods to the study of politics. Though not necessarily associated with right-wing projects, it has historically become associated with neo-liberal ideas because of its strongly individualist and rationalist assumptions, from which it has only relatively recently begun to emerge (in the form of 'new' Public Choice). While neo-liberals have sought to demonstrate that the market alternative works, New Right Public Choice has tried to prove that government does not.

Its two most important proponents, James Buchannan and Gordon Tullock, established the Center for the Study of Public Choice at the

Virginia Polytechnic University at the end of the 1960s, though the precepts had been developing since the early 1960s in the form of the theory of 'rational choice'. Though there are many debates about variants within rational choice theory, essentially humans are regarded as rational beings whose behaviour in all circumstances can be explained as the constant search for fulfillment of their own interests. Public Choice theorists applied this idea to politics. In essence, Public Choice Theory asserts that politicians and bureaucrats, as well as voters and economic actors, are seen to always act in a self-interested fashion. There is no insulated public sphere in which we make fair and disinterested decisions on social issues. Public Choice tends to highlight how, unlike in the market, self-interest in politics does not lead to the benefit of the public. These ideas were a useful 'cutting-edge' for the project of reviving the liberal political economy. They allowed the right-wing ambivalence towards democracy to resurface in intellectually respectable terms, although Public Choice theorists in alliance with neo-liberals would prefer to suggest they have not criticised the democratic ideal itself, but the mistake of elevating majority rule to a moral principle.

Public Choice may be complex and empirical, but critics point to its crude characterisation of human behaviour, and as a result its ignorance of issues of political culture, class and power. In particular, Public Choice theorists have been accused of ignoring the way in which large private organisations may be permanent centres of power in society, as well as overlooking the failures of market processes. However, Public Choice theory's attack on the way in which political processes fail to properly express preferences is powerful.

Libertarianism

It is important that a differentiation is made between neo-liberalism and libertarianism. Though both use similar language, libertarianism should not be seen merely as the extension of neo-liberal themes but as a radical school of its own. 'Right-wing' libertarianism is distinct from the New Right in that it pushes absolute individual freedom into the key areas of the family, internal and external national security, as well as the economy. As a result of the hostility this creates to its ideas in some quarters, the libertarian wing is not dominant in the New Right and the few genuine libertarians stand out.

Libertarianism represents, in essence, the triumph of 'freedom' over 'order'. It denotes absolute opposition to social and legal restrictions on the individual. Of course, support for the 'absolute' liberty of the individual is not only found on the margins of the right. 'Left' libertarianism and anarchism share many themes with the 'right' variant. But the thinkers noted here may be included in the New Right for two reasons: because of their strong defence of unrestricted capitalism, and their arguments against post-war social democracy.

Absolute rights to private property are regarded as fundamental, forming the basis for free contract and the free society. Robert Nozick[9] argues that if people have pre-social rights to property, then any social principles of justice via redistribution will violate citizens' rights. Just distribution is whatever results from free exchanges. Recognising peoples' 'self-ownership' (and consequently absolute rights to property ownership) is crucial to treating people as equals. Hence the key aspect of the libertarian agenda is a radically reduced state and the abolition or at least severe reduction of taxation.[10] For Nozick, the state should be limited to the narrow functions of protection against force, theft, fraud, and the enforcement of contracts. At the greatest extreme, the so-called anarcho-capitalist approach favours wholly unrestricted private property and free exchange.

The other three strands of the New Right have had an important social, political and economic impact. Genuine libertarianism has not. It does not, whatever the validity or otherwise of its arguments, fit into the mainstream of contemporary political debate in the way in which the other strands of the New Right do. This iconoclastic school, in which the notion of property rights reaches its zenith, constitutes a radically powerful set of ideas, but as a result divorces itself from even the most general assumptions that underlie everyday political life (and perhaps most people's basic sense of social morality).

Whatever the problems and inconsistencies in the libertarian argument, particularly its first principles and the assumption that free enterprise constitutes economic liberty, it does hold a vision of freedom which fully embraces human diversity. Hence, unlike the other strands of the New Right and other political ideologies, it takes genuine pluralism as the starting-point for its thinking. Whatever the commitment to political and social freedoms in other ideologies of left and right, they tend to offer uniform visions of possible future societies in a manner which true libertarians tend to resist.

Neo-conservatism
Neo-conservatism developed from the ideas of classical political philosopher Leo Strauss and his followers, and drew on economic

liberals such as Friedman and Hayek. There are two main types: the 'philosophic' defence of conservatism (which claims affinities with older traditions of conservative thought), and 'neo-conservatism' (more sociological and less philosophical), which is mainly American in origin. They share a mutual desire to prevent the erosion of social and political authority and the need for a return to 'traditional' moral and political values.

Philosophic conservatism's leading inspiration is Michael Oakeshott. He confronted what he called the 'politics of the book': politics in which traditions of behaviour have been replaced by rationalism, ideologies and abstract ideas. He argued:

> Politics is not the science of setting up a permanently impregnable society, it is the art of knowing where to go next in the exploration of an already existing traditional kind of society.[11]

Oakeshott asserted that to be a conservative is to be disposed to think and behave in a certain manners, to prefer the familiar to the unknown, and the actual to the possible. Despite the rejection of rationalist politics, a link can be seen between this form of conservatism and the neo-liberal desire for a limited state:

> ... the office of government is not to impose other beliefs upon its subjects, not to tutor or to educate them, not to make them better or happier in another way, not to direct them, to galvanise them into action, to lead them or to co-ordinate their activities so that no occasion of conflict shall occur; the office of government is merely to rule. This is a specific and limited activity, easily corrupted when it is combined with any other, and, in the circumstances, indispensable.[12]

The more recent expressions of the tradition upon which Oakeshott drew appear more authoritarian. They rest on the argument that the authority of social institutions derives from established, known and tried arrangements and thus should be met with our allegiance. The state is the embodiement of the three principles of authority, allegiance and tradition in this argument. The citizen is regarded as a 'subject' of the state, just as the child is tied to the family by natural necessity rather than by any mutually agreed contract as in liberalism. In addition, these neo-conservatives argue, society serves no great purpose, it simply exists as a natural form. Thus social discipline should be the central conservative concern rather than grand goals of liberty or equality.[13]

Ironically, this means that neo-conservatism, to some degree, has had to react to the rise of the other main New Right strand, neo-liberalism, with its project of individualism and markets, which seems to contradict neo-conservative concerns. Hence Letwin highlights 'conservative individualism' where society is regarded as the cradle rather than the enemy of individuality. For this kind of conservative, 'true freedom' resides in the *inheritance* of traditional rights and obligations, respected and acted upon by subjects.[14] This contrasts with, but does not necessarily stand in complete opposition to, liberalism, with its emphasis upon absolute and universal natural rights.

In America, neo-conservatives have addressed themselves to three specific problems: the breakdown of the traditional family structure; the poverty and 'underclass' problem; and the perceived 'cultural crisis'. As such, they aim to rehabilitate the work and family ethic (most obviously in the work of Gilder, for whom family is the 'great civiliser'[15]) and they may have an ambivalent attitude towards capitalism, since it has a tendency to subvert traditions[16] – their interest is in the promotion of civil society and political culture and their appreciation of its value to social order. They have defended in particular 'mediating structures': the organisations which come between the individual and the state (family, neighbourhood, voluntary organisations, church). These are seen as social resources for citizenship (or 'subject-hood'), and promote the development of civic virtues (such as concern for one's locality and the desire to aid the community) as well as allowing individuals to identify with the larger society.

While they have accepted criticisms of government failure[17] as well as the pervasive influence of capitalism, neo-conservatives see rampant individualism as destroying the traditional practices on which meaningful social existence depends. The primacy of state authority must be retained, though this may not necessarily mean an extended state. Neo-conservatives recognise the argument that through ineffective welfare programmes the state can contribute to poverty and 'moral dysfunction', and so erode the preconditions for social order itself. What is clear though is neo-conservatism's rejection of egalitarianism which is seen as permissive and a threat to the social hierarchy. This is connected to a deep antipathy to the supposed social and sexual liberation of the 1960s.

Common Themes Within the New Right

Prominent differences would seem to exist between strands of the New Right. 'Pure' neo-liberals may reject the notion that the public good requires a morally elevated and socially concerned citizenry, because social well-being can actually be an unintended consequence of individual action. Neo-conservatives argue that there must be a pillar of values other than those of the market to support proper citizenship, social morality and even individualism itself. Indeed, it is sometimes suggested that the neo-conservative strand concerns itself with addressing the sometimes disruptive political consequences of liberal economic policies.[18]

Despite such tensions, there are important linkages between the strands. Both worship at the altar of the 'religion of inequality' (as Tawney, the British socialist political philosopher, called it). Both agree on the importance of maintaining a system of inequality: the market for neo-liberals, social stratification for neo-conservatives. The neo-conservative emphasis on personal responsibility allies with the neo-liberal attack on welfare rights. Neo-conservatives have given neo-liberals a conception of nationhood and the value of duties and obligations, while neo-liberals have taught neo-conservatives the value of markets. Both are anti-progressive in that they resist feminist and multi-cultural agendas. Both see dangers in the politicisation of the social order which these and others threaten. Neo-liberalism tries to relegate decisions to the market, neo-conservatives to assert a heavily social and particularly cultural conception of the individual.

Liberal-Conservatism

Few New Right thinkers combine explicitly the themes of both main strands, but Hayek's thought is the most coherent and extensive example of 'liberal-conservativism'. Though ultimately he suggested he was not a conservative because he disavowed the characteristically conservative project of using the power of the state to protect endangered moral traditions and social hierarchies, he did draw on many conservative themes. For this and for the range and coherence of his work he is perhaps the most important thinker of the New Right, if not necessarily its most typical one.

To Friedman, and neo-liberals who followed in his wake, a reduction in the power of the state is the fundamental condition for greater freedom, but Hayek's principle target is state monopoly, thus state welfare services would be acceptable if offered in competition with private alternatives. Compared to Friedman, Hayek is a thinker who has analysed much more deeply the nature of what makes a free social order - the 'Great Society' - and, in the eyes of his admirers, has produced a non-rationalistic defence of individual liberty which can be reconciled with tradition.

Hayek suggests that human individuality is a tradition. The framework of the free society allows the fullest scope to experiments in living, thus promoting the competition which drives change and progress. Hayek's value to some conservatives is that he shows why they have been wrong in the past to think that conservative values could be protected by the successful capture of the expansionist state. He argues their pragmatism must be ditched for a dogmatic and inflexible commitment to liberty. Tradition is not a god to be revered (as for some conservatives), but it is crucial in ensuring stability and giving individuals knowledge of the social world around them. Socialist planning fails because the social order is a spontaneous formation. It can never be centralised and directed: this leads inevitably to its decay.

To Hayek, there may be general rules, but not absolute rights or preordained just outcomes. The type of law prevailing in the modern (especially welfare) state poses a threat to individual liberty because it is driven by the false idea that in an age of the universal franchise, constitutional limits on governments have become unnecessary. For Hayek, the 'Great Society' cannot agree upon desired ends (such as the vague notion of 'social justice' enshrined in the welfare state), but only means - liberty under law.

A similar blend of neo-liberal and neo-conservative themes has been particularly important in the UK, where the main vehicle for New Right reforms has been the Conservative Party. 'Liberal-conservative' approaches have been necessary because British conservatism has been affected irrevocably by the revival of neo-liberal political economy, which has argued that the market economy entails and depends on socially responsible citizens. Therefore moral choices made by citizens, particularly for economic independence and moral restraint, are not only private but of public concern. The individual is also a social being, and must be prevailed upon to recognise legitimacy in traditions and institutions, and to observe the existence of community.[19]

Criticisms and Recent Developments

Conservatism - a 'dead' ideology?

One of the strongest criticisms of the New Right, and one that has grown in stature in the last few years, is that all its ideals have been undermined, partly by their own 'success'. Conservatism of course has a far longer history than the New Right, and has been very good at adapting to new social, political and economic conditions, helped partly by the claim that it has never been a dogmatic ideology. However, it has been suggested that whatever its former status, conservatism has no future.

There are two inter-related arguments here. First, traditional conservatism has little purchase on the modern world. Societies are too complex, pluralistic, (globally) market-oriented and essentially liberal for an anti-rationalist and moralistic defence of existing institutions, practices and traditions.

Second, it has been suggested that, in the interests of its own survival, conservatism has become infected by the dogmatic and idealistic neo-liberalism of the New Right, but the price has been too high. This is not a new criticism, of course, and has been voiced previously from the 'One Nation' conservative position.[20] The New Right unleashed de-traditionalising forces, and the Left is now the traditional conservative force.[21] Post-New Right conservatism has inherited the unstable feature of classical liberalism: the inability of a free market to generate a sense of social and political obligation, allegiance and affinity. As a result, it has been suggested that neo-liberalism has hollowed out the conservative bases of support, especially in institutions and civil society.[22] There is no possibility of a return to traditional conservatism. Consequently, the British Conservative Party may have forfeited electoral fortune for a generation.

Neo-liberalism - a self-defeating force?

These arguments rely on the notion that neo-liberalism is inherently contradictory. It is hostile to tradition and is one of the forces sweeping it away (via market forces and aggressive individualism), but it relies nevertheless on the persistence of tradition for the legitimacy provided to New Right governments by conservative themes of nation, religion, gender and family.[23]

As a result, it is suggested that the New Right has been 'proved' to be a self-defeating project. It has unleashed dangerous de-traditionalising forces and scuppered its own chances as a political project by undermining social cohesion and stability. The effects are both theoretical (ever more dogmatic and authoritarian propositions) and practical (the erosion of assumed bases of support for the British Conservative Party and the exacerbation of its internal divisions). As a related group of contemporary ideologies over the last few decades, the New Right may have been born, and burnt fiercely, but now only the embers remain to be picked over.

This critique has been encouraged by the growth of interest in ideas of civil society and social capital, the lamented erosion of community and its resulting problems of anomie and crime. It is connected to the revival in communitarian and civic republican thought which, it is argued, the New Right, and in particular neo-liberalism, has neglected.

Recent Developments

There are two main reasons why these arguments can be seen as misguided. First, they ignore two recent developments in conservative thought. The first is a kind of 'softening' - the attempt to integrate belief in 'free markets' with concern for community and social cohesion, perhaps in response to the fear that the apparent primacy of free markets may be connected to social fragmentation, decline and disorder. For example, David Willetts argues in *Civic Conservatism*, for an attempt to place conservatism between neo-liberalism and 'traditionalist communitarianism'.[24] True civic-minded conservatism entails a commitment to the free market, limited government and strong institutions; he argues:

> the trouble with the neo-Liberals is that they simply think in terms of the individual economic agent without any understanding of the institutions, values and ties which are not just good in themselves but are anyway essential for any real free market to thrive.[25]

But this form of civic conservatism still seems to trust the market far more than the state to foster conditions favourable to community life. Government passivity seems prominent. If communities are fragile, civic conservatism proposes an apparent expansion of market exchange.

Nevertheless, this form of conservatism lacks the cutting edge so powerful for the earlier New Right. It becomes very descriptive, whereas the strength of the New Right was that it seemed very prescriptive. But it does improve upon the neo-liberal assumption that there is only one precondition for the growth of a sense of responsibility by citizens - a reduction in the scope and size of the state. They recognise the 'non-contractual element in contract', in other words, that market institutions rely on norms and forms of trust not stated in the economic contract itself. This realisation is important: social cohesion is crucial for the flowering of market processes, though critics might suggest the realisation has come too late. It also underlines the sense that there has been a collapse of socially progressive conservatism: it is unable to offer convincing intellectual foundations, political support or an effective governing project, unlike the Right.

The second direction right thought has taken in the 1990s is to become more 'hardline': to urge continuing reform of the welfare state, further reductions in the size of the state, and the introduction of more authoritarian social order measures. This can be witnessed in the pull of the neo-liberal New Right on recent Conservative Party politics. From its own perspective, the New Right agenda is hardly finished, particularly with regard to the role and size of the state. The think-tanks remain active and vigorous, if currently largely frustrated.

Whichever direction exerts more influence, a growing body of opinion is convinced that the New Right project, and its political focus - the Conservative Party - are doomed. A sea-change is thought to be occurring in British politics, as manifested by the 1997 general election. This seems like a profound error, similar to the one which suggested that New Right ideology would not find a broad audience in the 1960s and 1970s because of its 'dogmatism'. The analysis misreads the link between theory and political practice, and how the problems in the Conservative Party relate to (or are caused by) the direction of conservative/New Right thought over the last decade.

The current critiques of the state of contemporary conservatism appeared to capture the 'political reality' of a deadlocked, corruption-riddled and exhausted government and now a deflated party. But the relation between New Right thought and the Conservative Party's problems since 1992 is far from clear and simple. Even though some of the present critiques admit the possibility of a New Right-led second-wave, few think it a viable course for the Conservative Party. But these conclusions are based, to varying extents, on too crude a characterisation of the Conservative Party and its ability to sense the practicability of its governing ideology (this mistake was made before with

Thatcherism). Neo-liberalism has not collapsed as a significant intellectual force in the last five years, as these critiques often imply. The British Conservative Party may have lost power, and indeed may find itself out of power for some time, but this does not necessarily mean that the New Right has lost its dominance over contemporary political debate.

The Triumph of the New Right?

Another reason to be sceptical of critiques predicting a long walk in the wilderness for the New Right, is that from a certain perspective, the New Right has largely succeeded in its project. This conclusion is supported by Karl Polanyi's *The Great Transformation*,[26] which contains particularly relevant arguments in the context of a revival of economic liberalism. Polanyi developed a critique of economic liberalism both as a political creed and as an account of the nature of industrial society. His dispute with economic liberalism focused on the issue of whether primacy should be accorded to the economic over the social and political. He argued that a market economy can only exist in a market society. He traced the historical development of that society, and argued that the consequences of the market economy for human welfare were so extreme that they generated political movements which demanded change and led eventually to the successful imposition of regulation and control.

The value of Polanyi's approach lies in the recognition that market societies are not natural, but are made, and made by the state. The 'free' market is an institutional structure which does not emerge spontaneously from human nature but is planned and state-sponsored. 'Homo Economicus' is a product of the market society and not the other way round. A market society is not merely one in which resistance to the market principle is prevented through legislation, or in which the free market project is dominant, but one in which most institutions and the everyday orientation of social actors are brought into line with the principles of the market: individualism, competition, and self-interest. These are not givens, but social constructs. Polanyi developed his thesis in the age of the supposedly irreversible advance of collectivism at the expense of economic liberalism, but it appears pertinent in the counter-age of 'liberal market utopianism'.

Thus the neo-liberal idealisation of the market hides its more authoritarian current: its project to impose the 'principles' (rules) of market behaviour on us by arguing that markets are inevitable. Privatisation is not the only route to this. It is important to recognise the significance of the introduction of market principles in key institutions: the National Health Service, the BBC, schools, universities, housing associations, and so on. The purpose is not just to ease the way for privatisation, and the reduction of the state sector, but to benefit from the way in which the principles of the 'market society' act on agents within these institutions, ensuring that even those critical of the developments have to adjust. Those who point to the size of the state, and the scale of its continuing responsibilities in, for example, health-care and education, as evidence of the 'failure' of the New Right, fail to understand the degree to which market principles have been imposed upon those within these institutions. This development fundamentally challenges neo-liberalism's self-image and exposes the purpose of the New Right - the 'great market re-transformation'. Its project was not just about the power of the state, the size of its budget, and the type of welfare policies suitable for a better society, but the type of subjects and the way they thought. At times, neo-conservatism may be explic-itly authoritarian, often admittedly so. Neo-liberalism warrants more attention though because the discipline it seeks to impose - the 'market' - is more covert and pervasive.

Oakeshott was half right, then, when he suggested famously with regard to Hayek's *Road to Serfdom*, that: 'A plan to resist all planning may be better than its opposite, but it belongs to the same style of poli-tics.'[27] Neo-liberalism represents a form of 'planning', in a social sense, as invasive in many ways as any collectivist society, but a 'planning' for the protection of *property* (and in particular established property). In this respect, given conservatism's historical attachment to the protec-tion of property,[28] the divide between neo-liberalism and 'traditional' conservatism seems less solid.

Thus, despite the critiques of the demise of the New Right, its main project as perceived by Polanyi - the imposition of market behaviour, and the marginalisation of contrary thought - has been broadly achieved. While it may be that the state is still too large for neo-liber-als, and too amoral for neo-conservatives, while society is still not entrepreneurial and diverse enough for neo-liberals, and not morally cohesive enough for neo-conservatives, the New Right continues to succeed. Many details still frustrate it, but it has achieved in large part the framework of the modern social order it desires.

Conclusion

The New Right and conservatism are still dominant ideologies. They have not yet been challenged effectively by a formidable opponent after the collapse of state socialism. As John Dunn has suggested, the new feature of the political environment is:

> ... the effective disappearance of any systematic, or even widely credited, conception of how, for many generations to come (or even for ever), it [capitalism] could stand in any danger of being replaced by anything more edifying or less dismaying. What has been deleted from the human future, almost inadvertently but still with remarkable decisiveness, is any form of reasonable and relatively concrete social and political hope. [29]

Whether one thinks the New Right-inspired programmes of the last two decades have wrought a genuine reversal of economic and social decline, or merely wrought havoc, the New Right, on its own terms, has been a significant success. Where is the alternative political hope? The New Right has altered the nature of politics itself.

Despite the problems facing the British Conservative Party – extremely weak electoral position, public disenchantment and its own strategic dilemmas – can it really be suggested at the moment that the New Right hegemony is at an end? For while the newer ideologies dealt with elsewhere in this volume have provoked important critiques of the New Right, and to some extent have undermined the authority and legitimacy of conservative thought, ironically they have also strengthened the hold of right-wing ideas on domestic politics, by fracturing progressive forces and thus allowing the Right to retain a powerful ideological hold over mainstream politics. Institutional and social, if not perhaps current party political, conditions still provide New Right ideas with dominance. As such, the perceived 'endgame' of contemporary conservatism is far from being played out.

Notes

1. A. Gamble, *The Free Economy and the Strong State, The Politics of Thatcherism*, Macmillan, London 1988, p.32.
2. For the development and influence of the New Right think-tanks see: R. Cockett, *Thinking the Unthinkable, Think-Tanks and the Economic*

Counter-Revolution, 1931-1983, Harper Collins, London 1994;A. Seldon (ed), *Think-Tanks in Contemporary Britain*, Frank Cass, London 1996.

3. F.A. Hayek, *The Road to Serfdom*, Routledge and Kegan Paul, London 1944.

4. K. Popper, *The Open Society and Its Enemies*, Routledge and Kegan Paul, London 1962.

5. E. Powell, *Freedom and Reality*, Batsford, London 1969, p.10.

6. J.M. Buchannan and G. Tullock, *The Calculus of Consent*, University of Michigan Press, Michigan 1962.

7. According to Friedman there are four areas in which state action is legitimate – the guarantor of the legal framework for the efficient functioning of the market system, natural monopolies which the state may provide without adversely affecting the market, services too expensive or impracticable for market provision, and paternalistic provision for those unable to assume full responsibility for themselves, such as the mentally ill. See: M. Friedman, *Capitalism and Freedom*, University of Chicago Press, Chicago 1962.

8. K. Joseph and J. Sumption, *Equality*, John Murray, London 1979.

9. R. Nozick, *Anarchy, State and Utopia*, Basic Books, New York 1974.

10. M. Rothbard, *For a New Liberty: The Libertarian Manifesto*, Collier Macmillan, London 1978.

11. M. Oakeshott, *Rationalism in Politics and Other Essays*, Methuen, London 1962, p.58.

12. *Ibid.* pp.186-7.

13. M. Cowling (ed), *Conservative Essays*, Cassell, London 1978; R. Scruton, *The Meaning of Conservatism*, second edition, Macmillan, London 1984.

14. S. Letwin, 'On Conservative Individualism' in M. Cowling (ed.), *Conservative Essays*, Cassell, London 1978.

15. G. Gilder, *Men and Marriage*, Pelican, Louisiana 1986.

16. I. Kristol, *Two Cheers for Capitalism*, Basic Books, New York 1978.

17. Nigel Ashford identified six causes of such failure – the unintended consequences of many policies, the limits of knowledge, the pursuit of conflicting policies, the destruction of traditional problem-solving institutions and mediating structures, the existence of a 'New Class' with vested interest in expanding the state's role, and a utopian view of the ability of government to change the nature of man and society. See: N. Ashford, 'The Neo-Conservatives', *Government and Opposition*, 16 (3), pp.353-369, 1981.

18. D. King, *The New Right, Politics, Markets and Citizenship*, Macmillan, London 1987.

19. J Gray, *The Moral Foundations of Market Institutions*, Institute of

Economic Affairs, London 1992; R. Harris, *The Conservative Community – The Roots of Thatcherism and its Future*, Centre for Policy Studies, London 1989.

20. Most prominently: I. Gilmour, *Dancing With Dogma. Britain Under Thatcherism*, Simon and Schuster, London 1992.
21. A. Giddens, *Beyond Left and Right – The Future of Radical Politics*, Polity Press, Cambridge 1994.
22. J Gray, *The Undoing of Conservatism*, Social Market Foundation, London 1994.
23. A. Giddens, *Beyond Left and Right – The Future of Radical Politics, op. cit.*
24. D. Willetts, *Civic Conservatism*, Social Market Foundation, London 1994. See also: D. Willetts, *Modern Conservatism*, Penguin, London 1992 (especially chapter seven).
25. D. Willetts, *Civic Conservatism, op.cit.*, p257.
26. K. Polanyi, *The Great Transformation*, Octagon, New York 1944.
27. M. Oakeshott, *Rationalism in Politics and Other Essays, op.cit.*, p.21.
28. R. Nisbet, *Conservatism*, Open University Press, Milton Keynes 1986.
29. J. Dunn, *Western Political Theory in the Face of the Future*, Cambridge University Press, Cambridge 1993, p.122.

The Christian Right

Martin Durham

Introduction

In discussing the Christian Right, we are examining one particular instance of a broader transnational phenomenon, religious fundamentalism. Much as it annoys American conservatives to be compared with the Ayatollah Khomeini or Hezbollah, the Christian Right is far from unique in asserting traditionalist religious convictions against the disruptions of modernity.[1] But while it can be compared with other movements, the Christian Right has distinct characteristics; above all, it is a product of American political history. This is not to lessen its importance: as a force of some strength within the dominant power in the world, the Christian Right has a global significance even if it is not itself a movement of international dimensions. In one sense, indeed, it does have a presence outside the USA, in its involvement in the charitable work that American religious institutions conduct overseas (for instance, aid to the Nicaraguan contras in the 1980s).[2] There are also a number of cases where organisations in other countries have forged links with American Christian Right organisations or where American organisations have set up foreign subsidiaries.[3] But to focus on developments within the United States is crucial for our understanding of a movement which is defined by three characteristics: its roots in the evangelical community, its focus on issues of family and sexual morality and its overt commitment to a broader conservative politics. In other countries, for instance in Britain, there are movements that have the first two characteristics, or, as in France, that have the last two.[4] It is the American Christian Right, however, that has moulded a distinct politics by its combination of all three.

Forged within the USA, the Christian Right is also a relatively new development. Organisations of the 1920s and 1930s within the evangelical subculture (from which the Christian Right did ultimately spring) were significantly different from the contemporary movements. Not only did they subordinate concerns with the family to other questions but some also shared marked similarities to European fascism. Post-war movements bear greater resemblance to the Christian Right of today, both in their overall politics and, on occasion, in emphasising the family and morality. However, they proved unable to forge a sustained mass movement and never made a 'pro-family' stance the cutting edge of their appeal. As such, when the Christian Right came into existence in the late 1970s, it felt itself to be a *new* political movement.

Roots of a Movement

Modern American politics cannot be understood without a clear sense of religious differences. Between one in five and one in four Americans are white evangelicals in a religious landscape composed of three major blocs – white evangelicals, Catholics and so-called mainline Protestants – and a number of smaller groupings, notably black Protestants, Jews and a growing group without religious commitment.[5] Some of the central beliefs of evangelicals, that Christ was the Son of God or that the faithful will be rewarded in Heaven, are also to be found among Catholics, among mainstream Protestants and among black Protestants. Historically, however, it is a particular segment of white Protestantism that recognises itself in such terms as evangelical, fundamentalist or 'born again'. In understanding this, we need to go back to the late nineteenth and early twentieth century when a bitter dispute within Protestantism divided those who believed in the literal truth of the Bible from those who saw it as a guide to living that needed to be interpreted in the light of modern scholarship. The former group, fundamentalists, held to what they saw as the fundamentals of God's Word; the latter, they declared, were no longer Christians. Over time, this dispute saw many of those who championed biblical literalism leave the dominant churches of Protestantism and seek to build separate churches. Some remained as dissidents within the mainline churches. However, in the South it was the modernisers that were weak and it was not until recently that the Battle over the Bible, as some have called it, broke-out within the massive Southern Baptist Convention.[6]

Much of the energies of fundamentalists after the First World War took the form of opposition to the teaching of Darwinism in schools – a concern that continues to animate the Christian Right today. But if Christian conservatives both then and now demand that God's creation of the world should be taught in school, there is far less continuity in the politics of the two periods. The rise of fundamentalism took place in a largely segregated white church and the early days of the movement saw rich evidence of this in the enthusiastic support of many preachers and their flocks for the Ku Klux Klan, which in the 1920s was a genuinely mass movement. Bitterly anti-Catholic and vehemently opposed to sexual immorality, the Klan would decline by the latter part of the decade and while the much weaker extreme Right of the 1930s involved some evangelicals, it also exercised an appeal among Catholics. Within politics in general, during the 1930s and for years to come, white evangelicals were little noticed. Many voted, but there was no particular connection between theological conservatism and political conservatism, and for a significant section religious conviction rendered political involvement pointless. The task of Christians, they argued, was to save souls and prepare for the next world, not be distracted by the lures of this.

Differing amongst themselves in their views of politics, evangelicals also differed in their theology, and here it is important to appreciate the implications of the existence of three groupings within the broad evangelical movement. In the beginning, to use an appropriate turn of phrase, there were fundamentalists, but over time a significant grouping took the view that the faithful's insistence on separation from the 'unsaved' and their impressive ability to split over doctrinal issues was counterproductive to the bringing of Christ's message to the world. Wishing to differentiate themselves from their more sectarian colleagues, in 1942 they organised the National Association of Evangelicals. Smaller groupings of fundamentalists continued, although over time they too in some cases would prove amenable to cooperating with those outside of their particular tradition. Finally, in a separate development from the battles between fundamentalists and modernists, a movement that emphasised the outpouring of God's gifts upon His followers also emerged in the early twentieth century. This movement, the Pentecostals, emphasised speaking in tongues and faith healing as central to an experience of being 'Spirit-filled', and from the mid-twentieth century this experience would spread across many different denominations in the shape of the charismatic movement. All three of these movements, along with many members of the Southern Baptist Convention, can be defined as evangelical Protestants. That is not, however, how they would all see themselves or each other, and many of the problems that have troubled the Christian Right need to be seen in light of the differences among its immense but diffuse potential constituency.[7]

Birth of a Movement

In both of the crucial issues for the American Right in the late 1950s and early 1960s, the fight over segregation and the struggle against Communism, evangelicals were highly visible. In the South, white Christians were often willing to sanctify the separation of black and white while at a national level such groups as the Christian Anti-Communism Crusade and the Christian Crusade played a vociferous part in the Right's campaigning against the Soviet Union. For Christian Crusade, opposition to sex education (as in its celebrated pamphlet, 'Is the Little Red Schoolhouse the Proper Place to Teach Raw Sex?') was a major issue, and its equally pioneering battle against the sexuality and rebellion of rock music would also be taken up in later years by the Christian Right. But these early groups were to decline drastically and it was not until the 1970s that a substantial political mobilisation of evangelical Christians was finally to be achieved.[8]

This is often taken to be a direct reaction to the US Supreme Court's decision in January 1973 to strike down state laws restricting access to abortion. Yet while this decision was the launching-pad for a national anti-abortion movement, this was a preponderantly Catholic movement concerned with what it saw as the right to life. Several more years would elapse before the large-scale influx of evangelicals into politics, and while they too would oppose abortion, it was not the issue that precipitated their mobilisation. Instead, we need to see evangelicals as a subculture that over decades has grown not only in numbers but in resources, with its own schools and colleges and its own media, ranging from magazines and book publishing to radio and television. Seeking to win people out of the wider culture, it sought at the same time to protect itself from that culture, and in the 1970s that became increasingly difficult. The legalisation of abortion, the proliferation of pornography, the emergence of a gay movement, the changing role of women in society, were all an outrage to a community which believed the Bible set down the rightful relationship between men and women and society and sexuality. A variety of groups were established in opposition to feminist efforts to secure an Equal Rights Amendment to the Constitution and a number of organisations likewise emerged to oppose local gay rights ordinances. But it was two developments that finally created a national movement. Firstly, the state was seen as increasingly intrusive. In the early 1960s, the Supreme Court's ruling against prayer in state schools had not resulted in widespread opposition. In the late 1970s, however, Internal Revenue Service investigations into the tax status of religious institutions, and government concerns that Christian schools were educationally inadequate or racially segregated, convinced large numbers of evangelicals that an over-mighty élite was attacking the separate world they had tried to fashion. Secondly, where leading evangelicals were hesitant about entering politics, conservative activists were successful in persuading them that they should do so.[9]

For a number of writers on social movements, to mobilise people you need not only issues and resources but leaders or, as they are sometimes described, entrepreneurs.[10] The Christian Right had all three. Its issues and resources we have already touched on but what of its entrepreneurs? Here, we have the unusual coming together of elites from inside and outside the evangelical subculture. Within the community, the explosive growth both of religious broadcasting and of so-called 'superchurches' had given certain preachers a remarkable base of supporters and, significantly, contributors; while some were unwilling to enter politics others were more enthusiastic. This shift would have been far less likely had it not been for a conservative grouping that had emerged earlier in the 1970s, the New Right. For such figures as Paul Weyrich and Richard Viguerie, neither of whom were evangelicals, the conservatism which had been defeated in Barry Goldwater's unsuccessful bid for the presidency in 1964 could only triumph if it took up questions that were already agitating large numbers of Americans. In part, these involved such issues as opposition to gun control. But many of the issues the New Right believed would benefit conservatism, particularly opposition to abortion and to gay rights, were concerned with sexuality. When framed by such terms as 'pro-family', such overtly sexual issues could be linked in turn with what children were taught in schools or what they might see on television. The New Right itself would prove too intransigent in the years that followed and while many of its cadres would continue to be active, it itself would disintegrate. But for its offspring, the Christian Right, much more was to prove possible.[11]

Faith, Family and Polity

As we will discuss further later, the Christian Right would go through major changes, not least in its leading personnel. If, in its early years, fundamentalists such as Jerry Falwell and Tim LaHaye were particularly prominent, the movement's second decade has seen the rise of Pat Robertson, a charismatic, and James Dobson, an evangelical.[12] But amid such diversity, the Christian Right has been brought together around a particular view of the relationship between faith and politics. In order to best grasp this relationship, we need to look at four of the central elements in the movement's worldview: citizenship, the family, the nation and secularism.

Citizenship
In constructing the Christian Right, one particular obstacle has been the continued opposition of some evangelicals to any involvement in politics. Falwell himself in the mid-1960s reacted to the civil rights movement by arguing that the sole task of Christians was to 'preach the Word'.[13] This has sometimes been seen simply as a defence of white privilege but it is important to note that Falwell applied his argument not only to black demands for equality but to involvement in anti-Communist campaigns too. Subsequently, he was to characterise his earlier pronouncements as 'false prophecy'. Rather than avoid politics, he now believed, 'it was my duty as a Christian to apply the truths of Scripture to every act of government.' In declaring that we should render to Caesar the things that were Caesar's and to God the things that were God's, Christ was now seen as referring to the human predicament, of living in one and the same time in the world of God and of man. When there is a conflict between these worlds, the first takes precedence. When man's law is wrong, 'we must work tirelessly to change it'.

However, in arguing against those who continued to insist that piety was incompatible with politics, the Christian Right has been far from clear in explaining the purpose of its political project. In part, as we have already suggested, it is posed in terms of the defence of an embattled community. LaHaye, for instance, talks of resources that 'God has given us ... with which to insulate the Christian home' against attack. Hitherto, Christians had neglected political action but to take part in elections was to exercise 'good citizenship that helps to insulate the home'.

Yet to engage in political activity is not merely a matter of protecting a subculture against an intrusive state. America, LaHaye declared, needed to be brought back to traditional moral values and the righteous placed in positions of authority. Similarly, for Falwell, Christians were beginning to recognise that the actions of government affected their lives and that policies to which they objected could be challenged at the polls. But he also argued that the task of the mobilised Christian was to lead America 'back to basics, back to values, back to biblical morality'.[14]

In the tension between these two different perspectives, protecting an enclave and reclaiming a national culture for God, there is room for considerable confusion. To liberal opponents of the movement, it is trying to impose a monolithic religion upon a pluralist society, to replace democracy with theocracy. Yet for some, who represent a strand known as Christian Reconstructionism, the problem with the Christian Right is precisely that it declines to follow through the logic of God's command that the faithful should have dominion over the earth. The Old Testament, they argue, contains detailed guidelines for the creation of a Christian social order in which homosexuals, adulterers – and incorrigibly disobedient children! – would be subject to capital punishment.[15]

The ambiguity of the movement's conception of Christian citizenship has an additional complication. So far we have insisted on the Christian Right's evangelical roots but, as we have noted, evangelicals are restricted to a minority of the American people. While its leaders are formed in and shaped by their community, they seek to reach beyond it. By invoking notions of a common morality or shared Judeo-Christian values, the Christian Right attempts to bring together white evangelicals with Catholics, Orthodox Jews and others. In doing so it runs the constant risk of denying what evangelicals must necessarily assert, that it is through adhering to *their* beliefs, and theirs alone, that one can be saved. In this sense, the Christian Right cannot be seen as the political expression of the evangelical community because it includes non-evangelicals.

Furthermore, the Christian Right does not encompass *all* evangelicals. For example, in the early 1970s, the signatories of what became known as the Chicago Declaration of Evangelical Social Concern contended that Christians had failed to demonstrate 'the love of God to those suffering social abuses' or to proclaim 'his justice to an unjust American society'. While at the other end of the evangelical spectrum there are strict fundamentalists who believe that to ally with the followers of false gods is to betray the true faith.[16] The Christian Right has had more impact than either of these alternatives, but the ambiguity of its political purpose – whether it intends to participate or to rule – is accentuated both by its failure to speak for all evangelicals and its success in reaching out to other religious traditions.

The Nation

Much of the rhetoric of the Christian Right is linked with a notion of taking America back, in the sense both of recapturing its defining ethos and going back to an earlier less irreligious time. This commitment is linked in turn to a frequent belief in the specialness of America. Thus, for Robertson, God promised ancient Israel that if it remained faithful, He would make it rich and powerful. So too, he argues, with America.

> We have had more wealth than the richest of all empires. We have had more military might than any colossus. We have risen above all the nations of the earth.

This was because those who had

> founded this land made a solemn covenant that they would be the people of God and that this would be a Christian nation.

Yet today, faced with the nation's immorality, God has turned away: America lost the Vietnam war, is in economic decline and has lost its children to drugs and disease. God has so far withheld his full judgement. But if Christians are not victorious (not least in electing a conservative President in 1996), then 'this once proud, richly blessed Christian nation' will fall.[17]

The Family

At the core of the Christian Right's agenda is a notion of 'pro-family' politics. Thus, according to LaHaye, writing at the beginning of the 1980s, a war had been declared, and what was at stake was 'the traditional family'. Legalised abortion had resulted in the 'mass murder' of 'unborn babies', San Francisco had become 'like Sodom and Gomorrah', and 'unmarried teens' were being encouraged to have sex. The image of a nation at war was to appear almost a decade later in Dobson's description of America as facing a new Civil War in which the struggle was 'for the hearts and minds of the people'. Once again, it was the church and the family that were seen as beleaguered strongholds, and rather than being a war of weapons it was a war of discourse. In this conflict

> the forces hostile to family, faith and tradition seem to have the inside track. Controlling most of the major instruments of communication, they are able to manipulate words and their meanings over time, in order to advance the modernist agenda.

Words like virtue are replaced by values ('and, of course, we are constantly reminded that they are relative'). Homosexuality is no longer considered abnormal and a new term, homophobia, is coined to be 'levelled at anyone who opposes the gay rights agenda ... Through these semantic changes, normalcy is put on the defensive.' The most important of all the battlegrounds in the war over the culture, Dobson declared, concerned such issues as school curricula because those who controlled the young would decide the future of the nation. In Britain it was already too late: 'For them, the civil war is over. Traditionalists lost.' Now, in America, Judeo-Christian values were under attack. If the family collapsed, Dobson warned, then 'the heartland of the nation is wide open to cultural revolution'.[18]

The conviction that the family is under attack necessarily raises the question of attack by whom? In part, the answer is feminism. Thus, for Falwell, feminists believe 'that God made a mistake when He made two different kinds of people'. They refuse to accept that men and women rightfully occupy different roles in society. Women were intended to be wives and mothers, men to be the head of the family, giving 'their wives honor as unto the weaker vessel'.

But feminism is only one source of the onslaught upon the family. Another is homosexuality, a 'rebellion against God', which for Falwell represents a second facet of the rejection of divinely ascribed roles. The family, in which men must be dominant and women submissive, is 'God's order in Creation' and homosexuality, like feminism, rejects that order.[19]

Secularism

Ultimately, however, the source of the attack transcends either feminism or the gay movement. In LaHaye's account, the attack originates from those who have abandoned God and absolute morality. It is secular humanists, he declares, who are at war with church and family and it is they who have 'infiltrated the most important institutions in our culture' until they had come to dominate America. Likewise, for Dobson, where traditionalists believe in Scripture, premarital chastity and fidelity, their opponents reject God and define right by what *seems* right. It was the values of the latter that now dominated the power centres of society and if Christians failed to defend 'the beliefs and values that were handed to them by their ancestors', then 'immoral, atheistic bureaucrats and educators' would be victorious.[20]

Earlier, we cited Dobson's reference to an attempt to 'advance the modernist agenda'. The Christian Right in many ways can be seen as continuing not only the earlier Battle over the Bible but as waging an even older war. For Robertson, the nineteenth century was 'an age of intellectual rage', an era which brought forth

> three major figures: Karl Marx, Charles Darwin, and Sigmund Freud . . . committed to debunking the Bible, turning against the supernatural, and teaching their own rationalistic theory that man and all the creatures of the animal world are mere products of blind evolution.

The inevitable result, he holds, was the murderous Russian Revolution, just as the pernicious ideas of the Enlightenment, which 'sought to remove God from His Throne and to crown Reason in His place', were to lead to 'the horrors of the French Revolution'. For LaHaye, the evils of humanism are to be traced back even further to the Renaissance glorification of man and even further to Thomas Aquinas and his admiration for ancient Greek thought which, in the thirteenth century, gave new life to a reliance on human understanding rather than biblical revelation.[21]

The Christian Right can be seen as a social movement engaged in a fight with other social movements. In a wider sense, it sees itself as championing a religious worldview that has long been in conflict with an increasingly powerful secular antagonist. For some, however, the argument is taken further still. If America's moral decline is to be attributed to the machinations of an enemy within, then in turn it must be connected with the ceaseless strivings of the greatest Enemy of all.

The time will come (and soon, many evangelicals believe) when they will be taken from this earth while those left behind will suffer a terrible tribulation. An awesome tyrant, the Anti-Christ, will preside over all the nations of the earth until in a mighty battle – Armageddon – the forces of evil will be conquered and Christ return to rule over the faithful. In such a scenario the workings of anti-Christian conspirators have to be seen in the light of apocalyptic prophecy. In the early period of the movement this was particularly evident in the writings of Tim LaHaye, while in the 1990s Pat Robertson has been a forceful advocate of the view that the humanist 'fifth column' is working towards 'one world government' as part of Lucifer's age-old plan.[22]

The Christian Right and the Republican Party

Of the several organisations which emerged on the Christian Right at the end of the 1970s, the most important was Jerry Falwell's Moral Majority. Vehemently opposed to both feminism and the gay movement, Moral Majority saw itself as defending the traditional family but did not restrict itself to this concern. A strong defence policy, it argued, was the only way to keep America free from 'godless Communism', and a crucial part of the defence of freedom was to protect the state of Israel against Arab attack. Furthermore, free enterprise was seen as 'clearly outlined in the Book of Proverbs', although Moral Majority did not give the same attention to this (or to Falwell's condemnation of welfare spending) that it did to sexual politics and foreign policy.[23] Widely credited with mobilising significant numbers of voters for Reagan and other Republicans, the Christian Right was to find the 1980s a disappointing period. While much of what it shared with the broader conservative movement was (at least partially) attained, its specific concern with such issues as abortion or sex education were far from prominent on Republican politicians' agendas.

Thus, believing that God had told him to run, Pat Robertson challenged George Bush for nomination as the party's presidential candidate in 1988. He was defeated and did not even receive the support of many on the Christian Right. (Here, although concerns over electability were paramount, the tension between Robertson's charismatic beliefs and the fundamentalism of Falwell was important.) Coinciding as this did with sexual and financial scandals within the evangelical community and Falwell's decision to dissolve Moral Majority and concentrate on his ministry, Robertson's defeat left the Christian Right in seeming disarray, which some mistook for terminal decline.

Instead, however, it was to lead to the rise of Christian Coalition. Founded by Pat Robertson but under the day-to-day leadership of a former Republican student activist, Ralph Reed, the new organisation had become a major force within the party by the 1992 Republican convention. As with the earlier wave, the Christian Right in the 1990s is made up of a number of organisations with important strategic (and theological) differences. In the 1980s, however, the Christian Right was not yet a major part of the Republican party. In recent years, this has changed so that one estimate claims that it is the dominant force in eighteen state parties and a significant force in thirteen others. (In terms of sheer numbers, in 1995 Christian Coalition claimed a membership of 1.6 million.) But this has not been achieved without some compromise, and the future of the movement has been a matter of some dispute.[24]

The 1992 Republican convention produced a party platform that was strongly influenced by the concerns of the Christian Right. Attempts to move away from a strongly anti-abortion position were defeated, gay rights legislation was denounced and same-sex marriages opposed. But it was not George Bush but Bill Clinton who won that election. One response to this defeat was to re-examine what a 'pro-family' strategy might involve, and the following year Ralph Reed published an article in which he argued that rather than 'concentrating disproportionately on issues such as abortion and homosexuality', the movement needed to develop a broader agenda, taking up such issues as taxes, crime and government waste. The primary concern of evangelicals and Catholics, he declared, was 'not to legislate against the sins of others, but to protect the health, welfare, and financial security of their families'.[25]

In the months that followed, Christian Coalition supported Republican candidates who did not, for instance, wholeheartedly oppose abortion; and when the Republican leadership issued its Contract With America in a successful attempt to present a national platform for many of its congressional candidates, Christian Coalition threw itself into the fray despite the Contract's omission of any reference to such issues as abortion or gay rights. After faithfully supporting Newt Gingrich's strategy through the first hundred days of the new Republican Congress, Christian Coalition did issue its own distinct set of policies in the shape of a Contract With The American Family. But this, it emphasised, should be seen as ten suggestions not Ten Commandments and where abortion (unlike gay rights) figured, it was a restriction of abortion, not its banning, that was proposed.[26]

This approach came under fire from elsewhere on the Christian Right. One group, the Christian Action Network, which had already criticised the earlier call for a broader agenda, produced a rival contract to Reed's. More importantly, Dobson's organisation, Focus on the Family, and an allied group, the Family Research Council, was increasingly vociferous about the danger of the movement collapsing into the arms of Republican politicians. With a mailing list of over two million, this alliance posed a real threat to Christian Coalition's dominance and where Reed and Robertson remained committed to a Republican strategy, Dobson and Gary Bauer, the Family Research Council head, made it clear that they would support a third party if the Republicans failed to prioritise their concerns.[27]

Opposing the Christian Right

Divided internally, the Christian Right has also had to face opposition from without. Organisations such as People for the American Way have been established to campaign against it, and long established organisations, such as the American Civil Liberties Union, have similarly been active. Feminist and gay organisations have mobilised in opposition to a movement that seeks to roll back many of the gains they have made since the 1960s. Jewish organisations have accused Robertson and other Christian Right leaders of anti-semitism, mainline Protestant and Catholic leaders (and some evangelicals) have described the movement as heartless towards the poor and leading Democrats have denounced it for presenting the Republicans as God's Own Party. The issues that concern the Christian Right's opponents involve both the nature of rights and the nature of the American experiment itself. The Christian Right, they argue, is a danger to liberty and is incompatible with the separation of religion and the state that was established in the Bill of Rights over two hundred years ago.[28]

How are we to evaluate these arguments? The Christian Right does not believe in the right to abortion, or gay rights, and often its activists appear to doubt the value of any right to do anything they see as wrong. They are, as they say themselves, opposed to modern liberalism. But are they seeking to impose a religious morality on a secular state? The Christian Right rejects the claim that the Constitution erects a wall between faith and government. According to Reed, the most sophisticated of its advocates, religious conservatives have been unjustly attacked when all they demand is a 'place at the table'. The First Amendment, he argues, was never intended to deny believers their right to take part in politics. Their goal is a better land with safer streets, improved schools and stronger families. 'America would look much as it did for most of the first two centuries of its existence'; but, he added, in one way it would be importantly different: white evangelicals had once supported slavery and segregation. They should now break with their past and 'build a genuinely inclusive movement that embraces the full racial diversity of America'.[29] If, for opponents, such sentiments should be seen as rhetoric rather than genuine moderation, then this attempt to reposition the Christian Right is a measure of Reed's ambition to expand the movement's base. As well, of course, as raising once more the question of whether the Christian Right is to be seen as a defensive movement or as one which seeks to assert a religious hegemony.

Conclusion: Triumph or Tribulation?

In the years since its inception, the Christian Right has become a massive and, more importantly still, a sophisticated movement. Wielding considerable influence within the Republican Party, it has become central to Republican politicians' calculations, as is well demonstrated by the appearance of so many of them at Christian Coalition's annual Road to Victory conferences.[30] But it is not a united movement, and even if there is little likelihood of a significant exodus from Republican ranks, Ralph Reed's willingness to compromise and to rethink the very meaning of a 'pro-family' politics does not necessarily accord with the outlook of his followers.[31] Whether the present strategy will continue is far from clear. But the movement will not go away. For this is not conservatism as usual. Evangelicals entered politics with their own distinct language and their own defining concerns. Some may well be assimilated into conventional politics and others will retreat from the fray, to wait once more for the Lord while leaving politics to the Devil. But now they have been mobilised, the movement that calls itself God's Army will not easily leave the political process it has already so massively affected.[32]

Notes

1. See: M.E. Marty and R.S. Appleby (eds), *Fundamentalisms Observed*, University of Chicago Press, Chicago 1991.
2. See: S. Diamond, *Spiritual Warfare: The Politics of the Christian Right*, South End Press, Boston 1989, pp.17, 109-10.
3. For the establishment of a branch of the Christian Right legal organisation, the Rutherford Institute, in Britain, see: 'Religious Justice', *Evangelicals Now*, December 1995; for the Canadian branch of Focus on the Family, see: D. Herman, *Rights of Passage: Struggles for Lesbian and Gay Equality*, University of Toronto Press, Toronto 1994; for a recent discussion of American evangelical activity in the Third World, see: S. Brouwer, P. Gifford and S.D. Rose (eds), *Exporting the American Gospel. Global Christian Fundamentalism*, Routledge, New York 1996.
4. For moral crusades in Britain, see: M. Durham, *Sex and Politics. The Family and Morality in the Thatcher Years*, Macmillan, 1991; for Catholic family campaigning in France, see: C. Lesselier, 'Apocalypse now', *WAF Journal*, Winter 1992-1993.
5. L.A. Kellstedt and J.C. Green, 'Knowing God's Many People: Denominational Preference and Political Behaviour' in D.C. Leege and L.A. Kellstedt (eds), *Rediscovering the Religious Factor in American Politics*, M.E. Sharpe, Armonk 1993, p.56.
6. See N.T. Ammerman, 'North American Protestant Fundamentalism' in M.E. Marty and R.S. Appleby (eds), *Fundamentalisms Observed, op.cit.*
7. *Ibid.*; D.M. Oldfield, *The Right and the Righteous. The Christian Right Confronts the Republican Party*, Rowman and Littlefield, Lanham 1996, chapter 1.
8. *Ibid.* pp.89-95.
9. See: N.T. Ammerman, 'North American Protestant Fundamentalism', *op.cit.*, pp.40-41; D. M. Oldfield, *The Right and the Righteous. The Christian Right Confronts the Republican Party, op.cit.*, chapter 2.
10. See: S. Bruce, *The Rise and Fall of the New Christian Right. Conservative Protestant Politics in America, 1978-1988*, Clarendon Press, Oxford 1988, pp.20-21.
11. See: M. Durham, 'Family, Morality and the New Right', *Parliamentary Affairs*, Spring 1985; M. Durham, 'Abortion and the Politics of Morality in the USA', *Parliamentary Affairs*, April 1994.
12. See M. Moen, *The Transformation of the Christian Right*, University of Alabama Press, Tuscaloosa 1992; D.M. Oldfield, The Right and the Righteous. The Christian Right Confronts the Republican Party, *op.cit.*

13. P.D. Young, *God's Bullies. Native Reflections on Preachers and Politics*, Holt, Rinehart and Winston, New York 1982, pp.310-13.

14. F. Fitzgerald, *Cities on a Hill. A Journey through Contemporary American Cultures*, Picador, London 1987, p.170; J. Falwell, *Strength for the Journey*, Simon and Schuster, New York 1987, pp.337, 343-4; J. Falwell, *The Fundamentalist Phenomenon*, Doubleday, Garden City 1981, pp.194-5; J. Falwell, *Listen, America!*, Bantam Books 1980, p.17; T. LaHaye, *The Battle for the Family*, Fleming H. Revell, Old Tappan 1982, pp.206, 224-25; T. LaHaye, *The Battle for the Mind*, Fleming H. Revell, Old Tappan 1980, p.10.

15. S. Diamond, *Spiritual Warfare: The Politics of the Christian Right, op.cit.*, pp.135-39; N.T. Ammerman, 'North American Protestant Fundamentalism', *op.cit.*, pp.49-54.

16. M. Cromartie, 'Fixing the World', *Christianity Today*, 27 April 1992; S. Bruce, *The Rise and Fall of the New Christian Right. Conservative Protestant Politics in America 1978-1988, op.cit.*, p.173.

17. P. Robertson, *The Turning Tide. The Fall of Liberalism and The Rise of Common Sense*, Word Dallas 1993, pp.292-303. For a more extended discussion of America as God's chosen nation, see M. Lienesch, *Redeeming America. Piety and Politics in the New Christian Right*, University of North Carolina Press, Chapel Hill 1993, chapters 4-5.

18. T. LaHaye, *The Battle for the Family, op.cit.*, pp.32, 49; J. Dobson and G.L. Bauer, *Children At Risk. The Battle for the Hearts and Minds of Our Kids*, Word, Dallas 1990, pp.19-20, 35-36, 43-44, 217-23.

19. J. Falwell, *Listen, America!, op.cit.*, pp.130-31, 157-59.

20. T. LaHaye, *The Battle for the Family, op.cit.*, pp.32-33, 43; J. Dobson and G.L. Bauer, *Children At Risk. The Battle for the Hearts and Minds of Our Kids, op.cit.*, pp.20-22, 41.

21. P. Robertson, *New Millennium*, Word, Milton Keynes 1990, pp.10-11, 50; T. LaHaye, *The Battle for the Family, op.cit.*, pp.28-30.

22. T. LaHaye, *What Everyone Should Know About Homosexuality*, Tyndale House, Wheaton 1978, pp.203-204; P. Robertson, *The New Millennium, op.cit.*, pp.136, 13; P. Robertson, *The New World Order*, Word, Dallas 1991, pp.252-56, 92, 37.

23. J. Falwell, *The Fundamentalist Phenomenon, op.cit.*, pp.189-90, 212-16; J. Falwell, *Listen. America!, op.cit.*, pp.12, 11.

24. M. Durham, 'Abortion and the Politics of Morality in the USA', *op.cit.* M. Durham, 'The Road to Victory? The American Right and the Clinton Administration', *Parliamentary Affairs*, April 1996; D. M. Oldfield, *The Right and the Righteous. The Christian Right Confronts the Republican*

Party, op.cit.

25. Oldfield, *ibid.*, chapter 6; D. Balz and R. Brownstein, *Storming the Gates. Protest Politics and the Republican Revival*, Little, Brown and Co., Boston 1996, chapter 7; R. Reed, 'Casting A Wider Net', *Christian American*, July-August 1993.

26. *Contract with the American Family*, Moorings, Nashville 1995, pxi; M. Durham, 'The Road to Victory? The American Right and the Clinton Administration', *op.cit.*

27. W.L. Anderson, 'Onward Christian Soldiers?', *Reason*, January 1994; J.H. Birnbaum, 'The Gospel According to Ralph', *Time*, 15 May 1995; C. Curtis, 'Putting Out a Contract', *Christianity Today*, 17 July 1995.

28. See: D. Cantor, *The Religious Right. The Assault on Tolerance and Pluralism in America*, Anti-Defamation League, New York, 1994; R. Boston, *The Most Dangerous Man in America? Pat Robertson and the Rise of the Christian Coalition*, Prometheus Books, Amherst 1996.

29. R. Reed, *After the Revolution. How the Christian Coalition is Impacting America*, Word, Dallas, 1996, pp.40, 75-80, 28-32, 37, 236, 241.

30. See: 'Presidential candidates address conference attendees', *Christian American*, October 1995.

31. See: Anderson, 'Onward Christian Soldiers?' *op.cit.*; C. Wilcox, *Onward. Christian Soldiers? The religious Right in American Politics*, Westview Press, Boulder 1996, p.139.

32. See: 'God's Army Plans for War', *Montana Christian*, January-February 1992.

Islamist Political Thought

Phil Marfleet

Introduction: God and Change

In 1985 unusual graffiti appeared in North London. Large letters on road signs and railway stations proclaimed 'JIHAD!'. A few years earlier the Arabic word would have had no significance outside Muslim communities and even here it would have been subject to dispute about its meaning and context. In the mid-1980s, however, Islamic activism was an emerging force. The Iranian revolution had suggested that religion might be investing Third World politics with new energies and *jihad* was being widely interpreted as political struggle or even war against secular authorities. As Muslim activists challenged state structures across the Middle East and spread their influence into Africa and Asia there was the first suggestion that 'political' Islam might have a global reach. Activist currents began to grow rapidly in Europe and North America, especially among urban youth, provoking media interest, anxiety and often great hostility: an 'anti-muslim panic'.[1] But in proportion to such hostility, Islamic activism seemed to prosper. By the early 1990s it had become a strong pole of attraction within Muslim communities in the West and was drawing converts from the wider society. What is the substance of the politics that has caused such reactions and what is the status of the activist movement today?

Since the Iranian revolution of 1979, notions of a new Islamic politics have spread across the world. These can be identified as a politics of religious activism, or Islamism,[2] differentiated from the mainstream of Islamic thought by the vision of radical change and a strong emphasis on political action. Although Islamism emerged over a hundred years ago and has had profound influence in predominantly Islamic regions throughout the twentieth century, its wider impact is a more recent development.

In most countries in which Islam is the dominant tradition, religious ideas and institutions are of a conservative character. As with all the major religions, they have tended to endorse existing social and political arrangements and to discourage efforts to bring them into question. Islamism has challenged this orthodoxy. Although it has a highly conservative aspect to its ideology, Islamic activism has in general expressed the unease or discontent of subordinate sections of society, those who aspire to a share in power or to a dominant role in the political system. Hence Islamist movements are often referred to as manifestations of 'political' Islam.[3]

Islamists are usually highly critical of secular authorities and of Muslim rulers whom they believe to have compromised religious principles. Such rulers are often accused of injustice, collaboration with non-Islamic (usually Western) forces, incorrect application of *shari'a*[4] and of encouraging disunity among Muslims. The call for action is usually directed against such rulers on the basis that the political system requires realignment with 'true' Islamic principles or should even be replaced with an authentically Islamic state. Islamist political thought therefore focuses on a number of interrelated themes: the assertion of divine over secular authority; the requirement for social harmony under Godly supervision; the achievement of Muslim unity; and the obligation to work actively for assertion of Islam, usually associated with *jihad*, meaning 'striving' or 'exertion'.

For most Islamist movements these issues are common ground. Activists disagree sharply, however, on political strategy. On the one hand there are movements focused on reform which attempt to bring change by developing their influence over structures of the state. Thus in Egypt, Jordan and Algeria the Muslim Brotherhood has attempted to construct parliamentary blocs which will legislate for a new social order. In Turkey, the Refah (Welfare) Party, which formed a government in 1996, also represents this current – an Islamic gradualism which aims at the erosion of secular power, largely by means of legal reform. Here the attempt to reshape legal structures is itself the focal point of the struggle for Islam.

More insistent Islamist currents have adopted an insurrectionary strategy. Thus the militants of the *gama'at islamiyya* (Islamic groups) and the Jihad organisation in Egypt have attempted to wrest the state from secular authorities. Emphasising the need to destroy secular structures and to construct a new, wholly Islamic polity, they have organised for 'revolution' of the Muslim masses led by an Islamic vanguard – a framework which has been seen as reminiscent of Leninist-type parties of the Left.[5] A somewhat similar strategy was followed by Khomeini and his supporters in Iran and has been attempted by some activist groups in Algeria. All these radical movements view the obligation to assert Islam as fully satisfied only by confrontation with *kufr* ('unbelieving') institutions. Here *jihad* implies conflict, even war.

The gradualist and radical currents mark opposite extremes of the Islamist political spectrum between which are a host of other movements. Some shift their political strategies between these models, as with the Islamic Resistance Movement (Hamas) in Palestine[6] and Hezbollah in Lebanon, or follow highly conspiratorial militarist approaches like those of the underground opposition groups in Saudi Arabia or Libya. The basic distinction between the two wings is, however, echoed in the West. In Britain, for example, activists have been drawn largely by two currents. The Muslim Brotherhood's Young Muslims emphasise *da'wah* (proselytising and conversion) and the accumulation of influence. On the radical wing, Hizb al-Tahrir (The Party of Liberation) and Al Mujahirun (The Emigrants) are fiercely critical of secular authority and foresee a more traumatic confrontation with the state.

What this pattern conceals is the range and complexity of sects, groups, movements and parties. Understanding of their specific character, and of relations between them, requires that each is situated in a social, political and cultural context and in relation to the dominant currents. In fact such analysis is seldom carried out, overwhelmingly because of the tendency of Western media and academics to treat Muslim activism as one undifferentiated bloc, usually dubbed 'fundamentalism'. Here, religious activism is viewed as a primordialism – an assertion of basic or essential values – and there is little room for consideration of the political perspectives advanced by the movements.

The Problem of Orientalism

There is a long record of Western hostility towards Islam. This invariably inhibits understanding of Islamic history and of developments which have produced the activist movements.

Over the past twenty years there has been growing awareness of the problem of Orientalism – the set of assumptions about 'the East' which has long encouraged notions that Islam is backward and inferior.[7] Orientalism has not only dismissed Islam as a perverse and irrational challenge to the enlightened traditions of Christian Europe but has also made Muslims themselves merely bearers of the Islamic impulse – base, violent and 'fanatical'.[8] Despite increased awareness of the distorting effect of this perspective, highly prejudicial accounts of Islam continue to appear. A few titles among the many books written during the 1980s illustrate the problem: *Sacred Rage, Holy Terror, Holy War* and *The Dagger of Islam* all present 'fundamentalism' as violent and threatening, an offence to 'civilisation', which is invariably identified with the West.

Contemporary Islamism is often made to represent Islam as a whole. To give just one example, Conor Cruise O'Brien, a prominent European journalist and commentator, stated that:

> 'Fundamentalist' Islam is a misnomer which dulls our perceptions in a dangerous way. It does so by implying that there is some other kind of Islam, which is well disposed to those who reject the Koran. There isn't. ... What is going on today in the Muslim world is not the aberrant thing called Muslim fundamentalism but a revival of Islam itself – the real thing – which Western ascendancy and Westernised post-Muslim elites no longer have the capacity to muffle and control. The jihad is back.[9]

In this view Islam is war and Muslims are unthinking bearers of its violence. In fact such an approach invites 'us' – a Western audience assumed to possess superior capacities of understanding – to suspend critical faculties, bringing down a curtain of misunderstanding between Muslim and non-Muslim. It becomes impossible to comprehend Islamic traditions or to approach an understanding of contemporary Islamic movements.

A very different approach is needed, one which recognises that religious ideas and institutions, like other traditions and structures, are shaped and reshaped by human agents. It is the interaction between such social and political actors, and the structural factors that constrain their lives, which makes religion various and flexible. Islam, then, is no more fixed or essential than any other complex of ideas about the divine or other-worldly. The emergence of Islamic activism can be comprehended as a movement with specific roots and indeed as a development which is itself in part an expression of relations between societies of the Middle East and those of the West.

Roots

Islamic history is replete with schisms and factionalisms in which groups of believers challenge rulers and religious authorities on the basis that they possess sacred authority or have special access to scriptural knowledge or tradition. The Sunni-Shi'a split, for example, which had its origins in the earliest years of Islam[10] and became institutionalised in the eighth century CE/AD, has been the basis of all manner of claims about the legitimate exercise of power. In addition, the messianic character of some aspects of Islam has encouraged mobilisation around the figure of the *mahdi* – one whose just rule is said to herald the approach of the end of time. Dissident movements throughout the vast areas influenced by Islamic traditions have organised around such figures for centuries. What distinguishes Islamism from these revolts is its engagement with political structures associated exclusively with the modern world. It is this political modernism that has shaped the religious activism of today.

'Proto-Islamists' first appeared in Egypt in the 1860s when junior *'ulema* – members of the religious establishment – began to criticise the impact of European colonialism upon societies of the Middle East. They deplored the policy which had been adopted by local rulers in the face of European advance – a 'defensive' or 'imitative' nationalism which set out to reproduce structures of the European nation state. Such rulers had been strongly supported by senior *'ulema*, whose families were often closely linked to those in power and whose value to the latter lay in the authority they could convey by sanctifying and celebrating state policy.

In fact, imitative nationalism served only to accelerate European penetration. Among those most negatively affected were the merchants and artisans who were at the heart of the region's urban economy and who had always been closely connected to the religious establishment. It seemed to them that the social and political fabric of local society and even the institutions of Islam were under threat. Hussein al-Marsafi was one of the writers who articulated their anxiety and anger, attributing much of Egypt's plight to its rulers, officials and religious leaders, whom he believed to have been complicit in the European offensive. He contrasted their conduct as Muslims with that of the Prophet Muhammed and the first *umma* or community of believers. He maintained that Egyptians should reassert 'the faith in all its truth and purity' and drive out those who merely exploited religion to serve their own interests.[11]

This move towards an Islamic/Egyptian nationalism was sharpened by the seminal figure in Islamist political history, Jamal al-Din al-Afghani. An Iranian who agitated and organised in Egypt, India, Turkey and Iran during the last quarter of the nineteenth century, Afghani originated the idea of pan-Islam, a unity of all Muslims which would be capable of resisting European advance.

Afghani was not opposed to European culture as such but formally rejected Western political structures; in particular, he was hostile to the colonising activities associated with the nation state and to the fragmentation of the *umma*. Moazzam comments that:

> In view of the growing political penetration of the European powers, especially Britain, Afghani called on the Muslims to forget their internal rivalries, political and religious, and unite themselves against outside dangers. Declaring that 'there is no nationality of Muslims except Islam', he reminds his fellow believers that unity and power are the two chief pillars of Islam.[12]

Rather than imitate European nationalism, Afghani maintained, Muslims should reassert their own values, mobilising around uncorrupted Islamic principles to be determined by reference to the Prophet's *umma*. He called for a new leadership of scholars and suitably qualified Muslim rulers who would be capable of enforcing the *shari'a*. They were to be supported by the mass of Muslims in a struggle to reform society. Engineer comments: 'He [Afghani] wanted Muslim masses to take their destiny into their own hands'.[13]

Afghani thus became the first Muslim leader to argue for political action on the basis of Islamic tradition but in the context of modern politics. His pan-Islam envisaged an increasing unity of believers, although he assumed that in its initial stages this would be mobilised *within* the nation state he so mistrusted.[14] By the end of the nineteenth century his work had had a profound impact, especially upon anti-colonial movements in Egypt and Iran. As these movements gathered strength, however, the pan-Islamic element was subsumed by the emerging current of secular nationalism and across the Middle East Islamism became a marginal current. By the end of the First World War and the great anti-colonial upheavals in Egypt, Iran and the Arab provinces of the Ottoman Empire, religious activism was hardly significant within regional politics.

Mass Action and the Gradualist Approach

What gave Islamism new life was the failure of secular nationalism. This was most apparent in Egypt of the 1920s, where the nationalist government tolerated by the British occupying forces proved to be no more than a token of independence. When Hassan al-Banna founded the Society of the Muslim Brothers (Muslim Brotherhood) in 1928 he soon discovered a huge audience for a new politics of mass activism. Banna saw his inspiration in the teachings of Afghani and of the latter's disciples, notably Muhammed Abduh and Rashid Rida,[15] but his own contribution was decisive. In effect Banna projected Islamism into the arena of political contest defined by the modern state. He built the Brotherhood as a political party, an organisation that constructed an elaborate network of community organisations, trade unions and professional associations, schools and charities. By the 1940s it had become the largest participatory organisation in the region, with a membership estimated at 500,000[16] and it dominated the anti-colonial movement in the Arab states.

Banna's political thought anticipated much of the Islamist politics of today. He attacked 'external colonialism' – the rule of European powers in Islamic regions – which he believed had produced only decay and humiliation for Muslims. He also targeted 'internal colonialism' – what he saw as the collaborative role of local rulers and leading *'ulema*. It was the submissive Islam of senior *'ulema* which 'supported and sustained the imperialists', he argued.[17] They had damaged the Muslim collective so seriously that its much-weakened political structures had been easily fragmented by the colonial powers. These representatives of Islam, wrote Banna's associate Muhammed al-Ghazali, had sold their opportunity to speak on behalf of the mass of Muslims.[18]

As against these alien forces within and without Muslim society Banna proposed a reassertion of Islam:

> We believe the provisions of Islam and its teachings are all-inclusive, encompassing the affairs of the people in this world and the hereafter.

> And those who think that these teachings are concerned only with the
> spiritual or ritualistic aspects are mistaken in this belief because Islam is
> a faith and a ritual, a nation and a nationality, a religion and a state, spirit
> and deed, holy text and the sword . . . the glorious Qur'an . . . considers
> [these things] to be the core of Islam and its essence . . .[19]

This was indeed a call for assertion of the 'essence' – the fundamentals
– of religion. But there was no requirement for a *new* Islam – on this
point Banna was insistent. He maintained: 'The noble Qur'an is an
inclusive book in which God has gathered the fundamentals of faith,
the foundations of social virtues and all the worldly legislation'.[20]
Twentieth-century Muslims should not, therefore, attempt a 'return' to
the origins of Islam in the seventh century; those who suggested this,
Banna argued, were confusing 'the historical beginning of Islam with
the system of Islam itself'.[21]

Banna called for 'a vast spiritual awakening' among Muslims.[22] By
means of a great collective effort, he maintained, it would be possible
to bring into being *al-nizam al-islami* – an 'Islamic order'. This was
only vaguely defined: sometimes Banna referred to a future 'Muslim
state'; more often the new polity was presented as a set of legal principles. Mitchell observes: '*The shari'a* – its implementation or non-
implementation – was the determinant in the definition of a true
Islamic order'.[23]

Egypt could not be 'Islamised' overnight, Banna maintained, and
much had to be done to pave the way towards the final goal. The
Brotherhood was therefore active in the anti-colonial struggle and also
pursued political, legal and administrative reform. In effect Banna
argued for Muslims to exert an irresistible pressure on the colonial state
while they attempted to introduce legal reforms which could lay the
basis for a new order. But the Brotherhood proved unable to replace
the secular nationalists. Despite his scorn for the government, in the
late 1940s Banna attempted to negotiate a series of compromises with
its leading members and with the King, Faruq. The Brotherhood never
recovered from the mistrust this seems to have generated among its
many supporters and in 1952, with Egypt in turmoil, the army seized
power. Over the next decade the Brotherhood faced intense repression
and again became a marginal force. Islamist influence diminished across
the Middle East as the region seemed to embrace a secular model of
change.

Banna had an immense influence on later generations of religious activists. In the 1980s, for example, supporters of Ayatollah Khomeini traced their own 'revolutionary' Islamist heritage through the Brotherhood.[24] Banna's importance lay in his clarification of what had remained half-formed in the thought of Afghani: the idea that Muslim engagement with the political structures of the modern world should have an activist dimension. For Afghani, pan-Islamism was notionally an activism but one that operated essentially at a propagandist level, for Muslims were to be awoken to their tasks primarily through education. With Banna, this approach was given momentum by full entry into the political field. Although he was fiercely opposed to political parties on the secular model, claiming that they created 'disunity' in the nation and were therefore incompatible with Islam, the Brotherhood became a party in all but name and it was through this structure that activism was channelled. Such activism was *jihad*, not merely the personal exertion or 'inner struggle', which was the *jihad* of the religious establishment, but a *fight* for Islam which might even end in martyrdom when Muslims confronted the forces of the state. In effect, this new and more effective religious activism was shaped against the national political framework but also operated within it. It has remained the model for all the main 'reformist' or 'gradualist' currents.

The Radical Turn

The Brotherhood failed to bring change, however, and among some of its disillusioned supporters there developed a new activism. One current which emerged in the Arab East – Palestine, Syria, Jordan and Lebanon – formed around the Palestinian intellectual Taqi al-Din al-Nabahani. He identified the central problem facing Muslims as that of the destruction of the Caliphate – the political structures of the Ottoman Empire which had its centre in Turkey, and until the early twentieth century, ruled much of the Arab world. Since the seventh century political authority in the Sunni world had been invested in the *khalifa* ('caliph' – successor) to the Prophet. Under Ottoman rule, the *sultan* – the head of the Empire – was also caliph and, with the dismantling of the empire by Britain and France, the much-weakened structures of Islamic political authority finally collapsed. Nabahani sought to re-establish the *khilafa* (caliphate) as an Islamic state under authentic leadership which was capable of bringing a renaissance in Muslims' fortunes. He presented a detailed account of a prospective Islamic system and in 1952 established Hizb al-Tahrir al-Islami (The Islamic Liberation Party) to bring it into being. But Nabahani's influence in the Middle East was short-lived, perhaps because his political strategy focused on the immediate task of implementing a grand pan-Islamic order. Although he was later to have an unexpected influence among Muslims in the West,[25] in the Arab world the agenda was now set by a further radical activism which emerged in Egypt. The new generation of Egyptian activists drew upon ideological developments that had been taking place outside the Middle Eastern 'heartlands' of Islam, especially upon the ideas of Indian Muslim scholars, of whom the most prominent was Abu'l-A'la Mawdudi.

Two key ideas elaborated by Mawdudi had a profound impact upon Arab Islamists. First was the reassertion of a principle which had a long history in Islamic tradition but which Mawdudi invested with new significance: that of the notion of a universal battle between Islam and un-Islam – the world of *kufr* or unbelief. He maintained that this struggle would result in the triumph of Islam and the establishment of an Islamic state capable of introducing reforms in line with the *shari'a*. This would constitute Banna's 'Islamic order' – a society on the model of the Prophet's *umma*. What was new in Mawdudi's interpretation of tradition was identification of the modern state as a means of resolving the conflict between belief and unbelief, for once 'Islamicised', he maintained, the state itself could be the means of bringing universal order.

A second key idea absorbed by Arab activists from Mawdudi was that of the modern *jahiliyya*. In mainstream Islamic tradition, Arabian society before Muhammed had been characterised by its 'ignorance': it was a *jahili* or unenlightened order which had been transformed by the Prophet's transmission of God's instructions for human conduct. Mawdudi maintained that the materialism, corruption and Godlessness of contemporary society made it nothing less than a modern *jahiliyya*, one far worse than the pre-Muhammedan state of ignorance precisely because it flouted the principles contained in God's message.

These ideas were adopted and given further specific meaning by the Egyptian Sayyid Qutb, the most influential figure of the past fifty years among Sunni activists. Qutb had been an enthusiastic member of the Brotherhood under Banna but had been distressed at its failures and appalled at the conduct of those Brotherhood sympathisers who had come to power with the army in the early 1950s. Incarcerated by the nationalist government for over a decade, Qutb spent his years in prison developing a new theory of activism. He depicted Egyptian society as in a state of ignorance which amounted to barbarism:

> It is clearly visible that the entire world is steeped in *jahiliyya* and that too of an order whose evils are not diminished or attenuated even by the marvellous material comforts, luxuries and high-level inventions. The basis on which the edifice of the *jahiliyya* rests is the rebellion against the sovereignty of God on earth.[26]

The 'rebellion' against God, Qutb argued, should be met with a new rebellion of Muslims committed to liquidate *jahiliyya* and to introduce a new order. Their means of struggle must be that of *jihad* against those who flouted God's will. This struggle, which must be vigorous and consistent, was to be a political activism which contested the ungodly state, seeking to replace it with an Islamic state. Committed Muslims should be prepared to advance 'through the vast ocean of *jahiliyya*, which has encircled the entire world'.[27] Their reward would be in transforming *jahiliyya* into Godliness in an exercise which paralleled the Prophet's defeat of ancient unbelief.

Qutb viewed the Brotherhood's strategy as having been deficient in that it allowed the secular state to contain *jihad*. It was necessary to organise differently, by bringing together a 'vanguard' of activists which would begin the struggle for change by isolating itself from the contamination of *jahili* society. Small groups of believers should distance themselves from ungodly influences by 'migrating' from the mainstream of society into associations of Muslims whose harmonious activities would prefigure the new order. The 'vanguard' was identified with the Prophet's *umma* and their 'migration' with his *hijra*, the journey of Muhammed and the first Muslims from Mecca to Medina which laid the basis for the original Islamic community.

Qutb's radicalism was determinedly subversive: he contested the state itself and it is in this sense that he has been seen as an Islamic 'revolutionary'. Following Mawdudi he proposed an Islamic polity to be brought into being by righteous activity that itself negated secular structures. When in the mid-1960s Egypt began to move into a period of increased instability, the secular authorities were quick to move against him and in 1966 he was charged with attempting to overthrow the government by force, found guilty and hanged in prison.

Only after his death did Qutb's teachings have their full impact. From the late 1960s Egypt experienced a decade of political turmoil during which his followers attempted to put the strategy into practice. Prominent among them were Shukri Mustafa, founder of the Society of Muslims, and 'Abd al-Salam Farag, a leading figure in the Jihad organisation which assassinated Egyptian President Anwar Sadat in 1981. 'Qutbist' theories have since been closely associated with the radical wing of contemporary Islamism. They have guided the Jihad organisation and the *gama'at islamiyya* in Egypt, where for the past 25 years the state has been engaged in undeclared civil war with the Islamist underground. They have also influenced radical currents associated with the FIS in Algeria and were founding principles for the Palestinian Islamic Jihad.[28] Although often regarded as the product of a specifically Sunni tradition, their importance has also been acknowledged by leading Shi'a ideologues such as Khomeini.[29]

The Iranian Paradigm

During the 1970s secular nationalism began to retreat and Islamism re-established itself as the most dynamic political force in the Middle East. This development was largely ignored in the West, where dominant theories of 'modernisation' still predicted development of Third World societies towards a North American/European model. In these theories, religion – or at least non-Western religion – was regarded as a mere remnant of traditionalism. Islam in particular was seen as a sorry example of pre-modern superstition: a complex of ideas that had at various times contested European rationalism only to be forced into new retreats.[30] As a result, much analysis of Middle Eastern politics failed even to note the Islamist advance. When this extended to Iran, where for the first time Islamists seized state power, there was disbelief among Western analysts as they struggled to come to terms with the Khomeini phenomenon.

The Iranian revolution of 1979 occurred in conditions which had already proved fertile ground for Islamist advance in Egypt and elsewhere. Rapid economic change, mass migration and urban growth had exaggerated already wide social inequalities. When protests against the excesses of a strongly pro-Western regime were met with extreme state violence a broad opposition movement began to emerge. In earlier years such movements had come under secular radical influence but by the 1970s, with nationalist and Communist currents much weakened, some sections of the religious leadership rapidly came to prominence.

What gave them special appeal was the apparently radical character of their politics and their intransigence in the face of the regime.

Many analyses present the Shi'a *'ulema* as historically independent of the state and well fitted to articulate mass discontent. In fact, although some sections of the Iranian clergy (usually among its lower ranks) had been associated with movements for change, senior clerics had long been closely identified with the structures of privilege. From the earliest years of Iran's Pahlavi dynasty in the 1920s, prominent religious figures had been apologists for the regime. Standing in the tradition of 'quietism', they endorsed the activities of the state, even during periods of political turmoil. Khomeini himself, for example, offered only the most muted criticisms of the regime, observing that even the Pahlavi administration had virtues, being 'better than [no regime] at all'.[31] It was not until the 1960s, when the modernisation programme of the Shah – the monarchical ruler of Iran – began to affect seriously those sections of society most closely associated with the *'ulema*, that a fraction of the religious establishment under Khomeini's leadership asserted its independence and moved into opposition.[32]

During a long period of exile Khomeini developed a new Shi'a radicalism. As in the case of Qutb, who experienced the internal exile of imprisonment in Egypt, such development seems to have been associated with physical isolation from the religious establishment. From the early 1970s Khomeini began to depict Iran as a state which had fallen into the hands of 'traitors, usurpers and the agents of foreign powers' and called for both *'ulema* and the mass of believers to confront the Shah.[33] The latter was *taghut*, he argued, the sort of impious ruler who was an obstacle to implementation of the *shari'a* and therefore one whom Muslims should oppose as a matter of duty.[34] Such opposition should be highly active: scholars and the Muslim masses should intervene directly in social and political affairs and only the irreligious contested their duty to do so.[35]

Khomeini suggested that mass action against the regime was a 'sacred *jihad*'.[36] It was to be directed towards establishment of a new polity – an 'Islamic republic'. He argued, in effect, that notwithstanding the ungodly character of the Pahlavi state, it could be seized and used to forge a new order. This would be based upon rigorous application of the *shari'a*, definition of which would rest upon judgement by the most senior cleric. Even within the modern state, he argued, sovereignty belonged to such a cleric by virtue of his knowledge of Islamic tradition and his expertise in implementation of the law.

In a nation state transformed into an Islamic order, Khomeini maintained, all Muslims would willingly acknowledge the rule of such a jurist, the *vilayat-i faqih*:

> The two qualities of knowledge of the law and justice are present in countless *fuquha* [jurists] of the present age. If they would come together, they could establish a government of universal justice in the world.

> If a worthy individual possessing these two qualities arises and establishes a government, he will possess the same authority as The Most Noble Messenger [the Prophet] (upon whom be peace and blessings) in the administration of society, and it will be the duty of all peoples to obey him.[37]

While Sunni ideologues, notably Qutb, had argued for Muslims to follow the Prophet's conduct in *jihad* and to engage in *hijra* which emulated his exile from Mecca, Khomeini took the far more dramatic step of proposing that a cleric could rule in ways which might be 'the same' as that enjoyed by Muhammed. In the modern age, he argued, God had conferred upon governments the same powers and authority held by the Prophet in military, administrative, financial and welfare matters, and it was an obligation on the senior cleric to supervise them in his role as 'guardian of the nation'.[38]

Although this plan for rule as *vilayat-i faqih* was well known among Khomeini's immediate supporters, during the revolution his public pronouncements on the future Islamic republic presented it quite differently: as an open, participatory system which would guarantee the rights of all its citizens. Urging the mass of Iranians to remove the Shah, Khomeini promised that in the new Iran, 'the weak will be triumphant over the powerful ... the downtrodden will supplant the rich'.[39] This apparently radical vision was far more relevant to the masses of Iranians who were deeply engaged in the tumultuous events of revolution and was probably decisive in projecting Khomeini to leadership of the movement. He was soon in control of a new government, implementing a highly centralised rule based upon a loyal section of the *'ulema* and his own authority as *vilayet-i faqih*. Some former supporters and many analysts of the Iranian events have described this ascent to power as both brilliantly flexible in its execution and grossly opportunistic.[40]

Khomeini's assertion of divine rule through the nation state marks the full accommodation of Islamic political tradition with the structures of modernity. The nation state becomes a realisation of God's intentions for human conduct in this world: it resolves immediate divisions among Muslims, brings social harmony and creates the basis for further unification of the community of believers. Here the nation state itself is an instrument of *jihad*.

'Global' Islam

The Iranian events were enormously significant. They were widely perceived in the Third World as a triumphant insurgency against the West which paralleled the achievements of the earlier nationalist movements in Algeria or Vietnam but were distinguished by their religious dimension. Islam, it seemed, had empowered the Iranian masses, providing both spiritual resources to guide their struggle and an intransigent and successful leadership. At this stage the character of the post-revolutionary state was less important than the fact of its existence.

Islamists took heart from Khomeini's triumph. Between 1979 and 1982 they mounted insurrectionary challenges to the regimes in Saudi Arabia, Egypt and Syria, while in Iraq, Afghanistan, Lebanon, Sudan and all the North African states radical currents grew rapidly. Pro-Western regimes in the Middle East were particularly fearful that Islamism had succeeded in seizing the anti-imperialist credentials that had earlier marked the secular nationalist movements. At the same time, rulers of the Soviet Union were perplexed by the Islamist threat to the communist regime in Afghanistan and by the impact of the Iranian events in the predominantly Muslim regions of Central Asia. By the mid-1980s, the enthusiasm stimulated by the Iranian events was being felt in West and Central Africa, South and South-East Asia, and Europe and North America. Politicians and academics began to talk of a 'global' Islam: a religion in which the vision of a universal mission was congruent with economic, technological and other unifying processes said to be taking place at a world level.[41]

The new influence of Islam in the West has been a shock to those who assumed that it was a reassertion of 'alien' and outdated beliefs. For some Muslims in Europe and North America it has in fact taken on a particular significance as a tradition *uniquely* capable of dealing with the political problems of the modern world. As Abdelwahab El-

Affendi comments, many Muslims see themselves as 'the conscience of humanity':

> This role has been enhanced by the collapse of communism, which failed in its attempt to assume that role in the past. The Muslim voice is now the only dissenting voice in a fast homogenizing world.[42]

The 'Muslim voice' can become a voice of protest against Western domination of the Third World; at the same time it can be a protest against conditions faced by many communities of Muslim background and tradition resident in the West. Here, the vision of a universal *umma* which gives a place to every believer becomes especially powerful in the context of discriminations on the basis of colour, language, place of origin or religion which marginalise a large minority of the population. Thus Islamists in the West have projected *jihad* as a political strategy – simultaneously a struggle against the perceived evils of imperialism and against the exploitation, injustice and prejudice of daily life.[43]

Criticisms and Failures

The hopes generated among activists by the Iranian revolution and Islamist advances of the 1980s have not been realised, however. 'Khomeinism' has not had the impact that its supporters had anticipated; indeed, the record of the Iranian regime *vis-à-vis* its own population has alienated many Muslim activists.[44] During the 1990s the gradualist current associated with the tradition of Banna and expressed by the Muslim Brotherhood has retreated in strongholds such as Egypt and Algeria. The radicals, in the tradition of Qutb or of Khomeini, have been violently repressed almost everywhere and are a less significant factor than a decade earlier.

This reduced momentum has led some commentators in the Western media to suggest that 'fundamentalism' may have had its day. Up to the early 1990s Islamism was often presented in lurid terms: in the US, newspaper headlines such as 'The Muslims Are Coming' echoed a 'War of the Worlds' theme, with Islamism constituting a planetary invasion of aliens.[45] A few years later such media had swung towards triumphalist assertions of Islamist retreat. Even the more measured analyses now ask if the tide has turned: in 1996, the *Washington Post*, for example, considered whether 'the surge of Islamic militancy of the last 25 years has begun to abate', pointing to evidence that states such as Egypt have secured 'victory' over the radicals.[46]

It is unwise to suggest that the movement as a whole is in some sense defeated. At several points over the past hundred years it has been forced to the margins of politics in the Middle East, only to make dramatic recoveries from which it has reached even higher levels of mobilisation. What seems clear, however, is that Islamist politics has passed through a crucial phase. Islamist activists have recently seen unprecedented opportunities to realise their vision of a sacred polity but in country after country they have failed to secure their goal. Only in Iran have they managed to seize the state on the basis of mass mobilisation, apparently realising the idea of united Muslim self-activity. With the partial exception of Sudan,[47] the movement elsewhere has proved ineffectual, even in the face of the most vulnerable secular regimes, seeming to hesitate and retreat when the prospect of power becomes imminent. Indeed, the higher the level of mass engagement, the more the movements seemed to vacillate. In Algeria in 1992, for example, faced with the prospect of taking power on the basis of an electoral majority and with widespread popular backing, the movement's leadership appeared paralysed, unsure of its strategy. When the army then gambled on military means to retain power in secular hands, the Islamists proved unable to meet the challenge.

The Algerian case points up a contradiction in Islamist politics which has been present since Afghani laid out the basis for his pan-Islam. This lies in the simultaneous hostility to and orientation upon the nation state. The social core of all Islamist currents has been drawn from middling social layers best described as the new petite bourgeoisie. These professionals and functionaries, identified by Mitchell as 'the emergent Muslim middle class'[48] are themselves closely associated with the structures of modern capitalism and with the state. Therefore, although they may express intense hostility to secular political currents which have monopolised state power, they are seldom prepared to challenge the state itself. Roberts observes how, in the Algerian case, the radical rhetoric used to mobilise support for an 'Islamic alternative' was modified when Islamists faced the challenge of assuming power.[49] In 1992, he comments, 'we do not find an uncompromising, all-out, revolutionary Islamist onslaught on the state':

> ... the mainstream of Algerian Islamism has never had a revolutionary attitude to the Algerian state in the sense of an uncompromising hostil-

ity to this state and its corollary, the determination to overthrow it. On the contrary, the Islamist movement has always sought to advance its cause *within* the framework of the Algerian state and, whenever its rhetoric has suggested a revolutionary ambition, its practice has invariably belied this. Because of this, the real, as opposed to apparent, strategy of the Islamist movement has always been a strategy of alliances. Thus, while the FIS's rhetoric denounced the actual Algerian state as *un etat impie* [an ungodly state] run by *les voleurs du FLN* [the FLN thieves] and counterposed to this the radiant vision of an Islamic republic, *dawla islamiyya*, its practice was another matter altogether. Far from adopting a revolutionary and correspondingly uncompromising practice of refusing to have anything to do with the actual state, the FIS persistently operated an unacknowledged alliance with some of the most powerful elements of the state, including those whose policies might reasonably be held responsible for the economic distress of the electors the Islamists were appealing to.[50]

As a result, when the FIS retreated from the contest for state power – as Banna had done in the 1940s – its many supporters were disoriented and quickly disillusioned. The Islamists' mass base eroded and the army consolidated its hold on power.

The case of Iran provides the sole example of a direct Islamist challenge to state power under conditions of mass mobilisation. But even here, what Roberts calls 'the radiant vision of an Islamic republic' proved, under Khomeini, to be strikingly different from that anticipated by the revolutionary movement. As Roy has observed, one of the characteristics of the Khomeini regime has been its unwillingness to modify the state structures it inherited, even though these were earlier vilified as the very expression of unGodliness.[51] Indeed, it soon abandoned the notion of a new polity based upon divine principles in favour of an 'Islamo-nationalism'[52] – a capitalism with religious colouring constructed on the foundations of the Pahlavi state. This provided a framework around which the regime's own power could be measured in terms of control of everyday conduct among the mass of Muslims. Hence dietary matters, dress, relations between the sexes and the definition of cultural 'authenticity' become matters of overwhelming importance.

The Iranian experience emphasises the extent to which Islamist politics has systematically marginalised women. Western accounts of the movement tend to focus on this issue, sometimes to the exclusion of all other matters and often with the result that the status of women within the Islamic tradition as a whole is misrepresented. In fact, women's status has not been a central issue within Islamist politics conceived as the vision of a new polity. Although women have invariably been subordinated within Islamist movements, many have embraced their broad aims, especially during periods of political turmoil when religious activism has seemed to offer an alternative to the failures of secularism. As Haleh Afshar observes in the case of Iran, a 'throng of women' supported the revolution of 1979,[53] sharing the expectations of male participants that an 'Islamic Republic' would deliver new freedoms. Under the Khomeini regime they were soon to face laws and decrees aimed at driving women to the margins of social and political life. Such legislation is itself an expression of retreat. Unable to realise the vision contained within their populist project, Islamist leaders have directed their energies towards elaboration of restrictive codes of conduct based upon highly selective readings of the religious tradition. Here, the radical component of Islamism is rendered ineffective by the movement's inability to initiate genuine change and its ideological conservatism dominates the political agenda.

Women have strongly challenged these developments. Arguing that there are multiple interpretations of the religious tradition, they have maintained effectively that specific rights can be defended against programmes of legislation such as that in Iran. Afkhami comments:

> Iranian women can challenge the claim that there is something unique in Islam that separates it from other human experiences. The goal is to contest the right and legitimacy of Iran's patriarchal clerical order to be the sole interpreters of the values, norms and aesthetic standards of Shii Islam . . .[54]

Similar developments are taking place across the Middle East, notably in Egypt and Morocco. One unexpected outcome of recent Islamist activity, in fact, has been the emergence of a contemporary 'Islamic feminism'.[55]

Conclusion

Islamism is less a movement in terminal decline than one again afflicted by an inability to realise the promises laid out in its visions of radical change. It is likely to reappear in modified forms, especially where secular alternatives fail to provide a point of reference for those excluded by existing power structures. Esposito recently observed that, since the collapse of communism, Islam has become 'the most pervasive and powerful transnational force in the world'.[56] He might have phrased it differently: the collapse of secular alternatives has indeed opened wide the *prospect* of Islamist advance – but such a prospect goes unfulfilled. Islamism remains a politics of aspiration.

Notes

1. For reactions in the United States see: J. Esposito, *The Islamic Threat: Myth or Reality?*, Oxford University Press, New York 1992, chapter 6.
2. Here the term Islamism is used to suggest an activist politics directed to radical change which is defined by reference to Islamic tradition. This should be distinguished from the uniformly conservative politics of forces such as the monarchies of the Arab world, where the claim to religious authority is used expressly to inhibit political activity.
3. N. Ayubi, *Political Islam: Religion and Politics in the Arab World*, Routledge, London 1991, chapter 1.
4. *Shari'a* – literally the 'way' – is usually defined as the holy law of Islam.
5. O. Roy, *The Failure of Political Islam*, I.B. Tauris, London 1994, p.3.
6. The Palestinian case is an unusual one. Here Islamism confronts what its activists perceive as an intrusion into the Islamic world which is indistinguishable from colonialism. As an expression of national aspirations, Hamas has much in common with the Islamists of the colonial era, such as Hassan al-Banna's Muslim Brotherhood.
7. See: E. Said *Orientalism*, Penguin, London 1978; A. Hussain, R. Olson & J. Qureshi, *Orientalism, Islam and Islamists*, Amana, Brattleboro 1984.
8. Viscount Milner, the British colonial administrator of Egypt in the 1890s, summed up these views by describing Egyptians as 'most docile and good tempered' (*sic*) but 'in the grip of a religion the most intolerant and fanatical' in Viscount Milner, *England in Egypt*, Edward Arnold, London 1920, p.4.
9. C.C. O'Brien, *Independent*, 6 January 1995.
10. In a dispute within the Muslim community over who had inherited the Prophet's authority and rights to leadership.
11. J.M. Ahmed, *The Intellectual Origins of Egyptian Nationalism*, Oxford University Press, London 1960, p.22.
12. A. Moazzam, *Jamal al-Din al-Afghani: A Muslim Intellectual*, Concept, New Delhi 1984, p24.

13. Asghar Ali Engineer, *The Islamic State*, Vikas, New Delhi 1994, p.8.

14. This contradiction has been noted by several analysts of the Islamist movement, notably by Afghani's biographer, N. Keddie. See: N. Keddie, *Sayyid Jamal al-Din 'al-Afghani': A Political Biography*, University of California Press, Berkeley 1972, p.64.

15. Both are significant as key figures in the *salafiyya* movement, which focused on 'return' to the Islam of the 'ancestors' (*salaf*), the generation which followed the Prophet. Today *salafiyya* is often taken as a synonym for *usuliyya* – 'of the roots' – the contemporary rendition in Arabic of the English 'fundamentalism' or French 'Integrisme'.

16. R. Mitchell, *The Society of the Muslim Brothers*, Oxford University Press, London 1969, p.328.

17. *Ibid.* p.213.

18. *Ibid.* p.213.

19. *Ibid.* p.233.

20. *Ibid.* p.234.

21. *Ibid.* p.234.

22. *Ibid.* p.234.

23. *Ibid.* p.235.

24. Hamid Algar, *The Roots of the Islamic Revolution*, The Open Press, London 1983, p.5.

25. Hizb al-Tahrir al-Islami grew among young Muslims in Europe from the mid-1980s. Named by its British adherents 'Hizb ut-Tahrir', its influence was greatly exaggerated by a hostile media. In 1996 an internal split produced Al Muhajirun (The Emigrants).

26. Sayyid Outb, *Milestones*, International Islamic Publishers, Karachi 1988, p.49.

27. *Ibid.* p.51.

28. On Algeria, see: S. Labat, 'Islamism and Islamists', in J. Ruedy (ed), *Islamism and Secularism in North Africa*, Macmillan, Basingstoke 1994; on the Palestinian experience, see: Ziad Abu-Amr, *Islamic Fundamentalism in the West Bank and Gaza*, Indiana University Press, Bloomington 1994.

29. Khomeini, *Islam and Revolution*, Mizan, Berkeley 1981, p.365.

30. Encapsulating the Orientalist approach, in the 1950s the historian Gustav von Grunebaum described Islam as 'absolutely defenceless' in the face of the 'rationalist and positivist spirit' of the West. Quoted in D. Lerner, *The Passing of Traditional Society: Modernising the Middle East*, Free Press, New York 1964, p.45.

31. Shaul Bakhash, *The Reign of the Ayatollahs*, I.B. Tauris, London 1985, p.23.

32. There was a gradual movement towards political radicalism across Iranian society, within which new fusions of Islamist and secular leftist politics were attempted. The role of Muslim 'socialists' such as Ali Shari'ati was particularly significant in creating a current of liberal-leftist opinion within which Islamist ideas had a wide audience. See Ervand Abrahamian, *Radical Islam*, I.B. Tauris, London 1989.

33. Khomeini, *Islam and Revolution*, *op.cit.*, p.50.

34. Discussion about power within the Islamic tradition long centred upon the extent to which rulers facilitated implementation of the *sharia* and the appropriateness of submission or opposition to them. See: Hamid Enayat, *Modern Islamic Political Thought*, Macmillan, Basingstoke 1982.

35. M. Moaddel, *Class, Politics and Ideology in the Iranian Revolution*, Columbia University Press, New York 1993, p.128.

36. Khomeini, *Islam and Revolution*, *op.cit.*, p.116.

37. *Ibid*. p.62.

38. *Ibid*. p.62.

39. Engineer, *The Islamic State*, *op.cit.*, p.181.

40. Zubaida writes of 'a fundamentalist revolution ... achieved with the full support of secular democratic forces who were later to become its victims'. Sami Zubaida, *Islam, The People and the State*, Routledge, London 1989, p.60.

41. See: P. Beyer, *Religion and Globalization*, Sage, London 1994.

42. Abdelwahab El-Affendi, *Who Needs an Islamic State?*, Grey Seal, London 1991, p.3.

43. Hizb al-Tahrir al-Islam has made an especially vigorous effort to link perceived 'anti-imperialist' struggles in the Middle East conducted by Islamist currents with those pursued by Islamists within what it has termed *kufr* nations like Britain: See: Hizb ut-Tahrir, *Programme of the International Muslim Khilafah Conference*, London 1994.

44. Azzam Tamini (ed), *Power-Sharing Islam?*, Liberty, London 1993, p.8.

45. The *National Review* of November 19, 1990 headlined its story on the Islamic 'threat', 'The Muslims Are Coming! The Muslims Are Coming!', J. Esposito, *The Islamic Threat: Myth or Reality?*, *op.cit.*, p.227.

46. *Washington Post*, 3 April 1996.

47. In Sudan the Muslim Brotherhood has pursued a tortuous strategy of forming blocs and alliances to win influence within the country's military regime. This is far from even the gradualist strategies of the Brotherhood mainstream. See: Abdelwahab El-Affendi, *Turabi's Revolution: Islam and Power in Sudan*, Grey Seal, London 1991.

48. R. Mitchell, *The Society of the Muslim Brothers*, *op.cit.*, p.329.

49. H. Roberts, 'Doctrinaire Politics and Political Opportunism in the Strategy of Algerian Islamism', in John Ruedy (ed), *Islamism and Secularism in North Africa, op.cit.,* 1994, p.127.

50. *Ibid.* p.127.

51. O. Roy, *The Failure of Political Islam, op.cit.,* p22.

52. *Ibid.* p.26.

53. Haleh Afshar, 'Women and the politics of fundamentalism in Iran', in Haleh Afshar (ed), *Women and Politics in the Third World,* Routledge, London 1994, p.125.

54. Mahnaz Afkhami, 'Women in Post-Revolutionary Iran: A Feminist Perspective', in Mahnaz Afkhami & Erika Friedl (eds), *In the Eye of the Storm,* I.B. Tauris, London 1994, p.18.

55. See: Leila Ahmed, *Women and Gender in Islam,* Yale University Press, New Haven 1992; Mahnaz Afkhami & Erika Friedl (eds), *In the Eye of the Storm,* I.B. Tauris London 1994.

56. *Washington Post,* 3 April 1996.

Communitarianism

Elizabeth Frazer

Introduction

Communitarianism can be briefly characterised as the view that the community, rather than the individual, the state, the nation or any other entity, should be thought of as the key focus of analysis, and should be at the centre of our value system. Communitarians emphasise the social nature of individuals, relationships and institutions. They tend to stress the value of specifically public goods, and to conceive of values as rooted in communal practices. None of these themes and concepts are new – they have featured in many kinds of political thought and programme, from Aristotle onward, forming a more or less important part of the ideas of a whole range of thinkers down the centuries: liberals, feminists, marxists, conservatives, socialists, republicans, greens, social democrats. However, communitarianism as a body of political thought is certainly new. In the last twenty years communitarianism as a distinctive theoretical position crystallised in the form of a critique of certain aspects of recent liberalism. In the last five or six years communitarian ideas have made their way into the speeches and platforms of a number of politicians and parties, and in the UK and the USA there have been attempts to launch communitarianism as a political and social movement.

What accounts for this recent crystallisation of ideas and themes into a full-blown 'ism'? Undoubtedly, the major factor was a gathering dissatisfaction with liberalism, and a shared emphasis on certain themes common to an otherwise disparate range of critics of liberalism. However, the emergence of communitarianism can also be understood as the result of a historical shift in the last few years.

In the context of the cold war, the apparent dangers of nationalism and collectivism were at the forefront of popular and academic consciousness. Hence, the appeal of political theories that emphasised individual rights rather than the interests of state and society. These historical experiences have faded in the last decade or so, providing a more fertile ground for communitarianism's growing appeal. More significantly, there has been a resurgence of anxieties about the state of modern and western societies. Prominent among these are fears that the alienation which seems to be expressed in disorder, crime, abusive social relationships, and so on, is linked to the dominance of market relationships and the emphasis on individualism. The final failure of the self-consciously command economies of Eastern Europe and the growing scepticism about the future viability of welfare states of the Western European kind means there has been a simultaneous loss of faith in the power of states to solve the problems that markets create. As such, communitarianism seems to offer a solution that is neither exclusively market-oriented nor state-centred. Only strong communities, communitarians assert, can repair the damage caused by both states and markets.

In the academic context the debate between liberals and communitarians has been generated by the liberal theory of John Rawls. Rawls's *Theory of Justice*[1] elaborates the principles of justice that should govern political, social and economic institutions – the principles that would be chosen by rational individuals were they to have the opportunity and the need to sort out such principles from scratch. His conception of justice features individual freedom guaranteed by rights, together with a measure of egalitarian redistribution of resources.

Rawls's model and his method of deriving it have been criticised from every side.[2] However, two works in particular – Michael Sandel's *Liberalism and the Limits of Justice* and Michael Walzer's *Spheres of Justice* can be identified as responses to Rawls from the particular standpoint that has come to be known as communitarianism.[3] They explicitly take issue with Rawls's conception of the relationship between individual and society, emphasising how an individual's identity, values and understandings are socially constructed and expressed. They also argue with the Rawlsian project of deriving principles of justice which are universal in their applicability. These two strands of argument – social constructionism, and particularism – are central to philosophical communitarianism. These and related themes have been elaborated in works by a range of theorists, not all of whom respond to

Rawls so directly. As the debates proceeded they came to be widely understood as between liberals or 'individualists' on the one hand, and communitarians on the other.[4] Later, perhaps inevitably, a number of contributions pointed out how the opposition between the two 'sides' was exaggerated, how each side tended to misrepresent the other, how important 'communitarian' themes are in liberal philosophy, and how important liberal values are to those who are identified as communitarian.[5]

If we trace the philosophical origins of communitarianism, we see that it is a coalescence of many diverse strands in the western philosophical tradition. It is important to remember these complex philosophical origins, and the diversity of concerns that are pulled together under the umbrella of communitarianism. Any close and detailed discussion ought to pull the various strands apart, and point out the tensions between them. In a brief presentation like this one I can only note this complexity and try to avoid presenting communitarianism as a monolithic whole.

The Philosophy of Communitarianism

As we have seen, communitarianism began as a set of rather abstract criticisms of certain features of recent, mostly US, liberal political philosophy. If we can discern a single key theme it is anti-individualism; this can be analysed into three distinct arguments. First it is asserted that the world is more than just a collection of individuals. Communitarians, like many other social philosophers, are likely to argue for the existence and significance of collectives, institutions, human relations, and so forth. Second, there is an ethical argument, which itself falls into two parts. Communitarians will argue that ethical values are not located in the individual but rather are to be found in the social individual or even in the community or society of which the individual is a member. They will also argue for the importance of a range of values that have tended to be neglected in individualist philosophies: reciprocity, solidarity, trust, tradition, and so on. Third, there is a methodological thesis: communitarians argue that the way to discover ethical principles is not to try to deduce and apply universally-valid fundamental principles, but to interpret and refine values that already exist in the ways of life of really living groups: societies and communities. This way, ethical principles can be accepted and owned by social actors.

These three arguments generate a number of other beliefs. First, communitarians take issue with the idea (– a powerful idea in modern societies – and one that has been to some extent promoted in the development of modern legal systems and welfare states) that the individual stands in a direct, straightforward relationship with the state and with society. Second, communitarians dispute the place of the market as the key social institution, and the idea that market exchanges are a particularly right and even *natural* pattern of human relationships. In place of the individual who has defensive rights against society, the individual who engages in self-interested transactions with others, communitarian philosophers focus on a variety of institutions and traditional ways of doing things which characterise the relationship between the individual and state or society. Communitarian literature is replete with references to corporations, voluntary organisations, occupational groups, families, religious institutions. In these institutions, individuals enter into relationships with one another that are governed by a variety of shared values and practices. When we consider this range of social institutions in total, it seems clear that self-interest cannot be said to be the dominant motivating factor in human life (although, of course, it may have its place). Even markets, it is observed, are founded on trust, shared understandings and conformity to norms.

Third, there is a difference in values. A good way of thinking about political traditions is to analyse their lists of cherished values (such as liberty, equality, fraternity, authority) and their ordering of these values (for instance, liberals tend to put liberty before equality, and socialists vice versa). Communitarians value community itself, and tradition. Apart from that, they will argue that we cannot say, without reference to a particular society, what the cherished values are and how they should be ordered: it all depends on the traditions and ways of life of the society in question. Furthermore, we cannot, without reference to a particular society, say what liberty, for instance, means. What are the criteria by which we judge whether an individual is free or not? The meaning of liberty can only be discerned from within the established framework of a society and its way of life.

This last point is clearly both very important and very controversial. The controversy centres on the extent to which communitarians are committed to saying that right and wrong, good and bad, can only be judged within the terms of a particular society; so that practices and relationships that seem to modern, western, liberal minds to be clearly wrong, like slavery, or the immolation of servants or dependants on the death of a ruler, have to be thought to be right for the society in question (or, perhaps, neither right nor wrong because of the necessity of taking up a particular standpoint before such a judgement can be made). I shall return to this issue of relativism later. For now, I want to note that we find a variety of responses to these issues in communitarian philosophy. For instance, in *After Virtue*, Alastair MacIntyre very much emphasises the value of tradition; Walzer's *Spheres of Justice* dwells on the importance of understanding the place and meaning of a good (such as healthcare, material well-being etc) in a culture before we can say how it ought to be distributed. For all communitarians a major preoccupation is the unthinking projection of liberal assumptions onto other cultures. But an equally important theme is the emphasis that liberalism, too, is a tradition whose central concepts and practices have developed in relation to one another and have to be understood as such. This undermines the approach, associated with Rawls, Nozick and Dworkin, which holds that liberal principles can be derived purely through deductive reasoning, as though existing society, history or current values have no influence on their conclusions.

The Politics of Communitarianism

I have remarked that philosophical communitarianism is directed mainly against liberal political philosophy. However, there can be no straightforward leap from the philosophy of communitarianism to one or another political programme. Although socialism traditionally features many themes that in the present context can be associated with communitarianism, the extent to which the two imply one another is controversial.[6] Socialists are likely to be suspicious of communitarianism's conservative implications, given the emphasis on tradition and settled patterns of relationships. Indeed, traditional conservative thought features the ideal of community and other communitarian themes.[7] And although there are many affinities between feminism and communitarianism, these conservative implications trouble feminists too.[8] Meanwhile, eminent philosophers to whom the label 'communitarian' is usually attached have affirmed their commitment to liberalism.[9]

However, a specifically political communitarianism has recently emerged. This takes two forms. First, there has been effort to generate and lead a communitarian social and political movement. In the UK a 'Communitarian Forum' has been established, and a 'Citizens'

Agenda' drafted.[10] In the USA 'The Communitarian Agenda' was launched by Amitai Etzioni and others.[11] Second, clear communitarian themes have been heard in political rhetoric (notably the speeches of Tony Blair, leader of the British Labour Party) and have been picked up and elaborated in journalism.[12] The work of the philosophical communitarians is relevant for these political discourses (even if political communitarianism is not relevant for the philosophers), although it is important to remember that political communitarianism also has other antecedents: in Britain, notably, the Christian Socialist and ethical socialist traditions and certain strands of conservatism.

The content of political communitarianism features two familiar themes. First, the social thesis, which insists that individuals are fundamentally connected to each other; that our relations are central to our personalities; that the networks within which we live deeply affect the quality of our lives; and that communities are valuable in themselves.[13] Second, communitarians mention the importance of interpretivism in ethics: the idea that ethical principles or values are only powerful if they are in some sense already part and parcel of ordinary people's ideas in and about their daily lives. Political communitarians appeal to people's tacit understanding that community really does matter, that our unchosen obligations are as important as our voluntary choices.[14]

But more important than these are rather more practical political projects. First, to ensure that serious consideration is given to the community as an alternative to both the state and the market as a mechanism for the distribution of goods such as care, welfare etc. Second, to establish a clear connection between individuals' enjoyment of rights, and their carrying out of obligations and duties. Third, and more controversially, is an emphasis on individuals' local relationships, the importance of organisations and associations being properly rooted in and responsive to their local people.[15] This last is controversial because the emphasis on locality can seem to smack of romantic nostalgia for the lost world of village life. It also raises very directly an issue we have not yet addressed: the actual conception and definition of community.

In my presentation so far, the notion of 'community' has been taken very much for granted. Readers might expect that communitarianism, philosophical and political, would offer a clear analysis of the concept and a theoretical elaboration of its functioning (that is, a set of hypotheses about how communities work, under what conditions they flourish, what the consequences of the establishment of communities would be for other aspects of human life and so on), as well as a defence of community as the key social formation and the key concept. It has to be said that, especially in respect of the first two of these, they are likely to be disappointed. Conceptions and theories of community are, for the most part, only evident to readers who engage in a good deal of close reading between the lines of the texts. Further, the conceptions and theories that do emerge are far from well worked out – on the contrary. Nevertheless, we can identify three distinct conceptualisations of community that emerge from the philosophical and political communitarians.

First, there is the conception of community as a set of relations between persons: the kind of relations of trust, mutual respect, generosity, mutual understanding, shared values, reciprocity and so forth that can support socially useful and desirable distributions of goods and resources. For example, if, as communitarians argue, goods like care for the ill and needy are better distributed by the mechanism of community than by either state bureaucracy or the market, then this implies that members of a community relate to each other in such a way as to enable a particular pattern of useful exchanges.

Second, there is the conception of community as an entity, with boundaries and a particular location. This is evident in numerous references to neighbourhoods and the like. However, as we have seen, there is ambivalence about community as locality: it seems important in the current political and cultural context to disavow the traditional conception of community, for fear of being accused of nostalgia. There is a concomitant emphasis on the kind of community surrogates that people seek to build in response to the atomism, alienation and anonymity of urban life: the urban village, the networks and associations made possible by technology, voluntary organisations, the non-geographical communities of ethnic groups and political and social movements.[16]

The third conception is of community as a thinking subject. In political speech there is a strong tendency to talk of 'the moral voice of the community', 'the feelings of the community', and so forth.[17] In addition, political communitarianism pays a good deal of attention to the various institutions which exemplify, or provide the foundation for, community: educational and religious organisations, and most important of all, the family. In philosophical communitarianism the family is mentioned in two ways. First as an instance of community: an example of the kind of association in which the relation of community can be enjoyed. Second, as the basis of community – a necessary building block in a society where community can be realised. These two senses are combined in the concept of the communitarian family, which is elaborated by both the US and the UK political communitarians. The communitarian family is characterised as one where both partners are actively and deeply involved in their children's upbringing, and where all members participate in the community. Parents' moral responsibility to bring their children up is a responsibility to the community.

Criticisms of Communitarianism

I am going to begin this account of the common criticisms of communitarianism with an issue I have mentioned several times – the communitarians' vagueness in their deployment and discussion of the concept 'community'. The first complaint is about the confusion between community as a kind of relation, community as an entity, and community as some kind of thinking subject. In addition to this, communitarians slip between a descriptive sense of 'community' (that is, they use it as a characterisation of certain important social formations or certain important social relationships, arguing that theorists and analysts who are wedded to individualism overlook this aspect of social reality) and a prescriptive sense (that is, they deploy an ideal model of how community might be in order to set political goals). On the whole, in this literature, community is more exemplified than analysed; for instance, writers will say something like '. . . the self has to find its moral identity in and through its membership in communities such as those of the family, the neighbourhood, the city and tribe . . .'.[18] What analysis does exist hardly approaches in either quality or quantity the analysis in political theory and philosophy of such concepts as liberty, equality, authority etc.[19]

This conceptual vagueness is matched in political communitarianism by what we might call sociological vagueness. We have seen already the ambivalence about place and the extent to which the community in question is a local community. Further than this, we might conclude from what the communitarians say that the important issue is the range and quality of networks and associations an individual is involved in, the quality of friendship and acquaintanceship. That is, it might look as though the desirable society is one in which an individual enjoys and moves between a variety of fluid relationships and networks. However, the political communitarians' agenda for the family, and the overweening importance of kinship (as opposed to acquaintanceship), tends practically to contradict this view.

This raises a further problem, of a somewhat more abstract nature. The question has been put by critics of communitarianism: is community to be built for the sake of social order and settled social institutions, or for the sake of individual autonomy and flourishing? This takes us back to the original debate between communitarians and liberals as it is liberals who have put this question. On the whole, philosophical communitarians have tended to affirm the value of individual autonomy, while insisting that community is a means to autonomy (and therefore that certain aspects of liberal theory have been wrong). It might be that what is at issue here is a matter of emphasis; the danger is that in emphasising the value of community itself, communitarians will end up by diminishing individual freedom.

And this takes us on to some substantial criticisms of communitarianism that focus on the way community can exclude large numbers of people and have difficulty with groups behaving differently to the community's norms.[20] One common way of demonstrating the distinctiveness of community as a relation, and of a community as a particular kind of social entity, is by alluding to 'we-ness' – the notion that we, as a group, have our own distinct ways and values.[21] The obvious difficulty with this is that 'we-ness' implies 'they-ness' – the group outside the community who do not share our ways and values. The question arises, then, about 'our' attitudes to and relationship with 'them'. The obverse of the efficiency of communities in generating and distributing goods is the fate (sometimes unpleasant) of those whose non-membership of the community excludes them from enjoyment of the relevant goods. One might think, for example, of the difficulties faced by immigrants to a new country.[22]

In partial response to this problem, most communitarian theories are consistent with individuals having a variety of memberships of different and overlapping 'communities' (even if this is not exactly spelled out.)[23] But theories do not address the complicated questions that arise from the fact that some communities can be joined or left by the exercise of choice while others cannot be easily entered nor easily escaped. This is particularly significant since membership of some communities confers on individuals a good deal of social power, while membership of others is rather power-diminishing. For example, membership of a wealthy aristocratic community and of a prison community are hardly comparable in this sense. Apart from this, communitarianism also needs an analysis of the power relations which must exist between competing and coexisting communities. If we can sum up the force of this set of criticisms, it is that communitarianism needs to be supplemented both by a supra-communitarian theory which explores the relationships between communities, and by an intra-communitarian theory which looks critically at the welfare and status of individuals within communities.

Now communitarians might respond, reasonably enough, that communitarianism is not a mega-theory of the world, the universe and everything; that it is perfectly reasonable for it to be combined with a theory of, say, individual autonomy and human flourishing, which sets limits to the subjection of the individual to the community, and with a theory of say, democracy, which regulates the relationships between communities and social formations like states. Communitarianism, it might be said, is a theory of the relationship between individual and society, which generates certain prescriptions: for instance, that communities as such must be allowed to flourish, but this prescription is constrained by other valid prescriptions which arise from wider considerations of justice or democracy. Unfortunately, this argument is somewhat weakened by the fact that communitarianism started out as a consideration of justice itself.

From the point of view of practical politics, the preoccupation of the political communitarians, the question of what, exactly, is being promoted when we promote community, is one that must be urgently answered. Otherwise, serious critics cannot escape the conclusion that the function of the term 'community' in communitarianism is its rhetorical force as a kind of feelgood word: one which partly allays the anxieties of socialists (because of its resonances with such values as solidarity, communality and so on), one which appeals to conservatives who are anxious about social order, and one which is not too threatening to liberals.

The Future of Communitarianism

Although any sensible political theorist would quail at the prospect of going into print with anything so concrete as a prediction, it is possible to offer some sketchy contours of how the controversies discussed here might develop.

Firstly, one can say with reasonable certainty that the term community will not lose its rhetorical force, its importance in political speech from left, right and centre. This is certainly not because all political concepts are by their nature enduring: look at the fate of 'equality' in contemporary British political discourse. Rather, I think it is because the emphasis on community addresses a real and pressing dilemma, one that I identified at the beginning of this chapter: that both the market and state bureaucracies have been discredited as effective mechanisms for distributing certain worthy goods. In addition to this we can add two further factors in favour of the term: first, its rhetorical strength, second, its vagueness.

Its rhetorical strength is clear enough. Much in the way that 'freedom' exists in different contexts, with a version for socialists, liberals, conservatives and for many other political positions, community has its place in a whole range of political ideologies or systems of thought: conservatism, anarchism, socialism, feminism, green political thought, and even liberalism. The implications for coalition building are obvious, and insofar as communitarianism is making political headway it is because of this potential for pulling diverse characters into an alliance. But 'community' has an added strength: it also has a central place in a whole range of non-theoretical, non-political discourses and practices that are important in many people's day-to-day lives: community centres, community work, community development – all of these are significant sites of daily interaction for many people.

This is not to say that the description 'community centre' has an unambiguous meaning for the people who work and go to meetings there. On the one hand, activists and participants know that a good way to mobilise people in a locality is to exhort them to become active in and for their community. On the other hand, these very same activists and the people they exhort, know that 'community' is at best an aspiration. The population to which they appeal is divided, by, for example, generation, or class or ethnicity; it is difficult to ensure that community resources are genuinely accessible to all members of the community; and to keep participation going in the long term requires a great deal of effort. These difficulties are evident to all but the least observant involved in 'community work' but I think that it is precisely the obviousness of these difficulties that keeps 'community' alive as a practical social and political aspiration.

The vagueness of the term is both a source of strength and a weakness. Community can mean all those who live in a locality, or those who share a particular set of religious or cultural values, or those who share a particular set of political aims, or those who share some other social characteristic, e.g. they are patients at the same hospital. This vagueness contributes to the rhetorical power of the concept, as I have already discussed. However, there are certain social and political purposes where a more precise sociological vocabulary is indispensable.

A particularly serious issue is the way the vocabulary of 'community' can be used by outsiders to homogenise the population in a particular locality in a negative way. All the inhabitants of certain areas are effectively criminalised so that the conflicts and inequalities within the population become invisible to outsiders like police, local councillors and officials.[24] Furthermore, social relations in a locality can be formed in such a way that 'bads' (such as threats, robbery, reprisals) rather than goods can circulate and multiply efficiently. The circulation of 'bads' (just like the patterns of circulation of goods) constitutes inequality and antagonism across divisions of generation, sex, race, ethnicity, etc. In all such cases, an over-emphasis on the value of community can potentially get in the way of a realistic and effective understanding of the social relations, and social conflicts, in play.

Conclusion

These ambiguities were identified and have attracted criticism since the first appearance of philosophical communitarianism, and in the transition to communitarianism as a political project the confusion has, if any thing, deepened. However, criticism of the use of the term community is emphatically not an argument against the communitarians' fundamental insight that individuals are deeply affected by the social and cultural structures that generate them; that our social relationships in some important sense are prior to our individualistic aspirations; and that social collectives are real, existing features of our world. These insights remain as valid as they ever were but if communitarianism is to respond to its many critics, such insights need to be developed into a more rigorous social theory.

Notes

1. J. Rawls, *A Theory of Justice*, Harvard University Press, Cambridge Mass. 1971. See the chapter on Liberalism in this volume for a more detailed account of Rawls's theory.

2. See, for instance, N. Daniels (ed), *Reading Rawls: critical studies of A Theory of Justice*, Basil Blackwell, Oxford 1975.

3. M. Sandel, *Liberalism and the Limits of Justice*, Cambridge University Press, Cambridge 1982; M. Walzer, *Spheres of Justice*, Basil Blackwell, Oxford 1983; see also: M. Sandel, 'The Procedural Republic and the Unencumbered Self', *Political Theory*, vol 12, pp.81-96, 1984.

4. The most often identified 'communitarians', apart from Sandel and Walzer, are A. MacIntyre, *After Virtue*, Duckworth, London 1981; Charles Taylor, 'Interpretation and the Sciences of Man' and 'Atomism' in *Philosophy and the Human Sciences*, Cambridge University Press, Cambridge 1981. For other relevant contributions see the papers and extracts collected in S. Avineri and A. de-Shalit (eds), *Individualism and Communitarianism*, Oxford University Press, Oxford 1992.

5. For instance, M. Walzer, 'The Communitarian Critique of Liberalism', *Political Theory*, vol 18, pp.6-2, 1990; Charles Taylor, 'Cross-Purposes: the Liberal Communitarian Debate' in N. Rosenblum (ed), *Liberalism and the Moral Life*, Harvard University Press, Cambridge Mass. 1989. Later works by Rawls and Dworkin are characterised by themes that can be associated with communitarianism; in Dworkin's case an emphasis on 'interpretation' (specifically legal interpretation), and in Rawls's case an emphasis on liberalism as a tradition, and the applicability of his theory of justice only in the context in which it is built. See: R. Dworkin, *Law's Empire*, Fontana, London 1986; J. Rawls, *Political Liberalism*, Columbia University Press, New York, 1993.

6. D. Miller, 'In what sense must socialism be communitarian?', *Social Philosophy and Policy*, vol 6 pp.51-73, 1989.

7. R. Scruton (ed), *Conservative Texts: an anthology*, Macmillan, Basingstoke 1991.

8. E. Frazer and N. Lacey, *The Politics of Community: a feminist critique of the liberal-communitarian debate*, Harvester Wheatsheaf, Hemel Hempstead 1993.

9. M. Walzer, 'Communitarian Critique of Liberalism', *op.cit.*, p.22; R. Rorty, *Contingency, Irony and Solidarity*, Cambridge University Press, Cambridge 1989.

10. H. Tam, *Citizen's Agenda for Building Democratic Communities*, Centre for Citizenship Development, Cambridge 1995.

11. A. Etzioni, *The Spirit of Community: Rights, Responsibilities and the Communitarian Agenda*, Crown Publishers Inc, New York 1993.

12. P. Mandelson and R. Liddle, *The Blair Revolution: Can New Labour Deliver?*, Faber, London 1996.

13. A. Etzioni, *Spirit of Community, op.cit.*, pp.116-122; H. Tam, *Citizen's Agenda for Building Democratic Communities, op.cit.*, p1.

14. A. Etzioni, *Spirit of Community, op.cit.*, pp.101, 258-259.

15. P. Mandelson and R. Liddle, *The Blair Revolution, op.cit.*

16. A. Etzioni, *Spirit of Community, op.cit.*, pp.116-118, H. Tam, *Citizen's Agenda for Building Democratic Communities*, p.1.

17. A. Etzioni, *Spirit of Community, op.cit.*, p.54; P. Mandelson and R. Liddle, *The Blair Revolution, op.cit.*, p.34.

18. A. MacIntyre, *After Virtue, op.cit.*, p.221.

19. An exception is R. Plant, 'Community: concept, conception and ideology', *Politics and Society*, vol 8, pp.79-107, 1978.

20. I.M. Young, 'The Ideal of Community and the Politics of Difference', in Linda Nicholson (ed), *Feminism/Postmodernism*, Routledge, London 1990.

21. For instance, Report of the Commission on Social Justice, *Social Justice: Strategies for National Renewal*, Vintage Books, London 1994, p.306: 'A good society depends not just on the economic success of I, the individual, but the social commitment of we, the community'.

22. For an empirical discussion which illustrates this point see: A. Crawford, 'Review Article: The Spirit of Community', *Journal of Law and Society*, 1996.

23. The political communitarians mentioned most here – Etzioni and Tam – do spell it out briefly, but they do not discuss adequately the implications and complications. A. Etzioni, *The Spirit of Community, op.cit.*, p.116-118; H. Tam, *Citizen's Agenda for Building Democratic Communities op.cit.*, p.1.

24. See, for instance, B. Campbell, *Goliath: Britain's Dangerous Places*, Methuen, London 1993.

Post-Marxism

David Howarth

In 1982, the Marxist academic Alex Callinicos was prompted to write a book entitled *Is there a Future for Marxism?*. He was confident enough to provide 'a reasoned defence' and 'clarification' of its basic concepts and political commitments.[1] However, at the end of the 1990s, following the collapse of 'actually existing socialism' in the former Soviet Union, Eastern Europe and elsewhere, coupled with strident assertions regarding the universal triumph of liberal capitalism,[2] there is scepticism about the viability of even posing a question concerning the future of Marxism. Is it not presumed to be dead and buried? Is it worth resurrecting as a theoretical approach and guide to political action? One response to these questions, though strongly disputed by many within the Marxist tradition, has been the construction of a post-Marxist alternative. The aim of this chapter is to describe and evaluate this nascent post-Marxist approach, especially as it pertains to political theory.

The chapter begins with a brief discussion of classical Marxism, after which I shall revisit the 'crisis of Marxism' as it has developed in this century. I shall then seek to clarify the concept of 'post-Marxism' by looking at the debates about its precise meaning, before turning to the way in which Ernesto Laclau and Chantal Mouffe (the leading post-Marxist thinkers) have reformulated the basic ideas of historical materialism, and deployed them to express a novel theory of contemporary politics. I conclude by assessing the prospects for post-Marxist political thought.

Classical Marxism

At the outset, simplifying considerably, I want to highlight a number of important aspects of classical Marxist theory. First, Marxism is based on the belief that the way in which human beings interact with nature, and each other, to produce their material conditions of existence – such as food, shelter and clothing – is the most important aspect of human behaviour. All else in life – religion, art, politics – is shaped by the nature of this material production. As Marx puts it:

> The mode of production of material life conditions the social, political and intellectual life process in general.[3]

In this context Marxist thought argues that societies which base their material production on the exploitation of one group by another will necessarily be subject to conflict and contradiction and thus crisis-ridden. Why should this be so? Marxists identify two important contradictions in any particular system of production.

The first is between the forces of production (comprising the means of production: machinery, technology and human labour power) and the relations of production (the way in which ownership of the forces of production is arranged, i.e. usually one small group possessing ownership and one much larger having no such ownership). In the capitalist system of production – a system in which the workers' labour-power is bought and sold through the paying of wages and the power of an employer to hire and fire – this contradiction manifests itself in the tension between the need of capitalism for completely unfettered expansion in the power of the forces of production and the private ownership of the means of production, which prevents this full development of the productive forces. This incompatibility appears in a series of crises, such as the tendency for the rate of profit to fall, the growing imbalance between production and consumption, the increasing centralisation of production in the hands of the dominant capitalist class, and the impoverishment of the working classes.[4]

The second contradiction concerns the struggle between social classes, each defined by their ownership or non-ownership of the means of production, which Marx suggests is the key political dynamic of history.[5] In capitalist society, it is the struggle between its two principal social actors – the bourgeoisie and the proletariat – which constitutes the main class antagonism. And it is the victory of the latter which abolishes all social divisions based on property ownership and brings about a socialist society.[6]

The combined effect of these two contradictions is the inevitable and apocalyptic downfall of capitalism and its replacement by a new rational mode of production, structured around the common ownership of the means of production. How is this to be brought about? What are the obstacles to its achievement? These questions bring us to Marx and Engels's political theory. As Marx puts it in a classical expression of the view:

> In the social production of their life, men enter into definite ... relations of production which correspond to a definite state of development of their material productive forces. The sum total of these relations of production constitutes the economic structure of society, the real foundation, on which arises a legal and political superstructure and to which correspond definite forms of social consciousness.[7]

The main elements of Marxist political thought, including the analysis of social relations, the critique of liberal democracy, and the alternative to capitalism, follow directly from this famous base/superstructure model. Thus, 'political power ... is ... merely the organised power of one class for oppressing another',[8] and the modern bourgeois state is seen as the major institutional means of maintaining class domination, and 'managing the common affairs of the whole bourgeoisie', through a combination of force and ideology.[9] This means that the proletariat, as the most dominated class in capitalist society, has to overthrow the liberal democratic state through revolutionary struggle in order to dismantle capitalist relations of production and construct a new society in its own image.

To conduct revolutionary class struggle, the proletariat must transform itself from what Marx calls a 'class-in-itself' into a 'class-for-itself', by beginning to see itself as an exploited and dominated class. This entails the elaboration of a revolutionary ideology and the creation of an organisation by which to envisage and attain emancipation from capitalist rule.[10] While Marx was reluctant to elaborate detailed characteristics of an emancipated order and how it could be achieved – he cautions against writing 'recipes for the cookshops of the future' – the primary objective of communism is the removal of capitalist relations of production which structure man's relation to nature, and his fellow-men. The proletarian revolution abolishes the private ownership of the means of production, and the communist alternative involves their common ownership in the hands of the working class. This results in an overcoming of the division of labour, and the relations of domination that sustains.

Even so, Marx (and Engels) changed their views on the precise nature of a future communist society. The essentially pastoral description of communism in *The German Ideology*, in which 'society regulates the general production and thus makes it possible for me to do one thing today and another tomorrow, to hunt in the morning, fish in the afternoon, rear cattle in the evening, criticise after dinner ... without ever becoming hunter, fisherman, shepherd or critic',[11] gives way in *Capital* to a more realistic assessment of the possibilities of completely transcending the division of labour. Thus, by the time he wrote *Capital*, Marx had accepted the existence of labour as a necessity and had made the attainment of true freedom conditional upon a shortening of the working day.[12]

The Problems of Classical Marxism

Today, it is something of a cliché to speak of a 'crisis of Marxism.'[13] However, for reasons to which I have already alluded, the crisis of Marxism in the 1990s surpasses in intensity and scope anything which has gone before. In this chapter, I shall concentrate on the *theoretical* crisis of Marxist political thought, and the efforts to repair or replace the assumptions which have given rise to it. To do this, we need, initially, to identify the growing number of problems in the Marxist tradition showing how, during the past few years, they have crystallised into a theoretical crisis for Marxist thought.

Let us return to Marxism's two major contradictions of capitalist society. While Marx correctly predicted a series of booms and slumps in capitalist society, the essentially anarchic character of capitalist production pinpointed by Marx has, in the twentieth century, been gradually replaced by a more organised system.[14] The exploitation of new technologies, the plundering of new markets made available by imperialism, and the growing role of the state in providing the appropriate conditions for capital accumulation – thereby offsetting economic crises – have all meant that capitalism has proved more robust and durable than expected.

It is well-known that Marx was ambiguous about predicting exactly *when* the inevitable collapse of capitalism would occur, arguing that no time limit could be placed on a successful revolution since such a revolution requires the proletariat 'becoming conscious' and 'fighting out' the conflict arising from the contradictions of capitalism – processes which were faltering and unpredictable in their detail.[15] However, the relative impoverishment of the working class anticipated by Marx and Engels, which would be accompanied by a political radicalisation and eventually the revolutionary overthrow of capitalism, has proved very elusive in practice. Socialist revolutions, at least in the name of Marxism and the proletariat, *were* realised in the Soviet Union and China, for example, but these were the *least* developed of capitalist societies and the totalitarian outcomes were quite different from those anticipated by Marxists, and contrary to their goal of greater freedom.

In the more advanced capitalist societies of Western Europe and the United States a further historical direction not fully foreseen by Marx became evident. As against the predicted formation of the proletariat into a single revolutionary force with shared interests, there has been a fragmentation of the working class and a differentiation of its supposed economic and political interests.[16] Not only have there been splits *between* different sections of the working class, a tendency already noticed by Marx and Lenin in their discussions of the emergence of a privileged group of workers labelled the 'labour aristocracy',[17] but there were also splits *within* the working class: workers displayed multiple identities not based purely on their class. For example, the shocking chauvinism of the working classes towards other nations noted by the Marxist leader and writer Rosa Luxemburg during the Great War, and the centrality of nationalist values which followed in its wake, was a clear signal that divisive forms of identification such as nationalism rather than class were increasingly taken up by the proletariat.[18]

These tendencies were to some extent a product of social changes: the incorporation of workers into the political system through the extension of the franchise, the development of mass political parties, the attainment of social and economic rights, rising material prosperity, and the expansion of ideological mechanisms (such as mass communication and mass education) designed to uphold capitalism.[19] This also resulted in the separation of economic and political interests, as workers could pursue their economic interests via their trade unions, while voting for reformist political parties operating within the confines of the capitalist state.[20]

More positively, the blunting of the revolutionary aspirations and potential of the working class was accompanied by the growth of alternative forms of political protest, particularly in the post-1968 period. However, the emergence of political struggles around gender, racial and sexual divisions, as well as the activities of students, environmentalists, anti-nuclear campaigners, neighbourhood and citizens groups, ethnic and national minorities – collectively named the 'new social move-ments' – has further eroded the role of the working class as the only agent of emancipation.[21] Recently, these novel forms of political activ-ity have been supplemented by the 'politics of identity': politics focused on the complex construction of one's own and others' identi-ties in the gender, religious, cultural, and ethnic fields.[22] These demands for the realisation of 'multi-culturalism' and the 'recognition of differ-ence' have further exacerbated the fragmentation of class politics in the twentieth century.

Finally, and importantly, alongside the eruption of new political forces in the 'West' during the post-war period, there has been the intensification of growing anti-colonial and anti-imperial struggles in the 'Third World', as well as types of political movement, such as populism, religious fundamentalism and ethno-nationalism as in the Former Yugoslavia, which defy description in classical Marxist language.

What is important to note is that all these movements and political identities have not conformed to the classical Marxist model. They are not organised around the relations of production, and have not neces-sarily elaborated socialist demands and ideologies. In short, the increasingly organised and robust form of twentieth century capital-ism, the failures of revolutionary working-class politics, coupled with the novel forms of protest and struggle in the post-1968 period, have all resulted in an accumulation of problems for the Marxist approach.

The Difficult Emergence and Definition of Post-Marxism

There are four ways of defining post-Marxism. First, it might refer to thinkers and bodies of thought which have been *influenced* by Marx's writings, though this categorisation is so broad as to have very little analytical value. Second, it could designate those Marxists writing *after* Marx, though this conceptualisation, again, is meaningless as a means of classifying thought. Third, it might define those writers who have explicitly identified themselves as post-Marxist. Fourth, it might repre-sent an ideal to strive after, what I call, borrowing from Jacques Derrida, 'a post-Marxism to come'.[23]

I use a combination of the third and fourth definitions to characterise post-Marxism here. More specifically, I will focus on the influential writings of Ernesto Laclau and Chantal Mouffe. My reasons for this choice are fourfold. They have chosen to elaborate a self-proclaimed post-Marxist position, and have provided a clear rationale for this particular choice;[24] their decision has elicited considerable criticism, commentary and debate amongst Marxist and non-Marxists alike, concerning both the concept of post-Marxism and the substantive commitments entailed by it;[25] their writings have been closely associated with the emergence of the new social movements and identity politics, which they have endeavoured to understand theoretically; and they have proposed a novel left-wing political project arising out of this engagement, which they call 'radical democracy', so as to link together these new forms of protest.

At the beginning of *Hegemony and Socialist Strategy*, Laclau and Mouffe argue that 'we are now situated in a post-Marxist terrain', because it

> is no longer possible to maintain the conception of ... classes elaborated by Marxism, nor its vision of the historical course of capitalist development, nor, of course, the conception of communism as a transparent society from which antagonisms have disappeared.[26]

This change of terrain has provoked an enormous storm of protest from those still loyal to classical Marxist thought. Instead of a progressive and enriching '*post*-Marxism', Laclau and Mouffe have been labelled 'non' or 'anti-Marxists', and their approach an 'ex-Marxism without substance'.[27] Why is this?

Four main arguments have been used against Laclau and Mouffe's position: they deliberately misrepresent the Marxist tradition by removing its complexity and subtlety; their approach is simply part of a current fad for applying the prefix 'post' to existing concepts without offering any substantial improvement on the originals, and is doomed to fail along with other fashionable but mistaken trends in contemporary thought, such as postmodernism and post-structuralism; the content of their thinking is thus compromised by these associations, and they lose sight of what is specific to Marxism; their work is part of a general abandonment of leftist commitments in the wake of the emergence of Thatcherism and the political failures of left-wing parties and ideologies in the 1980s and 1990s.

Laclau and Mouffe's response has been to emphasise their *deconstructive* impulse.[28] They argue that their objective is not to abandon, but to rejuvenate Marxism, by exploring paths of thinking which have been closed by its dominant logics. They thus seek to recover its 'plurality' and vitality, which they see as 'heterogeneous and contradictory' and constituting its 'inner structure and wealth'. It is only in this way, they argue, that its 'survival as a reference point for political analysis' can be guaranteed.[29] Let us examine these claims in more detail.

Radical Materialism: The Primacy of Politics

The substance of Laclau and Mouffe's approach centres on the two major contradictions in the Marxist theory of social change. Laclau and Mouffe suggest that Marxism displays a contradiction between what they name the 'logic of necessity' and the 'logic of contingency'.[30] The former is the Marxist proposition that history is driven inexorably by the contradiction between the forces and the relations of production and that economic systems, such as capitalism, have certain inevitable outcomes that can be objectively discovered.[31] The latter is manifest in the class struggles Marx also identifies as historically central, but these introduce an unpredictability into Marx's understanding of social formations that sits uneasily with the idea of objective, inevitable changes as suggested by the logic of necessity.

However, while both logics are present in Marxist theory they do not have an equal status. On the contrary, Laclau and Mouffe argue that the Marxist tradition has systematically privileged the former over the latter. Even though the logic of contingency comes into play to explain processes that cannot be explained by economic determinism, this does not undermine the latter's primacy, as it is still the objective 'laws of history' which specify when the latter becomes significant.[32] Laclau and Mouffe's post-Marxism involves a thoroughgoing overturning of this opposition, and the construction of a new conception based on the interweaving of necessity and contingency.

Laclau and Mouffe also redefine the concept of antagonism itself and give it a primacy in their theory of social relations. As against the Marxist notion of economic contradiction as the source of social antagonisms (and against mainstream accounts of social conflict, in which antagonisms are either reduced to underlying structural tensions, or to

the clash of self-interests) Laclau and Mouffe insist that social antagonisms occur because of the *inability* of social agents to realise their
identity. Thus, an antagonism is seen to occur when 'the presence of
[an] "Other" prevents me from being totally myself'.[33] This 'blockage'
of identity is a mutual experience for both the antagonising force and
the force which is being antagonised.

A number of consequences follow from this definition of antagonisms. First, they are relations which grow out of the unpredictable
developments of the identities of groups and individuals of different
social positions (peasants and landowners struggling over access to
land, for instance), and they do not follow automatically from 'objective' laws of development. Further, they help form social relations
rather than being simply an effect of them. This is because the production of antagonisms involves the institution of boundaries between
social agents; what Laclau and Mouffe call the construction of political
frontiers. Finally, the creation of antagonisms introduces contingency
into social relations. This is because identities are always based on an
antagonistic relationship with another identity and hence can never be
complete in themselves.[34] This understanding of the role of antagonisms is based on a novel concept of 'discourse'. Let us look more
closely at this concept.

Laclau and Mouffe begin with the premise that reality is discursively
constructed, i.e. that social practices are only meaningful within certain
socially constituted contexts of meaning. For example, the secret ballot
only makes sense within a complex set of political and social values
relevant to developed liberal democracies. The political role of a
shaman, for example, would not make sense in this context but clearly
does in other complex discourses constructed in other societies. Laclau
and Mouffe reject the notion that discourses reflect an underlying
material reality, as it is the discourses themselves which *make up* the
social world. Furthermore, these discourses do not simply repeat an
already existing system of meaning, but constantly and actively transform it.

This implies that the elements which make up a discourse, and the
discourses themselves, do not have an unchanging essence, but can be
constantly altered by political actions. Thus, systems of social relations
– viewed as discursive orders – are precarious and unstable historical
constructions surrounded by other discourses which constantly challenge those systems and their own discourses.

It follows, in contradiction to the Marxist tradition, that there are no social or political forms which express an underlying essence. In this case, social formations are always 'open' systems, comprising many antagonisms, not reducible to any one point of society (such as the relations of production).

Radical Democracy

How does Laclau and Mouffe's post-Marxist perspective address the theoretical problems of Marxism, and the issues raised by contemporary politics? Their view of society as riven with numerous social antagonisms displaces the essentialist Marxist conception. This implies that there cannot, and ought not to be, one primary agent of social change – the proletariat – with an objective interest in removing capitalism. Instead, they make possible the idea of multiple positions and identities, none of which can make a claim to a superior knowledge or nature.

In the place of the privileged social force, Laclau and Mouffe introduce the idea of radical democracy.[35] In this proposed project for the Left, the struggle against capitalist relations of production by the working classes is only one aspect of the broader struggle for radical democracy. Socialist struggles are not the *foundation* of a radical democratic politics, they are just one important site of struggle against undemocratic domination in the sphere of production. Radical democracy, for Laclau and Mouffe, consists of the extension of demands for freedom and equality in ever greater spheres of society. In the political sphere, for instance, it is manifest in demands for equal citizenship rights and for the enlargement of the voting franchise, whereas in economic social relations it is manifest in struggles for better working conditions, higher wages, rights to form trade unions and participate in collective decision-making. In short, as they put it, the task of the Left

> cannot be to renounce liberal-democratic ideology, but on the contrary, to deepen and expand it in the direction of a radical and plural democracy.[36]

These ideas emanate in the main from Claude Lefort's idea of the 'democratic revolution', as well as Tocqueville's conception of democracy as the restless demand for an 'equality of condition' amongst all citizens of a democratic state. According to Lefort, these developments result in the emergence of a new, distinctively modern form of society characterised by an 'empty space of power' where a constant contest of ideas, interests and power occurs.[37]

Having briefly outlined Laclau and Mouffe's alternative political project, it is important to note their strategy for its attainment. This is centred on their own versions of the concepts of hegemony and radical democracy. For Laclau and Mouffe, many groups, despite their differences and even opposition to each other on some issues, can find common cause in their shared commitment to extending democracy and their shared hostility to anti-democratic forces such as the New Right. This shared set of values constitutes a hegemony, that is to say a dominant set of beliefs, aims and structures shared by and uniting a diversity of groups. However, to avoid the authoritarian connotations of the Leninist notion of hegemony (in which different groups are led by one political party chiefly to serve the interests of the proletariat), they also stress the necessary autonomy of the different groups welded together into a hegemonic project. What they call the 'logic of difference' is the maintenance of some separation between the various forces.

Evaluating Post-Marxism

To evaluate Laclau and Mouffe's attempt to resolve the theoretical crisis of Marxism, and outline a post-Marxist perspective, let us begin with their radical materialism, and the concept of discourse which informs it. Without considering the numerous philosophical questions which have been raised by this concept, notably its alleged idealism and relativism,[38] the key issue concerns the character of the concept of discourse proposed by Laclau and Mouffe. A key feature of Marxism is that social formations are *historically specific* combinations of economic and other aspects, i.e. they each have their own particular constraints and logics relevant to a particular point in history. The difficulty with Laclau and Mouffe's position is that this historical specificity is lost. Though they identify the existence of certain 'elements' in a discourse, i.e. the factors which constitute a discourse, they do not specify what these elements actually are.[39] Moreover, even if we accept that all practices are discursive, at least in the general sense in which Laclau and Mouffe use the term, it does not follow that they are all the same. On the contrary, they are structured differently by the systems (economic, political, cultural and so forth) which define and constitute them. Thus the primacy of one or other of these moments, and the precise relationships which are established between them, can and has to be examined in each particular historical point. This requires a set of concepts specific to these particular configurations. This work has not yet been done by Laclau and Mouffe.

However, the substantive question that emerges from Laclau and Mouffe's approach is whether or not it represents a return to a pluralist approach, which Marxists such as Ralph Miliband, Nicos Poulantzas and Claus Offe have criticised for failing to account for the way certain interests dominate the formulation of policy and decision-making.[40] Laclau and Mouffe's emphasis on the fragmentation of the state, and the consequent dispersion of power, makes them vulnerable to the charge that they neglect the power of vested interests and powerful economic forces, which seriously constrain the possibility of a successful radical democratic politics. A similar difficulty arises if we consider their account of the relationship between the state and civil society in which the state is portrayed as available to be employed by different political projects.[41] Again, however, this may underestimate the obstacles to a radical democratic project presented by liberal democratic states, in which the institutionalised separation of state and civil society serves to depoliticise and safeguard economic and social interests.

In addition, the writings of Steven Lukes raise the question of structural power in Laclau and Mouffe's account of social relations.[42] His critique of pluralist and elite views of power is premised on the existence of mechanisms in modern society which prevent the recognition of 'real interests' by certain oppressed groups. In this regard, Laclau and Mouffe distinguish between 'relations of subordination' – those in which agents are subjected to the decisions of another – and 'relations of oppression' – those relations of subordination which have been transformed into sites of antagonism.[43] This distinction needs to be supplemented by what Lukes would call the third face of power, that is, situations in which power is exercised precisely by preventing the transformation of 'relations of subordination' into 'relations of oppression'.

Finally, we come to Laclau and Mouffe's project for radical democracy and the means for attaining it. The novelty of Laclau and Mouffe's proposed political project lies in their effort to combine elements of liberal democracy with socialist demands, while retaining a productive tension between them. The attraction of defending traditional liberal values such as individual rights and freedoms, constitutionalism and democratic procedures, while adding demands for social and economic equality and participatory democracy, needs to take account of the limitations imposed on a radical project by the capitalist state and the social relations it sustains. As we have already noted, for Marxists, the division of the political and economic, and the public and private spheres, places inordinate difficulties on a substantial redistribution of power in capitalist society, as the principal function of these divisions is to legitimise class domination by providing the illusion of freedom amongst citizens who are only equal in a formal, legal sense.[44] This means that Laclau and Mouffe's proposals are confined to seeking modifications *within* a state system which is constitutively opposed to radical transformation. This problem is compounded by the complete absence of concrete proposals, particularly with regard to economic restructuring and policy.

Problems may also be evident in the strategy of hegemony. For Marxists the difficulty with this conception is the failure to outline the actual conditions in which different agents can be realistically linked together, as well as the basis of such links. In this regard, the contrast with Gramsci, the originator of the notion of hegemony as a part of Marxist strategy, is clear. Gramsci's concept of hegemony was intimately connected with the need for the working class to transcend its economic-corporate interests and create a historical bloc structured by the universal values of the proletariat – thus the condition and nature of such hegemony was clear.

To conclude, this chapter has charted the shift from Marxism to post-Marxism in the field of political thought. I have examined the growing series of problems with the classical formulations of Marx and Engels, and Laclau and Mouffe's radical post-Marxist alternative. Laclau and Mouffe's work represents an important, if as yet incomplete, reworking of Marxist theory. As I have indicated in my concluding remarks, whether their work has successfully addressed and transcended the problems bequeathed by the Marxist tradition is not yet clear. Nevertheless, it has opened up new avenues of research and thought which need to be explored further, if there is going to be a viable post-Marxism.

Notes

1. A. Callinicos, *Is there a Future for Marxism?*, Macmillan, London 1982.

2. See: F. Fukuyama, *The End of History and the Last Man*, Penguin Books, Harmondsworth 1992; A. Shtromos (ed), *The End of "Isms": Reflections on the Fate of Ideological Politics After Communism's Collapse*, Basil Blackwell, Oxford 1994.

3. K. Marx, 'Preface to *A Critique of Political Economy*', in D. McLellan (ed), *Karl Marx: Selected Writings*, Oxford University Press, Oxford 1977, p.389.

4. See: E. Mandel, 'Economics', in D. McLellan (ed.), *Marx: The First Hundred Years*, Fontana, London 1983, pp.189-190.

5. As Marx and Engels famously put it in the opening passages of *The Communist Manifesto*: 'The history of all hitherto existing society is the history of class struggles.' See: K. Marx and F. Engels, The Communist Manifesto, in D. McLellan, *Karl Marx: Selected Writings, op.cit.*, p222.

6. *Ibid.*, p230. See also: K. Marx, 'Towards a Critique of Hegel's Philosophy of Right: Introduction', in D. McClellan, Karl *Marx: Selected Writings, op.cit.*, pp.72-73.

7. *Karl Marx*, 'Preface to *A Critique of Political Economy*', in D. McLellan, *Karl Marx: Selected Writings, op.cit.*, p.389.

8. K. Marx and F. Engels, *The Communist Manifesto*, in D. McLellan, *Karl Marx: Selected Writings, op.cit.*, p.238.

9. *Ibid.*, p.223.

10. *Ibid.*, pp228-230.

11. Karl Marx and Friederich Engels, *The German Ideology*, in D. McLellan, *Karl Marx: Selected Writings, op.cit.*, p.169.

12. Karl Marx, *Capital*, Volume 3, in D. McLellan, *Karl Marx: Selected Writings, op.cit.*, p.497.

13. It can be traced back to Thomas Masaryk who coined the phrase in 1892, and has been deployed extensively since the late 1970s. See: E. Laclau and C. Mouffe, *Hegemony and Socialist Strategy: Towards a Radical Democratic Politics*, Verso, London 1985, p.18; for discussions in the 1970s and 1980s, see: P. Anderson, *In the Tracks of Historical Materialism*, Verso, London 1983, p28; B. Smart, *Foucault Critique and Marxism*, Routledge and Kegan Paul, London 1983, pp.4-10.

14. See: C. Offe, *Disorganised Capitalism*, Polity Press, Cambridge 1985, p.4-5; S. Lash and J. Urry, *The End of Organised Capitalism*, Polity Press, Cambridge 1987, pp.1-10. However, these ideas were presaged by thinkers within the Marxist tradition who were writing at the time. See: R. Hilferding, *Finance Capital*, Routledge and Kegan Paul, London 1981; V. Lenin, *Imperialism: The Highest Stage of Capitalism*, Progress Publishers, Moscow 1968; A. Gramsci, *Selections from the Prison Notebooks*,

Lawrence and Wishart, London 1971.

15. K. Marx, 'Preface to *A Critique of Political Economy*', in D. McLellan, *Karl Marx: Selected Writings, op.cit.*, p.390.

16. These processes did not go unnoticed by Marxists writing at the time such as Karl Kautsky, Eduard Bernstein, Rudolf Hilferding and Karl Renner. See: E. Bernstein, *Evolutionary Socialism*, Schocken Books, New York 1961; T. Bottomore and P. Goode (eds), *Austro-Marxism*, Oxford University Press, Oxford 1978.

17. V. Lenin, *Imperialism: The Highest Stage of Capitalism, op.cit.*, pp.244-246.

18. See: R. Luxemburg, *The National Question: Selected Writings of Rosa Luxemburg*, New York, Monthly Review Press. For a clear discussion of the devastating implications of nationalism for Marxism, see: E. Nimni, *Marxism and Nationalism: Theoretical Origins of a Political Crisis*, Pluto Press, London 1991.

19. Much twentieth century Marxist political and social analysis, ranging from the writings of Antonio Gramsci to critical theorists such as Max Horkheimer, Theodor Adorno and Jurgen Habermas and structuralists, such as Louis Althusser and Nicos Poulantzas, has concentrated on the political and ideological incorporation of the working class and the threats to its revolutionary potential.

20. T. Bottomore, *Political Sociology*, Second Edition, Pluto Press, London 1993, pp.19-27.

21. *See:* C. Boggs, *Social Movements and Political Power*, Temple University Press, Philadelphia 1986; M. Castells, *The City and the Grassroots*, Edward Arnold, London 1983; A. Scott, *Ideology and the New Social Movements*, Unwin Hyman, London 1990; A. Touraine, *The Voice and the Eye*, Cambridge University Press, Cambridge 1981. It should be noted that the term 'new social movements' is somewhat unsatisfactory because it implies that these movements are somehow separate and opposed to 'older' forms of struggle based on class interests.

22. See: R. Brunt, 'The Politics of Identity', in S. Hall and M. Jacques (eds), *New Times: The Changing Face of Politics in the 1990s*, Lawrence and Wishart, London 1989, pp.150-159; W. Connolly, *Identity/Difference: Democratic Negotiations of Political Paradox*, Cornell University Press, Ithaca 1991;A. Philips, *Democracy and Difference*, Polity Press, Cambridge, 1993; F. Piven, 'Globalization and the Politics of Identity', in L. Panitch and F. Wood (eds), *Socialist Register 1995*, Merlin Press, London 1995.

23. I borrow this expression from Jacques Derrida who, in his recent writings, has spoken about the promise of a 'democracy to come'. See: J. Derrida,

The Other Heading: Reflections on Today's Europe, Indiana University Press, Bloomington 1992, p.78.

24. E. Laclau and C. Mouffe, *Hegemony and Socialist Strategy: Towards a Radical Democratic Politics*, op.cit., pp.3-5. See also: E. Laclau and C. Mouffe, 'Post-Marxism Without Apologies', *New Left Review*, 166, November/December 1987, pp.79-106; E. Laclau, *New Reflections on the Revolution of Our Time*, Verso, London 1990.

25. See: S. Aronowitz, 'Postmodernism and Politics', in A. Ross (ed), *Universal Abandon: The Politics of Postmodernism*, Edinburgh University Press, Edinburgh 1988; M. Barrett, *The Politics of Truth: From Marx to Foucault*, Polity, Cambridge 1991, Chapter 4; S. Best and D. Kellner, *Postmodern Theory: Critical Interrogations*, Macmillan, London 1991, Chapter 6; D. Coole, 'Is Class a Difference that Makes a Difference?', *Radical Philosophy*, 77 May/June 1996, pp.17-25; T. Eagleton, *Ideology: An Introduction*, Verso, London 1991; N. Geras, 'Post-Marxism?', *New Left Review*, 163 May/June 1987, pp.40-82; N. Geras, 'Ex-Marxism Without Substance: Being a Real Reply to Laclau and Mouffe', *New Left Review*, 169 May/June 1988, pp.34-61 (both republished in his *Discourses of Extremity: Radical Ethics and Post-Marxist Extravagances*, Verso, London 1990); S. Hall, *The Hard Road to Renewal: Thatcherism and the Crisis of the Left*, Verso, London 1988, pp.10-11; D. Howard, 'The Possibilities of a Post-Marxist Radicalism', *Thesis Eleven*, 16, 1987, pp.69-84; E. Laclau and C. Mouffe, *Hegemony and Socialist Strategy: Towards a Radical Democratic Politics*, op.cit., pp.79-106; B. Jessop, *The Capitalist State*, Martin Robertson, London 1982; R. Miliband, 'The New Revisionism in Britain', *New Left Review*, 150, March/April 1985, pp.5-26; N. Mouzelis, 'Marxism or Post-Marxism'?', *New Left Review*, 167, January/February, 1988, pp.107-123; N. Mouzelis, *Post-Marxist Alternatives: The Construction of Social Orders*, Macmillan, London, 1990; M. Rustin, 'Absolute Voluntarism: Critique of a Post-Marxist Concept of Hegemony', *New German Critique*. 43 Winter, pp.147-173; E. Meiksens Wood, *The Retreat from Class: A New 'True' Socialism*, Verso, London 1986; S. Zizek, 'Beyond Discourse-Analysis' in E. Laclau, *New Reflections on the Revolution of Our Time*, Verso, London 1990, pp.249-260.

26. E. Laclau and C. Mouffe, *Hegemony and Socialist Strategy: Towards a Radical Democratic Politics*, op.cit., p.4.

27. N. Geras, 'Ex -Marxism Without Substance: Being a Real Reply to Laclau and Mouffe', *New Left Review*, 169, May/June 1988, p.p34-61.

28. In this respect, Laclau and Mouffe draw explicitly on Jacques Derrida's deconstructive readings of philosophical texts. See J. Derrida, *Positions*,

Chicago University Press, Chicago 1981.

29. E. Laclau and C. Mouffe, *Hegemony and Socialist Strategy: Towards a Radical Democratic Politics, op.cit.*, p.4.

30. *Ibid.* p.7, 110-114; E. Laclau, *New Reflections on the Revolution of Our Time, op.cit.*, pp.5-23, 182.

31. K. Marx, 'Preface to *A Critique of Political Economy*', in D. McLellan, *Karl Marx: Selected Writings, op.cit.*, p.389.

32. E. Laclau and C. Mouffe, *Hegemony and Socialist Strategy: Towards a Radical Democratic Politics, op.cit.*, pp47-48.

33. *Ibid.*, p.125.

34. E. Laclau, *New Reflections on the Revolution of Our Time, op.cit.*, p.183.

35. The idea is first elaborated in their *Hegemony and Socialist Strategy*, but developed further in: C. Mouffe (ed) *Dimensions of Radical Democracy*, Verso, London 1992; C. Mouffe, *The Return of the Political*, Verso, London 1994.

36. *Ibid.*, p.176.

37. C. Lefort, *The Political Forms of Modern Society*, Polity Press, Cambridge 1985; A. de Tocqueville, *Democracy in America*, 2 Volumes, Vintage Books, New York 1945.

38. See: D. Howarth, 'Discourse Theory and Political Analysis', in E. Scarborough and E. Tanenbaum (eds), *Research Methods in the Social Sciences*, Oxford University Press, Oxford 1997.

39. Although, in Laclau's earlier work, 'elements' are explicitly understood as ideological components such as 'militarism', 'anti-clericalism', 'nationalism', 'anti-semitic racism', 'elitism', and so forth, which make up concrete ideological discourses such as Italian Fascism or Peronist populism. See: E. Laclau, *Politics and Ideology in Marxist Theory*, pp.92-100.

40. See: R. Miliband, *The State in Capitalist Society*, Weidenfeld and Nicholson, London 1973; R. Miliband, *Marxism and Politics*, Oxford University Press, Oxford 1977; C. Offe, *The Contradictions of the Welfare State*, Hutchinson, London 1974; N. Poulantzas, *Political Power and Social Classes*, Verso, London 1983; N. Poulantzas, *State, Power, Socialism*, Verso, London 1978.

41. E. Laclau and C. Mouffe, *Hegemony and Socialist Strategy: Towards a Radical Democratic Politics, op.cit.*, pp.179-181.

42. S. Lukes, *Power: A Radical View*, Macmillan, London 1974.

43. *Ibid.*, pp.153-154.

44. See: P. Osborne, *op.cit.*, pp.214-215.

Postmodernism

Simon Thompson

Introduction

In the past twenty years or so, the idea of postmodernism has waxed and waned. While isolated uses of the word 'postmodern' have been traced back as far as the 1870s,[1] it only started its rise from relative obscurity in the 1960s when it began to acquire a popularity among American literary critics. In the next decade it moved steadily into other fields, including art and architecture. Then from around 1980 it entered a brief period of fame and notoriety, spreading out across a whole range of disciplines, including philosophy, politics and sociology.[2] But it is probably true to say that in the last few years it has begun a fairly marked decline. It has fallen, if not back into obscurity, then into a kind of limbo reserved for ideas still found fashionable only by their critics. A number of books have appeared with titles suggesting that they are 'after' or 'beyond' postmodernism;[3] and theories that until recently would have been proud to march under the postmodernist banner now go by names like 'radical democracy' and 'radical humanism'.[4] However, the influence of this strand of thought, in terms of ideas and concepts, if not in name, is still highly evident.

In this chapter, I try as much as possible to avoid the heated controversies that have marked debates about the origins, nature and significance of postmodernism in these various fields. My aim here is to consider its impact in the field of political ideas alone, and to sketch the central features of a postmodernist politics. By way of a provisional sketch map, then, consider four strands that will run throughout this discussion. Although not all those associated with postmodernism would endorse all of these themes, they can help here to get us underway. First, postmodernism accepts the contingency of political values, i.e. it does not feel the need to base political values on absolute, meta-physical foundations such as human nature or the dominant power of human reason. Second, it rejects simple monocausal stories of inevitable and straightforward social progress, and instead places its faith in a condition in which humans are always faced by alternative possibilities. Third, postmodernism celebrates pluralism, dismissing what it sees as the uniformity promoted by other types of politics. Fourth, rejecting the politics of class, party and state, it endorses a poli-tics of personal identity, as exemplified by new social movements such as feminism and the green movement. The main part of this chapter will explore each of these themes in greater detail, pointing out impor-tant internal disagreements within the postmodernist camp, and exam-ining the objections made to each theme by modernist critics.

Before beginning these tasks, I should issue a number of warnings. First, my account of postmodernism is highly selective. While I believe that all the themes I have chosen to discuss here are central to post-modernist political thought, it would be quite possible to argue that important ideas have been left out. Second, the themes considered are sometimes presented in somewhat simplified ways. In the space avail-able I can only lay out the principal lines of the debate in the hope of encouraging further reading. Third, the account of postmodernist political thought presented here must be seen as a composite model. It does not attempt to do full justice to any particular thinker associated with postmodernism. Fourth, lots of quotations are used in the text, which sometimes makes things look rather cluttered; the aim here is to try to give a flavour of the diversity of voices in the postmodernist debate. Finally, my discussion remains more abstract than most of the other chapters in this book. This is partly because, as I indicate, several of these other chapters serve to supply more concrete details about the various possible forms that a postmodernist politics could take.

The chapter begins by examining the philosophical commitments of postmodernism, and the principal elements of its politics. After this it lays out a number of critical issues at stake between postmodernism and its critics, before drawing the threads together in a brief conclusion.

Philosophy

In order to explore the philosophical aspects of postmodernist politics, I consider three closely entwined themes. Put negatively, these are postmodernism's rejection of modernist conceptions of metaphysics, history and human nature.[5]

Metaphysics

Modernist political philosophy believes that political values can and must be given metaphysical backup. It contends that it is possible and necessary to provide grounds capable of convincing any reasonable person of the merit of particular political values. The account of the nature of metaphysics on which such an assumption rests can be considered under three interrelated headings: representation, correspondence and foundationalism.

First, modernist philosophy holds that it is possible to represent the real; that is, it is possible to provide a true and accurate description of the nature of reality. Thus a well-founded scientific theory can provide an exact account of what there is in the world. On this account, language – the means we use to communicate our explanation – is a medium in which the world is accurately reflected. Second, such a philosophy of representation depends on a notion of correspondence, according to which a statement is true if it corresponds to a fact. Thus the statement, 'there are three chairs in this room' is true if there are three chairs in this room. Third, in its strongest version, modernist philosophy claims that political values can only be justified if they are anchored in universal, eternal and absolute foundations. For example, a well-founded account of human nature could provide grounds for the claim that people should be treated in a certain way. If it is argued that all humans are by nature selfish, violent and greedy, then this can be used as an argument for restrictive laws and a powerful state to prevent the descent into such behaviour.

Postmodernist philosophy criticises this sort of metaphysics. It argues that metaphysical backup for political ideas and values is unnecessary and/or impossible. Rorty, in particular, has developed a well-known critique of the modernist acceptance of correspondence, contending that our explanations cannot be seen to function simply as a 'mirror' of reality.[6] He argues in particular that the idea of correspondence itself makes no sense. The basic claim here is that there can be no relationship between our statements about things and the things themselves, so that a true statement somehow looks onto something out there in the world. In fact, since our descriptions of these things are actually part of our theory and not something external to it, there is nothing out there which our statements could be said to to correspond.

A strong version of this claim contends that, rather than being a passive reflection of the world, language actively constitutes it. As a result of this argument, correspondence is rejected in favour of a notion of contextualism. According to this theory, the best we can hope to do is to find coherence within the set of beliefs and values that we already hold. Thus a particular proposition is tested by seeing if it fits with others in which we, or our particular community or culture, presently have confidence. In practice, many postmodernists offer such a contextualist account to uphold political ideas and values.

However, while some postmodernists do talk happily of 'social practices' and even 'traditions', others are wary of the conservative implications of such an analysis. Here White contrasts 'communitarian' and 'post-structuralist' anti-foundationalists: the former hold that '[a]ll contexts are fictions, but the ones in which we find ourselves embedded have a special legitimacy'; the latter, by contrast, fear that this attitude 'allows us to settle too comfortably into the "soft collar" of our community's traditions'.[7] Both parties would agree, however, that these systems of meaning and value are open to challenge and revision at any time.

History

The emergence of modernism saw the eclipse of faith in divine providence and the rise of a new confident hope in purely human progress. Even if God was not around to offer guidance in human affairs, humanity itself could take responsibility for ensuring that its history was one of steady progress. The postmodernist rejection of such modernist notions of history, by contrast, arises from a rejection of the notion of progress itself.

The best and most frequently deployed way of thinking about this modernist belief in progress is Lyotard's notion of 'grand narratives of legitimation' or 'metanarratives'. Such narratives are large-scale explanations of human history that seek to uphold the modernist claims about gradual but continuing progress. At different times, Lyotard suggests that 'Christianity, Enlightenment, romanticism, German speculative idealism, Marxism'[8] have all served as narratives that have competed for the attention of modern societies. Each has offered an account of the nature of history, each suggesting that progress is driven by just one necessary cause, such as God, reason, nature, history or class struggle.

Lyotard has two closely related points to make about these modernist notions of history. First, he points out that in fact we no longer believe in metanarratives, that they have lost the authority that they once had for us. Thus he famously argues that, 'simplifying to the extreme', postmodernism can be defined as 'incredulity toward metanarratives'.[9] In a postmodern world it is no longer believed that metanarratives can provide an anchor for the particular beliefs and values that guide our lives. The reasons for this loss of credibility are many and various. Above all, it is the fact that society is fragmenting into a wide variety of different values, identities and ideas that forces us to acknowledge the diversity of ways of seeing the world.[10] It is impossible, Lyotard contends, to ignore the growing degree of social fragmentation by sticking to one overarching, dominant understanding of human history.

Following on from this, Lyotard offers other reasons for rejecting metanarratives. He argues that such narratives have imperialising tendencies, i.e. they seek to *impose* their explanation across a wide range of areas. For example, the metanarrative of science that came to dominate modern societies sought to reduce all legitimation to a matter of 'performativity', i.e. all theories were judged according to their ability to achieve concrete results, to get things done. This single form of legitimation came to be illegitimately applied in a variety of areas in which it had no rightful place, for example, quality control criteria and performance tables in education and healthcare.[11] Thus Lyotard argues that the effect of this extension of particular narratives has been to undermine pluralism, to destroy difference. Metanarratives attempt to create a unity where there is in fact diversity, and, by seeking to do so, that diversity is forcibly suppressed.

However, while a wide variety of thinkers associated with postmodernism would accept the broad thrust of Lyotard's argument, an important difficulty has been identified. It has been argued that the very idea of defining postmodernism as a condition *after* metanarratives is itself a highly modernist way of regarding matters. Lyotard is accused of offering 'a grand narrative account of the move to postmodernity and the eclipse of grand narratives'.[12] Clearly, if it's true that we now find such narratives incredible, then such an account would self-destruct. Lyotard has responded to this sort of criticism by suggesting that 'postmodern' should be regarded simply as a 'mood' or 'state of mind', rather than a grand explanation.[13]

Human Nature
With the notion of a human nature, modernist political philosophy endorses the belief that humans have certain immutable qualities.

Against this, some postmodernists deny that human nature exists, while others offer a rigorously anti-essentialist account of the self. To explore this theme, I adopt (and adapt) Hall's contrast between what he calls an 'Enlightenment subject' and a 'postmodernist subject' ('subject' can be taken here to mean broadly the individual human being both as an actor in the world and/or as an object of analysis[14]).

First of all, consider the principal features of each subject. As the name suggests, the idea of the Enlightenment subject emerges around the time of the eighteenth-century revolution in ideas. It possesses a number of distinct features. It is homogenous – all subjects share the same basic nature; unified – individual subjects do not possess internal contradictions; rational – characterised by the power of conscious reason; autonomous – able to exercise its reason in order to be self-governing; stable in identity – unchanging over time; and, finally, each subject is an individual – possessing unique qualities and abilities (although not different basic natures) that mark it out as distinct from all others.

The postmodernist subject can be defined by a series of contrasting features. It is heterogeneous or fragmented – patched together out of a variety of different bits of values, identities and beliefs; dispersed or decentred – characterised by all sorts of internal divisions, such as that between consciousness and unconsciousness; somatic – inseparable from the body and its needs and desires; creative – while lacking the modernist power of autonomy, it may be able to be inventive in ways unknown to the modernist subject; unstable – changing over time; and, finally, although not a self-contained individual, the patchwork of which it is composed may mean it is at least idiosyncratic. Thus, while modernism's Enlightenment subject is a sovereign individual, with a solid and stable core, possessing powers of rational autonomy, the postmodernist subject is regarded as a complex combination of relatively random components.[15]

Although there are different ways of understanding the reasons for this change of subject, I will look only briefly at one of the most significant. This is to see these two subjects as the products of different historical forces. On this account, to put it very crudely, modern societies produce modernist human beings, and postmodern societies, postmodernist human beings. Foucault can provide one part of this argument. He makes a rough distinction between classical and modern periods, suggesting that the break between them occurs in the early nineteenth century. He argues that, in the latter period, distinct forms of knowledge and power gave rise to a distinct type of subject. With regard to knowledge, he contends that it is only with the rise of the modern way of thinking that man can exist 'as a primary reality, with his own destiny', who is regarded both as the main object requiring explanation and the only being capable of understanding the truth of the world.[16] As far as power goes, Foucault's historical studies – for example, on insanity, criminality and sexuality – have traced the various ways of controlling the behaviour of others that have produced this subject. To Foucault's theory, it is necessary to add an account of the way in which contemporary historical conditions have undermined the modernist subject he analyses. Such an account draws, for example, on theories of social fragmentation to argue that contemporary social forces produce the divided subject of postmodernism.[17]

Politics

Now I want to trace the impact of these philosophical themes on postmodernist politics. To reduce this to a formula, it could be said that, with the rejection of metaphysics, history and human nature, it becomes necessary to live with contingency, pluralism and difference (and to adopt appropriate practices which enable this).

Contingency

First, consider how the rejection of metaphysics involves the embracing or at least the acceptance of contingency. For Heller and Fehér, for example, '[t]he world into which people are born is no longer seen as having been decreed by fate but as an agglomerate of possibilities'.[18] We must accept that the human world has no necessary order, neither God nor human reason nor class have destined the world to take one inevitable form. Everything could have been, and still could be, other than it is.

It should be noted that, in order for contingency to be accepted, it may be necessary to engage in a critique of existing ideas in order to prize people from their current attachment to particular beliefs and values. Thus Foucault seeks to demonstrate 'that the things which seem most evident to us are always formed in the confluence of encounters and chances, during the course of a precarious and fragile history'. By tracing the 'network of contingencies' from which they emerged, he hopes to convince us 'that since these things have been made, they can be unmade, as long as we know how it was that they were made'.[19] Put the other way round, if we understand how something was made, we know that it didn't have to be made that way, and so we gain the ability to change it, or to create something new. For example, if we discover, as Foucault claims, that the description of some people as 'mad' only came into being at a very specific point in recent human history in order to serve certain professional interests and in response to changes in other beliefs and in society, we can see that 'madness' is not an actually existing thing *discovered* by the medical profession but is constructed by it. This then opens the way for us to consider other ways of responding to 'mad' behaviour.

Now, following on from this point, consider the way in which this account of contingency encourages a political practice of *invention*. If we give up the search for foundations and embrace contingency, we shall be able to defend a politics which enables us to create new possibilities. As Laclau puts it, '[t]he possibilities of practical construction from the present are enriched as a direct consequence of the dwindling of epistemological ambitions'.[20] In other words, the less we think we *have* to know about our world, the more we can make up.

Less grandiose than the invention of new things, and even new worlds, is the practice Featherstone calls 'the act of *naming*'. This is the strategy used by groups engaged in struggle whereby they use new terms or phrases to highlight certain factors in order to shift debate or understanding and so aid their cause.[21] This is what happens, for example, when feminism persuades us that behaviour once labelled 'a harmless bit of fun' actually constitutes 'sexual harassment'.

Pluralism

The rejection of modernist accounts of history, and of the associated belief in one particular kind of progress, opens up other possibilities for a postmodernist politics. If history is not driven by one force, in one direction, toward one destination, it follows that multiple possibilities always exist. In short, the postmodern condition is one of pluralism.

Postmodernist thinkers characterise the increasing complexity of this postmodern world in different ways. Bauman, for example, describes 'the increasingly apparent plurality and heterogeneity of the socio-cultural world'.[22] Similarly, for Heller and Fehér, since the world is 'a plurality of heterogeneous spaces', there must be 'acceptance of the plurality of cultures and discourses'.[23] Developing this final point,

Touraine puts a slightly different twist on matters. Rejecting conventional (Western) accounts of progress, he contrasts the 'rich diversity of so-called traditional cultures' with the 'impoverishing homogeneity of modern civilisation'.[24] Both kinds of pluralism reject the idea that there is a single master plan suitable for all of humankind. Instead, there is a diversity of ways of being, and no one way can be judged superior or inferior to another.

From this account of pluralism, it's a fairly short step to the political practice of *interpretation*. Each particular social and political world is treated as a text, and, inside each world, the political theorist's job is to offer an interpretation of that text. In this manner, Walzer suggests that, instead of attempting to deduce the nature of justice from abstract metaphysics, one should aim 'to interpret to one's fellow citizens the world of meanings that we share'.[25] As Bauman points out, the interpreter can also play an important role between worlds by 'facilitating communication between autonomous (sovereign) participants' across different traditions.[26] In either case, the important point about interpretations is that, rather than being metaphysical judgements handed down from on high, they are complex, multi-stranded analyses always open to challenge from other interpretations.

Attention to pluralism also leads postmodernists to endorse a form of political action perhaps best characterised as one of *micropolitics*. To see what this involves, first consider how modernism could be said to endorse a 'macropolitics'. This has the following characteristics: first, it is based on ideas and values for which universal validity is claimed; for example, ideas of human rights are seen as a suitable benchmark from which *all* cultures can be judged. Second, it seeks universal solutions to universal problems; for example, a particular Western model of democracy is seen as a political ideal to which *all* societies should aspire. Third, if of a radical bent, it may endorse notions of universal struggle, asserting that only one single historical actor can be seen as the bringer and recipient of emancipation; for example, classical marxism believed that the working class fulfilled this role.

By contrast, then, a postmodernist micropolitics has the following features. First, its method of interpretation makes it sensitive to local rules and understandings. Second, it is attentive to the many different contexts of political action, believing that a wide variety of political practices can have validity. Thus Best and Kellner, for example, contend that Lyotard's postmodernism is for 'heterogeneity, plurality, constant innovation, and pragmatic construction of local rules and prescriptives agreed upon by participants, and is thus for micropolitics'. He reduces 'justice to a justice of multiplicities which is necessarily for him local, provisional, and specific'.[27] As such, a postmodernist conception of justice is one that moulds itself to local conditions rather than trying to mould those conditions to it. Third, accepting that there is a diversity of political actors, it is concerned with their local struggles and need for specific emancipations; for example, it may focus on the battles for recognition of particular groups and communities. As Smart puts it, it is now necessary to recognise that 'all social struggles are partial struggles and that their objectives are specific emancipations rather than the "global emancipation of humanity" '.[28] For example, anti-racist struggles are understood and valued on their own terms rather than attempting to reduce them to one part of a wider struggle such as the emancipation of the working class.

Difference

Postmodernists, rejecting all essentialist accounts of the subject, argue that identity is defined by, dependent on, and at the same time undermined by difference, i.e. our identities are formed and challenged by those with other or conflicting identities. (For example, a large part of what it is to be English is that the English regard themselves as different from the French, the Americans, etc.)

One sort of politics that this account leads to is what can be called the politics of identity. For example, Giddens talks about the emergence of a 'life politics' which is 'about how we should live in a world where everything that used to be natural (or traditional) now has in some sense to be chosen, or decided about'. According to this politics, not just 'orthodox areas of political involvement', but also everything from the contents of our shopping baskets to the nature of our relations with those we love becomes the substance of politics.[29] I want to concentrate here, however, on the other side of this account of the subject, and to focus, not on the politics of *identity*, but rather on various aspects of the politics of *difference*.

If we accept that the process of identity construction marginalises and suppresses different others, that in forming our identity we inevitably exclude and often ignore or even suppress the needs of those who do not share our identity, then we are involved in an ethical commitment to those others. We have a responsibility to those others oppressed by the construction of dominant identities. One task that becomes necessary in order to carry out this ethical commitment is to expose the methods by which identity is formed through the exclusion of others. I have already suggested how Foucault might be able to supply suitable tools for this job. Thus, following Foucault, Boyne contends that 'social philosophy' 'must continue to address the rights of the other. It must continue to expose those political practices which exclude the other in a multitude of subtle and not so subtle ways'.[30] He argues for a politics which agitates for the 'many voices' of those subordinated by power to be heard – including 'prisoners, homosexuals, the mentally ill, the unemployed, children, ethnic minorities, unbelievers, believers, women, the disabled, students, ecologists, conscientious objectors'.[31]

But there are also more constructive political practices that this account of the significance of difference might lead us to. Here the ethical imperative is to find ways of actually fostering difference. For White, the actual validity of difference,

> as opposed to mere tolerance, could give us grounds for a stronger commitment to public policies that do not merely protect the formal *right* of individual or collective concrete others to express themselves, but go further and do more to *empower* or to *foster* the emergence of such voices.[32]

This commitment to the fostering of difference has taken a variety of institutional forms. One is that of multiculturalism. Such a politics starts from the premise that respect is due to all individuals in light of a 'universal potential . . . for forming and defining one's own identity'.[33] For example, while linguistic and cultural minorities, indigenous and aboriginal peoples are very various in character, they do share a desire to secure appropriate acknowledgement and understanding of their needs and identities. Thus the politics of multiculturalism contends that all distinct individual and group identities should be recognised, and political forms should be devised that encourage and foster the development of those identities. The aim is to achieve 'integration through diversity' in what Smith calls an 'overarching political community'.[34]

A second and closely related form that such a politics can take is that most often called simply 'the politics of difference'. This politics contends that various groups must be given powers within the system of formal political institutions itself. Thus Young, in a well known example of this sort of politics, identifies a wide range of groups who, since they have suffered various forms of oppression, need formal political recognition. She also proposes a range of devices with which to incorporate groups into the political system, including institutional and financial support for groups to be able to organise themselves effectively; providing groups with the chance to generate and respond to policy proposals; and giving groups the right of veto over any policy proposal that affects them directly.[35] The aim in each case is to publicly acknowledge groups in order to empower them, and so to institutionalise the recognition of difference.

Critical Issues

Of course the elaboration of the sort of postmodernist politics summarised so far has not gone without vigorous response from modernist critics. Here I want to look, albeit rather briefly, at a number of important issues at stake in this debate. The presentation roughly follows the route already mapped. Criticisms are considered of the postmodernist commitments to contingency, pluralism and difference. These prompt charges of irrationalism, relativism and conservatism, and a critique of the politics of difference.

The Modernist Critique

A first criticism concerns the postmodernists' abandonment of foundations and acceptance of contingency. Habermas, for example, argues that postmodernism is *irrationalist*. He contends that because postmodernists do not try to provide any grounds or foundations for values and beliefs they 'can and want to give no account of their own position'.[36] For this reason, he calls them 'neoconservative'. As Rorty says,

> [t]he thrust of Habermas's claim that thinkers like Foucault, Deleuze, and Lyotard are 'neoconservative' is that they offer us no 'theoretical' reason to move in one social direction rather than another.[37]

At worst, this critique suggests that postmodernism implies that politics as no more than a battle between rival forces and that the claim to have right or justice on one's side is merely rhetoric concealing a fight for power. As Flax argues,

> [i]f there is no objective basis for distinguishing between true and false

beliefs, then it seems that power alone will determine the outcome of competing truth claims.[38]

A second criticism follows postmodernism's endorsement of pluralism against universalism. This leads critics straight to the charge of *relativism*, since reasons for choosing one action over another are only to be found in specific cultural contexts. It is then argued that this is unacceptable. First, it is a nonsensical position since it depends on a form of universalism that it officially rules out; that is, postmodernism calls for the toleration of the diversity of cultures – but what is this call based upon if not a universal position? There seems to be no *specific* cultural context which has given rise to that call. Second, it is a morally offensive standpoint, since it lends support to immoral cultures; that is, it permits violations of universal standards of human decency. If a specific society indulges in torture and cruelty, then according to the critics, postmodernists have no position from which to criticise such practices since they disallow universal values such as justice or human rights which exist outside of any one society.

The accusation of *conservatism* follows hot on the heels of irrationalism and relativism. If postmodernists offer no reasons or only local reasons for their values, then they are unable to take up a standpoint from which they could effectively question their own values – or challenge those of the currently dominant elite. Sandel summarises the case like this:

> If the notion of justice is to have any critical force ... it must be based on standards independent of any particular society; otherwise justice is left hostage to the very values it must judge.[39]

Without an external standpoint, postmodernism is condemned to mere approval of the status quo. To take one specific case, reflecting on Lyotard's penchant for what they call 'smallish, localised narrative', Fraser and Nicholson contend that '[t]here is no place in Lyotard's universe for critique of broad-based relations of dominance and subordination along lines like gender, race, and class'.[40] Such criticism, they conclude, is clearly still needed in face of the large-scale, systematic injustices that disfigure our societies.

Finally, a number of criticisms can be made of the politics of difference. First, a general point may be made about the sort of groups who form the core of this political approach. If, as one would expect, these groups operate according to a logic of identity, whereby an identity is forged in conflict with other identities, then, as Squires puts it, 'we must recognise that solidarity is often achieved at the expense of a two-fold strategy of exclusion and assimilation.[41] That is, the formation of such groups will involve the expulsion of some individuals from the group and the coercion of those left inside. If this is so, this may give us good reason for not basing a postmodernist politics on groups of this kind. Second, it may be asked whether *all* differences between groups carry the same moral weight, and whether some carry any moral weight at all. For example, should neo-nazis be able to demand rights to resources or representation on the basis of the claim that they possess a distinct cultural identity? Modernist critics argue that any attempt to draw a line between acceptable and unacceptable differences will depend on universalist premises. A final criticism questions whether sensitivity to difference can go too far. If we focus too closely on difference, it may be that the basis for any coherent politics will be undermined. For example, if a politics of difference splits 'women' into different fragments, and then those fragments into further fragments, it becomes difficult to know if any coherent constituency will exist for a feminist politics to represent.[42]

The Postmodernist Response

Since the development of the postmodernist politics sketched here took place against the background of a critique of modernism, it is not surprising that part of the postmodernist response to modernist criticisms will simply be to reiterate their original position. Thus, in responding to charges of irrationalism, postmodernists may try to switch the burden of proof back by asking modernists to prove that their sort of rationalism is viable. The charge of relativism will be met by the demand for a convincing justification of any form of universalism. Against the charge of conservatism, postmodernists will ask how it could be possible to stand outside any particular social context, to take up a 'God's eye view'. Critiques of the politics of difference will be countered by questioning whether any politics that ignores difference can avoid the oppression of others. Here, however, I want to look a little further at the more constructive responses that postmodernists can and have made to the modernist critique.

One response to attacks on postmodernism's irrationalism is to try to show that it is based on a false choice. Foucault, for example, argues that it is necessary to get around the 'simplistic and authoritarian alternative' of being either for or against Enlightenment rationalism. He contends that, while we are 'beings who are historically determined, to a certain extent, by the Enlightenment', we can nevertheless develop a 'permanent critique of ourselves' in order to determine what relationship we now want to have to the Enlightenment.[43] Amongst other things, a critique of this kind must address what could be called the question of value: by what means and to what extent can we defend our values in the absence of Enlightenment reason? This is the question taken up in a collection of essays which begins from the premise that '[a] post-Enlightenment defence of principled positions, without the essentialist or transcendental illusions of Enlightenment thought, is both possible and necessary'. Here Squires and her contributors seek to map out various ways in which it might be possible to reassert values 'without relinquishing the critical gains' made possible by postmodernism.[44]

The criticism of relativism could also be met by trying to show that, like irrationalism, it is based on a false distinction. Rorty's defence of a position he calls 'ethnocentrism' represents an attempt of this kind. Ethnocentrists assert the superiority of their values – so they are not relativists; but they do not believe that it is possible rationally to persuade all others of the rightness of their values – so they are not universalists either.[45] Alternatively, if, as seems likely, postmodernists find ethnocentrism unpalatable, then the 'rediscovery of value' suggest an alternative way of responding to criticisms of relativism. If any of these rediscovered values have validity beyond their particular place of origin, then postmodernism can endorse some kind of minimal universalism. For example, Walzer claims that there are 'basic prohibitions – of murder, deception, betrayal, gross cruelty' which 'constitute a kind of minimal and universal moral code'.[46] The important point about such codes is that they must express a 'contextualized universalism'. That is, they must be sensitive to, although not fully immersed in, local contexts and cultures.

Having got this far, various ways of responding to the charge of conservatism become apparent. For example, we *can* offer non-universal reasons for values which differ from those now dominant in a particular culture. Or we can criticise societies – including our own – if their values violate Walzer's minimal universal code. He suggests that in this case the prohibitions in this code provide a 'critical perspective' on such societies.[47] Other methods of critique which could be taken up by postmodernists can also be found in Walzer's work. In particular, he suggests that social critics can remain connected to their society so long as they occupy a marginal position in it. As he says, we should be 'in but not wholly of' our society since '[i]t is not connection but authority and domination from which we must distance ourselves'.[48]

The critique of the politics of difference offers a number of challenges to postmodernists. Let me just sketch the problems they need to work through here. First, an account of the nature of groups must be formed which is capable of showing how groups can unite people without suppressing any individual member's specific identity or values. Here Young's work is particularly useful. She has worked toward what she calls an 'emancipatory', rather than 'oppressive', account of 'group difference'.[49] Second, it is necessary to find a way of establishing the limits of acceptable difference, of putting justifiable constraints on otherness. Perhaps this could draw on the contextualised universal values hinted at above. Or perhaps it could find some internal rationale to limit difference; for example, we may respect all those who respect others' difference. Finally, in order to counter the criticism that the politics of difference leads to the fragmentation of any viable politics, it is necessary to show how and when it is necessary and justifiable to stress unity rather than fragmentation. Thus Best and Kellner contend that 'both in the theoretical and political spheres it is sometimes valuable to stress differences, plurality, and heterogeneity, while in other contexts it may be preferable to seek generalities, common interests, and consensus'.[50]

Conclusion

All too often, accounts of the debates between postmodernists and their critics have relied on parodies of each side's position. Postmodernists appear as playful and mocking jokers, wilfully neglectful of the realities of human suffering and oppression. By contrast, modernists are presented as tight-laced and grim-faced pessimists, whose opinions about such 'realities' have on occasion been twisted around and used to *legitimate* such oppression. In most cases, there is no more than a grain of truth in these images. Once we look at the details of the debates between postmodernists and their critics, neither side takes up the extreme positions that might justify these parodies. For example, most modernists are aware that reason has been used in the service of oppression, and most postmodernists do offer reasons for their values – just not the sort of reasons that modernists think they should offer. Similarly, modernists will generally concede that sensitivity is required when dealing with differences between groups, and in most cases postmodernists are prepared to admit that all groups have certain basic characteristics in common.

If differences between the defenders and critics of postmodernism are often not as extreme than they first appear, then what have the debates between them actually achieved? At the very least, it could be said that these debates have put a number of new issues on the political agenda. For example, there is now a greater sensitivity to the importance of the language of politics; unfortunately, this is seen at its most simplistic and unhelpful in debates about political correctness. In addition, a model of politics as a poetic, playful and inventive practice has grown in importance at the expense of a model which slavishly follows models of scientific inquiry and bureaucratic application.

There is also a greater awareness of the constructed and flexible character of 'human nature'; hence the increased importance of identity politics – seen, for example, in the various forms of the politics of sexuality. Finally, less traditional models of organisation have also developed a more significant role in contemporary political life. In particular, non-hierarchical social movements or networks – such as those seen in protests about road development and animal welfare – are more prominent today than ever before. For this reason, it would be fair to say that, even if postmodernism as a fashion has had its day, in a whole series of political ideas and practices, its influence lives on.

Notes

1. H. Bertens, *The Idea of the Postmodern: a History*, Routledge, London 1995, p.20; M.A. Rose, *The Post-modern and the Post-industrial: a Critical Analysis*, Cambridge University Press, Cambridge 1991, p.xi, note 1.
2. This stage of its history can perhaps be dated to the original French publication in 1979 of J.-F. Lyotard's *The Postmodern Condition: a Report on Knowledge*, Manchester University Press, Manchester 1984, or to J. Habermas's 'Modernity versus Postmodernity', *New German Critique*, vol 22, 1981, pp.3-14. Together these can be said to have set the terms of much of the subsequent debate.
3. H.W. Simons and M. Billig (eds), *After Postmodernism: Reconstructing Ideology Critique*, Sage, London 1994; H. Haber, *Beyond Postmodern*

Politics: Lyotard, Rorty, Foucault, Routledge, London 1994.

4. C. Mouffe (ed.), *Dimensions of Radical Democracy: Pluralism, Citizenship, Community*, Verso, London 1992; J. Weeks, *Invented Moralities: Sexual Values in an Age of Uncertainty*, Polity Press, Cambridge 1995.

5. Here the analysis is indebted to J. Flax, *Psychoanalysis, Feminism and Postmodernism in the Contemporary West*, University of California Press, Berkeley 1990, pp.32-34.

6. R. Rorty, *Philosophy and the Mirror of Nature*, Princeton University Press, Princeton 1979, pp.371-72.

7. S. White, *Political Theory and Postmodernism*, Cambridge University Press, Cambridge 1991, p.27.

8. J.-F. Lyotard, *The Inhuman: Reflections on Time*, Polity, Oxford, 1991, p.68.

9. J.-F.Lyotard, *The Postmodern Condition, op.cit.*, p.xxiv.

10. *Ibid*, pp.xxv, 17.

11. Compare J. Habermas, *The Theory of Communicative Action, Volume Two: Lifeworld and System – a Critique of Functionalist Reason*, Polity Press, Cambridge 1987.

12. M. Featherstone, 'In Pursuit of the Postmodern: an Introduction', *Theory, Culture and Society*, vol 5, nos 2-3, 1988, pp.195-215, at p.198; and see: S. Best and D. Kellner, *Postmodern Theory: Critical Interrogations*, Macmillan, London 1991, pp.171-72.

13. J.-F. Lyotard, 'Rules and Paradoxes and Svelte Appendix', *Cultural Critique*, no 5, 1986, pp.209-19.

14. S. Hall, 'The Question of Cultural Identity', in S. Hall, D. Held and T. McGrew (eds), *Modernity and its Futures*, Polity Press, Cambridge 1992.

15. Compare A. Lent, 'Radical Democracy: Arguments and Principles', in M. Perryman (ed.), *Altered States: Postmodernism, Politics, Culture*, Lawrence and Wishart, London 1994, who contrasts 'unitary' and 'divided' subjects.

16. M. Foucault, *The Order of Things: An Archeology of the Human Sciences*, Vintage, New York 1973, p.310.

17. See, for example, S. Hall, 'The Question of Cultural Identity', *op.cit.*

18. A. Heller and F. Feher, *The Postmodern Political Condition*, Polity Press, Cambridge 1988, p.17.

19. M. Foucault, *Politics, Philosophy, Culture: Interviews and other Writings 1977-1984*, Lawrence D. Kritzman (ed.), Routledge, London 1988, p.37.

20. E. Laclau, *New Reflections on the Revolution of Our Time*, Verso, London 1990, p.189.

21. M. Featherstone, 'In Pursuit of the Postmodern: an Introduction', *op.cit.*, p206.

22. Z. Bauman, 'Sociological Responses to Postmodernity', *Thesis Eleven*, no 23, 1989, p.53.

23. A. Heller and F. Fehér, *The Postmodern Political Condition, op.cit.*, p.5.

24. Quoted in B. Smart, *Postmodernity*, Routledge, London 1993, p.56.

25. M. Walzer, *Spheres of Justice*, Martin Robertson, Oxford 1983, p.xiv.

26. Z. Bauman, *Legislators and Interpreters: on Modernity, Post-modernitv and Intellectuals*, Polity Press, Cambridge 1987, p.5.

27. S. Best and D. Kellner, *Postmodern Theory: Critical Interrorgations, op.cit.*, pp.165, 178.

28. B. Smart, *Postmodernity, op.cit.*, p.29.

29. A. Giddens, *Modernity and Self-identity: Self and Society in the Late Modern Age*, Polity Press, Cambridge 1991, pp.90-91.

30. *Ibid*, p.158.

31. *Ibid*, pp.132-33.

32. S. White, *Political Theory and Postmodernism, op.cit.*, p.110.

33. C. Taylor, 'The Politics of Recognition', in Amy Gutmann (ed.), *Multiculturalism: Examining the Politics of Recognition*, Princeton University Press, Princeton 1994, p.42.

34. A.D. Smith, 'Towards a Global Culture?', *Theory, Culture and Society*, vol 7, nos 2 & 3, 1990, p.173.

35. I.M. Young, *Justice and the Politics of Difference*, Princeton University Press, Princeton 1990, p.184; and see pp.173-74.

36. J. Habermas, 'Modernity versus Postmodernity, *op.cit.*, p.336.

37. R. Rorty, 'Habermas and Lyotard on Postmodernity', in R. Bernstein (ed.), *Habermas and Modernity*, Polity Press, Oxford 1985, p.171.

38. J. Flax, 'Postmodernism and Gender Relations in Feminist Theory', in L. Nicholson (ed.), *Feminism/Postmodernism*, Routledge, London, 1990, p.42.

39. M. Sandel, Review article on Michael Walzer's *Spheres of Justice, New York Times Review of Books*, 24 April, 1983, p.20.

40. N. Fraser and L. Nicholson, 'Social Criticism without Philosophy: an Encounter between Feminism and Postmodernism', in L. Nicholson (ed.), *Feminism/Postmodernism*, Routledge, London 1990, p.23.

41. J. Squires, 'Introduction', in J. Squires (ed.), *Principled Positions: Postmodernism and the Rediscovery of Value*, Lawrence and Wishart, London 1993, p.7.

42. See: J. Butler, 'Gender Trouble: Feminist Theory and Psychoanalytic Discourse', in L. Nicholson (ed.), *Feminism/Postmodernism*, Routledge, London 1990, p.327.

43. M. Foucault, 'What is Enlightenment?', in P. Rabinow (ed.), *The Foucault Reader*, Penguin, Harmondsworth 1986, p.43.

44. J. Squires, 'Introduction', *op.cit.*, pp.1-2.
45. See, for example: R. Rorty, 'On Ethnocentrism: a Reply to Clifford Geertz', in his *Objectivity Relativism and Truth: Philosophical Papers, volume 1*, Cambridge University Press, Cambridge 1991.
46. M. Walzer, *Interpretation and Social Criticism*, Harvard University Press, Cambridge, MA 1987, p.24.
47. M. Walzer, 'Moral Minimalism'. in W. Shea and A. Spadafora (eds), *From the Twilight of Probability*, Science History Publications, Canton 1992, pp.9, 12.
48. M. Walzer, *Interpretation and Social Criticism, op.cit.*, pp.37, 60.
49. I.M. Young, *Justice and the Politics of Difference, op.cit.*, pp.168-73.
50. S. Best and D. Kellner, *Postmodern Theory: Critical Interrogations, op.cit.*, p.175.

Feminism

Moya Lloyd

Introduction

Radical, liberal, psychoanalytic, French, postmodern, socialist, Marxist, third world, lesbian; the peace camps at Greenham Common, protests at Miss World competitions, Take Back the Night demonstrations: from its inception feminism has been characterised more by internal variety in its theories and practices than by any semblance of unity. There is, thus, no such thing as feminism, only a plethora of feminisms drawing inspiration from a multiplicity of sources and producing a plurality of explanations of women's situation. To understand feminism one has to acknowledge this diversity and the vibrant role that it plays in the practical politics of the women's movement.

Historical Roots

Trying to determine the origins of the women's liberation movement is difficult. As we shall see below, ideas about the difficulties women face in a male-dominated world have been around for some time. In practical terms, however, the impetus for the new wave of feminist movements emerging in the 1960s derives from other sources. Many of the women who became feminists in Britain did so as a result of their experiences in other protest movements, particularly the New Left, the radical students' movement and the anti-nuclear and anti-war movements. Some came from women's peace groups, still others from an increasingly activist and militant working class.[1] However, two events are of specific interest. In 1968 a three week strike amongst machinists occurred at Ford Dagenham (and later at Ford Halewood) over the issue of equal pay for equal work. As a result of this action the short-lived trade union National Joint Action Committee for Women's Equal Rights was formed. It drew up a five item charter that included a demand that the TUC lead a campaign for equal opportunity and for equal pay.[2] If this strike raised national consciousness about women's situation, in 1970 the women's movement really took off in Britain with the National Liberation Conference at Ruskin College, Oxford.[3]

This conference attracted some 600 participants. Together they formulated a four-point programme of demands for equal pay; equal education and opportunity; twenty-four hour nurseries; and free contraception and abortion on demand.[4] By the mid-1970s, this 'women's rights policy "package" ',[5] added three more goals: financial independence for women; equal employment opportunities; and freedom from violence. These demands combined a focus on work (evidence of the close affiliation between feminism and the labour movement in Britain) with an emphasis on women's control over their own bodies. The British women's movement thus defined itself not only in terms of legal and economic rights but also in terms of personal and sexual rights. As such, it sought for women not only equality with men but also an end to 'male-dominated society'.[6] One of the very first activities of this newly born women's movement was a series of demonstrations at the Miss World Contest that aimed to denounce beauty contests as harmful to women and to highlight the current passivity of women in the face of male power.

In order to appreciate the history of current feminism, it is necessary also to have some sense of its indebtedness to the ideas of the past. Dating the origins of feminism is difficult. Many of the writings from which it might be said to derive have disappeared over the course of its history. The term itself, understood as the advocacy of women's rights, originates in France in the 1890s. Prior to this date, however, various texts appeared concerning women's lot in life.[7] One of the earliest is Christine de Pisan's *The Book of the City of Ladies* written in 1405. This is followed by a regular stream of writing across Europe and, later, the US. In 1792, Mary Wollstonecraft's *A Vindication of the Rights of Woman* appeared. Drawing on the Enlightenment ideals of equality, rationality and autonomy, Wollstonecraft makes an appeal on behalf of women for equality of rights with men. Observing that the mind has no sex, Wollstonecraft argues in particular for the extension to women of the right to education and thus the right to become intellectually independent. This argument for the equal treatment of the sexes, so important during second wave liberal feminism, is echoed by John Stuart Mill in *The Subjection of Women* published in 1869.[8] Continuing the argument that both sexes are rational and thus in need of equal education, Mill adds to this a demand for the same civil liberties and economic opportunities for women as for men. Central to both arguments is the idea that women's equality is impeded by social barriers and by custom, not by innate or natural differences between the sexes.[9]

Unlike these early liberal feminists who stress the sameness of male and female nature, their contemporaries, the utopian socialists, emphasised their differences. Women, they argued, were the more virtuous species (a sentiment that recurs in some second wave feminism). Their feminine qualities are not only vital to the egalitarian societies of the future, but the very progress of the whole human race depends upon the emancipation of women: 'The extension of women's rights is the basic principle of all social progress'.[10] In addition to women's inequality in the public sphere, these utopian writers (specifically William Thompson and Anna Wheeler[11]) drew attention to the simultaneous discrimination against women at home. Marriage far from enhancing human relations, is a hindrance to human development, a site of slavery (economic, emotional and cultural) for women and a block to progress in these same areas for men. The solutions: the abolition of private property; the eradication of the sexual division of labour and its replacement by the communal provision of household services; and the institution of societies founded upon mutual cooperation and common ownership. In place of the legal and social reforms suggested by liberal feminists, the utopian socialist feminists advocate social reconstruction at both the private and the public level.

In contrast to the Utopians' claim that women's rights are a measure of the advancement of society, Marxist analysis makes scant mention of women's specific plight. The so-called 'Woman Question' concerned Marx very little in comparison to the class dynamic underpinning capitalism. It was left to two of Marx's followers – Friedrich Engels and August Bebel – to fill in the blanks. In *The Origin of the Family, Private Property, and the State* (1884) Engels offers an account of the origins of women's oppression in the private ownership of property and in the exclusion of women from production. In *Woman and Socialism* (1885) Bebel provides an historical account of women's lot and a critique of the emerging 'bourgeois' women's movement. Despite different emphases, both authors are adamant that only the complete overthrow of capitalism could bring about the emancipation of women. If women are to contribute to this revolution, they must enter the workforce where their politicisation as proletarians will ensure their involvement in socialist revolution, a position echoed by Marxist feminists during the 1960s and 1970s. This class emphasis clearly has implications for the relations amongst women. Although Bebel recognises that women have interests in common that transcend their class differences, he continues to regard alliances between bourgeois and proletarian women as less effective than socialist revolution.[12] Women's interests as women are subordinate to women's class interests: an attitude that left its own legacy (see below and the chapter on Socialism and Social Democracy in this book).

Although feminism did not disappear in the period leading up to the late 1960s when its second wave begins, it did enter a period of relative quiet. This comparative silence was broken at least once by the appearance of a remarkable book entitled *The Second Sex* written by the French existentialist philosopher Simone de Beauvoir.[13] This vast and difficult text introduces a number of themes that have since preoccupied feminism: the idea of otherness, the difference between sex and gender and the question of woman-centredness. For de Beauvoir, a woman's biology does not exclusively determine or decide her destiny (although it has an effect); rather culture, society, law and so forth help to determine what a woman can be. As she puts it: 'One is not born, but rather becomes, a woman'. At present, this means that Man (the norm) is regarded as active, able to manipulate and change both nature and his environment whereas Woman (the Other) is passive, an object acted upon. The task for women is to repudiate and alter this view of womanhood. Although women are physically weaker than men, and although women are subject to their reproductive functions (menstruation, pregnancy) technology now exists (contraception and abortion), de Beauvoir argues, to enable them to free themselves from these disadvantages. They can take control of their bodies and liberate themselves to a future of economic and social equality. Like Marxism, de Beauvoir emphasises production as the arena for women's liberation. Like early liberal feminism she seems to endorse rationality over other qualities (such as emotion). However, with her emphasis on women's control of their own bodies and her account of the opposition between men and women, she also presages many of the sentiments of radical feminism.

Philosophical Aspects

Contemporary feminist inquiry partakes of many different forms: it critically evaluates existing ideologies, demanding to know where women fit; it develops its own specific, woman-oriented modes of analysis; it seeks out the silenced voices of women long dead. Whether it speaks from within an established ideological position or attempts to mould a new theory, feminism always fights for women. It is a movement for social transformation.[14] This is what binds first and second wave feminisms and what draws together women from around the globe.

However, one of the problems of this generalised definition is that it hides the fact that what is meant by fighting for women and, thus also by social transformation, differs depending on whether women are perceived as the same as men, or as different from them and on how the differences amongst women are treated. One of the key debates therefore concerns the notion of *Woman*. This in turn has focused attention on the concept of *gender*.

All forms of feminism are concerned with the fact that women are always subordinated to men socially, politically, economically. While some accounts acknowledge that there are also social, political and economic differences *amongst* women (grounded in racial or ethnic divisions, in class differences and/or in terms of women's different sexual orientations), feminism is mainly concerned with the differences between the sexes/genders. This has led to the emergence of the concept of *patriarchy* as a means of describing this phenomenon. It should be noted, however, that not all feminists adopt this term when talking about women's position. Thus, the following sections deal with the fundamental feminist concerns (and disputes) of difference and patriarchy.

However, before beginning this section of the chapter, it is important to note that although different forms of feminist theory and practice draw inspiration from different traditions, there has also, during the second wave in particular, been a great degree of cross-fertilisation between different feminisms. They take from, and respond to, each other in many, often innovative, ways.

Difference

From the start, feminists have been divided in how they regard women. Some – predominantly liberal feminists – argue that men and women are fundamentally the same: that is, that despite biological differences, men and women share the same capacity for rationality and the same rights to autonomous self-development. The capacities that the sexes share are the ones that liberals regard as central to human progress. The problem is that, in actuality, men and women are treated differently in respect of these traits and rights. Women suffer from discrimination on the basis of their sex. In order to resolve this situation, therefore, liberal feminists propose the removal of all hurdles preventing women being treated in the same way as men (prompting critics to observe that women are not valued for their own qualities and achievements). This emphasis on opening up opportunities for women focuses initially on the public social and political realm.[15]

Is this the best way to achieve equality? Those committed to equal rights argue that it is. However, those within liberal feminism inter- ested in welfare considerations (the fact that only women get pregnant; that they are also primarily responsible for childcare even if they work outside the home), surmise that it is also necessary to take account of women's biological differences from men, and the consequences of these in practical terms in the current world, by securing certain special concessions for women; that is to find mechanisms to deal with the specific disadvantages that women face. Such mechanisms may include state-funded crèche facilities, special training programmes etc (see section entitled Practical Goals below). The point of this is not to introduce any idea that the sexes are fundamentally different but rather to ensure that men and women can compete on equal terms for soci- ety's scarce resources so that everyone, regardless of their starting point in life, can take part in the 'race for society's goods and services'.[16] At the end of the day, the best person will win out.

In contrast to the claims of equal rights feminism, radical feminism, which emerged in the 1970s, asserted that women are not simply treated differently to men, but that they are different. Support for this claim is sometimes derived from biology, specifically, from women's capacity to bear children. This argument works in several ways. For some, motherhood and women's reproductive capacities generally are regarded as burdensome.[17] For others, motherhood is regarded more positively: as the site of women's good qualities that are, however, constrained under patriarchy from developing naturally – that is, in a fulfilling way for women.[18] At other times, women's innate differences are seen as a result of their closer connection with nature.[19] Where the differences between the sexes are regarded as innate it is assumed that the qualities that women (and indeed men) have are natural: that they have always existed, and that they always will. These arguments (about women's biology and/or nature) have been criticised for being essentialist.

For other radical feminists and for socialist and/or Marxist feminists, women's particular attributes are regarded as the result predominantly of their social and cultural environments, including their socialisation: that is, how they are taught to behave by schools, the media, church and family as children and adults.[20] Instead of discussing biological sex, these writers refer to gender or 'the sex/gender system'.[21] What is meant by gender is the acquisition of certain characteristics deemed culturally appropriate for one sex or the other (i.e. the characteristics of femininity and masculinity). Gender is not natural, but is the effect of social and cultural processes,[22] including, for some, psychological processes.[23] Thus, for instance, Ruddick claims that women learn to think in certain ways through their experiences as mothers.[24] The idea of 'maternal thinking', linked with women's tendency to pacifism, arises from their preoccupations with caring, empathy, co-operation and their sense of responsibility to others. Similarly, Carol Gilligan, rejecting the idea that men have a more developed moral sense than women, claims that men and women simply acquire different conceptions of morality on account of their different gender development.[25] In terms of Marxist feminism, these notions about gender can be said to be ideological; that is, they are the effect of ideas about the relations of men and women under capitalism; for socialist feminists they are the effect of capitalism and patriarchy combined.[26]

Within the context of post-structuralism, the leading French feminists (Irigaray, Cixous and Kristeva) offer a version of difference based on language. Here it is claimed that there is a masculinist style of writing and thinking that is phallogocentric (from 'phallus' indicating a masculine style and 'logos' meaning word). This can be contrasted with a specifically feminine form of writing (*l'écriture féminine*) that is multiple rather than linear, plurivocal rather than univocal, fluid rather than fixed. Some of these writers appear to regard these differences as innate while others regard both as open to either men or women. All agree, however, that women should develop their own distinctive and different voice(s).[27]

The usefulness of the concept of gender is that it allows, in theory, for the acknowledgement of differences between women in different cultures and at different historical periods and thus for changes in the factors producing women's particular characteristics. Instead of talking about differences between the sexes, feminists in the 1980s and 1990s, therefore, emphasise gender on the grounds that it forms an inescapable although variegated system[28] organised in such a way that it is '(more) defined and (imperfectly) controlled by one of its interrelated parts – the male'.[29] It is not, therefore, a monolithic system. Nevertheless, the concept of gender has also come under scrutiny, sometimes for smuggling in essentialist notions[30] that hide differences across race and culture; sometimes for ignoring the many ways in which gender operates within the same society to oppress groups such as lesbians and gays.[31]

Patriarchy

Liberal feminism (of the equal rights variety in particular) emphasises that women suffer discrimination on the basis of their sex: that is, they are restricted in ways that men are not. As such, sex discrimination violates the liberal belief in justice: men are judged on their ability while women are judged on their sex.[32] The sources of these inequalities are legal, customary, economic, social. Women have been legally barred from certain jobs; they have been discriminated against in the housing market (denied mortgages and so on); subject to more limited national insurance and tax benefits; they have often earned less for the same job or have been unable to move beyond particular rungs of the promotion ladder at work; they have been removed from employment on pregnancy and on marriage. Central to the liberal feminist case, therefore, are the concepts of *inequality* and *discrimination*. As Anne Phillips suggests, this has certain consequences.[33] By talking of inequality and discrimination, liberal feminism is arguing that women suffer from not being treated as/like men. Liberal feminism, for this reason, may be thought of as liberalism with women added in. To ensure equality, on this argument, it is important to deal with both sexes in identical terms. This raises a number of problems: it denies the specific needs and problems of women. For instance, currently at least, men cannot bear children. To treat women the same as men, means ignoring this sex-specific difference. This means that there need be no special provision for women who get pregnant: no maternity allowance, no maternity leave etc. For this reason, some liberal feminists have shifted to a welfare perspective that acknowledges the existence of particular needs. Instead of simply removing barriers to women's participation in politics, the workforce or whatever, welfare liberals are concerned with substantive equality.[34] This means that equality may be achieved only by treating people differently.

By contrast, radical, Marxist and socialist feminists tend to talk about women's *oppression*. As Phillips notes, oppression highlights not the anomalies of women's exclusion from certain realms but 'a complex of ideological, political and economic forces that combine to keep women in their place'.[35] The name that radical feminists give to this form of oppression is *patriarchy*. This is one of the most important concepts that feminism has produced. Deriving from the idea of rule of the fathers, in contemporary usage it refers to the fact that 'every avenue of power within society ... is entirely in male hands'.[36] Women's subordination is thus structural and systematic not accidental and *ad hoc*. As the Redstockings Manifesto puts it: '*All men* have oppressed women';[37] they all benefit from patriarchal structures while all women suffer. This mode of exploitation is universal: applying at all times in all places. Moreover, it may be the most fundamental form of human domination. This means that other modes of oppression (such as racism or class) are always secondary.[38] The mechanisms that men use to control and subdue women, according to radical feminists, are manifold. They include rape, domestic violence, pornography, control over women's bodies (over their access to contraception or abortion; their right to refuse sex or sterilisation); genital mutilation, and compulsory heterosexuality; factors relating principally to women's bodies, their sexuality and to violence against them. In contrast to the liberal feminist stress on women's lack of public equality with men, radical feminists assert that women are also oppressed in the private sphere.[39]

One criticism levelled at radical feminists is that they lack an understanding of the class nature of oppression. Within the context of Marxist feminism, women's oppression is usually treated as a subspecies of class oppression. It is women's function within the family, and her absence from the paid workforce that is the source of her condition. As such, Marxist feminists have focused on analysing domestic labour in order to highlight the economic nature of women's class oppression.[40] Just as radical feminism has a one-sided emphasis on patriarchal oppression, so Marxist feminism has a one-sided emphasis on class oppression. According to socialist feminists, however, the two things have to be considered in unison for women are subject to patriarchal and to class oppression. Analysis of women's economic exploitation (the feminisation of poverty included) is just as important as analysing male control of women's bodies. What is needed is 'dual systems' analysis.[41] Thus, for example, Juliet Mitchell contends that women's subordination is the effect of the interaction of four spheres: production, reproduction, sexuality and the socialisation of children.[42] Women's oppression is, therefore, a combination of gender factors and economic factors that can only be eradicated with a transformation of both spheres. Overthrowing either capitalism or patriarchy alone would not be enough to liberate women.[43]

Practical Goals[44]

Although all feminists concur that changes have to be made to secure an improvement in women's lives, the solutions they propose are, nevertheless, diverse: for some, piecemeal reform is sufficient to secure these changes, for others change can only be accomplished by a more radical restructuring of society at large. This diversity stems partly from the different ideological positions that feminists adopt, partly from the actual day-to-day operations of the women's movement. As noted at the outset, in Britain feminism has been characterised by a combination of both equal rights policies and policies aimed at eradicating male control over women's bodies.

By and large, liberal feminists emphasise reform, the aim being to secure women's access to and success in the same arenas as men. To attain 'gender justice' (parity between the sexes) liberals have pursued one of two strategies: (a) the removal of the barriers that impede women's participation in the labour market, education, politics and so on, in order to secure the same opportunities as those open to men; and/or (b) the provision of certain additional services necessary to enable women to participate on an equal footing with men. While the former has concentrated on removing constraints and securing equal rights, the latter has emphasised granting particular forms of assistance to women. Examples of initiatives in the UK that follow the first model of reform include the Equal Pay Act (1970; operative from 1975) and the Sex Discrimination Act (1975).[45] While on paper these acts establish equal legal rights for both sexes, in practice it has been more difficult to ensure adequate implementation of the law. This arises in part from the inadequate powers of the Equal Opportunities Commission who are charged with monitoring the two Acts in question. Instead of equal rights, the second kind of policy reform is geared to the provision of equivalent rights[46] through, for instance, affirmative action programmes, quotas, special training programmes to teach women certain skills, or the provision of state-funded crèche facilities for those with children. The point of this mode of reform is to generate positive help for women in order to allow them entry to the labour market or to education, for instance. In theory, the state will provide the necessary forms of compensation for women's biological or material disadvantage.[47] Currently under UK law, positive discrimination is unlawful – hence the Labour Party's inability to retain quotas for women candidates – however, practices such as Emily's List, where money is provided to train women in the skills necessary for practical politics, are not.[48]

For radical feminists, however, state-sponsored legislation is an inadequate means of improving women's position for the state is, itself, a patriarchal tool. Participating in its structures perpetuates rather than undermines male power. Women's liberation, therefore, requires women to unite to end male oppression by overthrowing patriarchy. The range of proposed strategies for women to achieve this is vast. According to Firestone, for instance, since male power is rooted in control of women's biological functions, women need to seize control of the means of reproduction. This alone can secure their freedom. This argument is premised on the idea that technological developments can liberate women from the burden of childcare. This view has been challenged more recently by others[49] who contend that women's dependence on reproductive technology would not weaken but would actually consolidate male power (since it is under men's control). By contrast, Millett argues for androgyny: the integration of the best features of both masculinity and of femininity. This involves an end to the current sex/gender system and the creation of a new society where men and women are equal at all levels. For others, such as Mary Daly, the essence of radical feminism is that it is woman-centred: what Daly calls a 'journey of women becoming'.[50] The stress here is on developing women's creativity. Only the end of patriarchy can create a society where women's essential selves are allowed to flourish. For some, this involves the development of separatist communities. For others, it requires a form of lesbian lifestyle. Here lesbian not only refers to same-sex sexual relationships but also to privileging friendships amongst women.[51] In practical terms, however, radical feminism is above all a grassroots movement. This is the idea of 'the personal is political' translated into activism at the level of personal relationships and women's daily experiences of violence and abuse. Thus women have been encouraged to withdraw sexual and domestic services at home, to attend consciousness-raising sessions, to establish self-help groups and to encourage woman-centred projects.

In the British context, the range of 'radical' measures in which the women's movement are actively involved is wide-ranging. With each successive onslaught on the 1967 abortion act, feminists have mobilised to support abortion on demand. From the Reclaim the Night marches of the late 1970s/early 1980s that aimed to make the streets safe for women to the setting up of WAVAW (Women Against Violence Against Women) at the first Sexual Violence Conference in Leeds in 1980, feminists have raised popular consciousness about the various types of violence that men perpetrate against women including the use and production of pornography. With the establishment of the first women's refuge in Chiswick in 1972 and the founding of the Women's Aid Federation, to the successful passage of the Domestic Violence Act in 1976, feminists highlighted the pervasiveness of the problem of domestic violence and helped to shift official thinking on this issue, symbolised, at present, by the Zero Tolerance Campaign adopted by a number of councils in Britain.[52] From the institution in 1976 of the first Rape Crisis Centre to provide practical advice, counselling and a sympathetic environment for female victims of rape, to the Sexual Offences (Amendment) Act (1976) to secure the privacy and anonymity of the victim in a rape trial, feminists have challenged professional (patriarchal) responses to rape and the media coverage of it. Some of these campaigns have resulted in legal changes. Most, however, operate through the establishment of woman-centred direct action organisations functioning at the grass-roots level. Many of these organisations are voluntary and frequently underfunded.

Criticisms

For the most part feminism has been criticised more from within its own ranks than by outsiders. Indeed, the very nature of feminism is such that it brings together under one umbrella advocates of socialist, Marxist, liberal and radical persuasion to debate the key issues affecting women today. In this regard, debates within feminism are like a microcosm of debates between the other ideologies.[53] There are, however, two areas that have posed serious challenges to feminism: the first concerns the question of race/ethnicity; the second concerns post-structuralism and postmodernism.

Race/Ethnicity

Central to many forms of feminism is, as we have seen, the claim that all women share either common experiences of sex or gender oppression, or an identical nature. It is this shared something that is perceived to give unity to the feminist movement. Feminism as identity politics stresses women's commonalities. This is captured in the idea that 'sisterhood is global'. However, it is precisely this idea that all women are the same that has been a source of dispute over the last twenty years.[54] As many black feminists and women of colour, in particular, have shown, women as a group are, themselves, subject to differences. The claims made on behalf of women in general tend to ignore the fact that for black women and women of colour sexism is not the only form of oppression to which they are subject: they also suffer from racism, increased levels of poverty and so forth. Moreover, they do not suffer sexism as women and racism because they are black, because as Spelman observes 'sexism and racism do not have different "objects" in the case of women'.[55] Black women cannot separate their sex/gender from their race. They are subject simultaneously to multiple oppressions. For Audre Lorde this means that 'Black feminism is not white feminism in black face'.[56] The concerns of black women are simply different than those of white women. The problem with some feminisms is that they disregard these differences. They are guilty of what Rich calls 'white solipsism': the tendency to 'think, imagine, and speak as if whiteness described the world'.[57] While almost all black feminists would agree that all women suffer at the hands of patriarchy, most observe that they do not all suffer in the same way.[58]

This has a second effect. Although black men may oppress black women, they are themselves victims of the same structures of racism as black women. They are both enemies and allies; enemies in the context of gender, allies in the fight against racism. This means that a more sophisticated analysis of their oppression is required than one that simply blames all men equally. Some writers have, therefore, chosen to reject the label feminist or *the* feminist movement in favour of other labels. Alice Walker favours the term 'womanist' for it signifies a commitment to the 'survival and wholeness of the entire people, male and female'.[59] bell hooks chooses the term feminist movement (without the definite article 'the') to highlight the plural nature of feminist struggles and to emphasise the fact of inequality amongst men too within 'white supremacist, capitalist, patriarchal class structure'.[60] As a consequence white feminists have had to acknowledge the existence of power differentials between various groups and to attempt to develop ways of speaking about women that are more sensitive to difference. It is no longer possible to think of all women as identical, if indeed it ever was.

Post-structuralist and Postmodern Challenges

One of the defining features of the post-structural/postmodern theoretical complex is that it is radically anti-essentialist. It rejects the idea that there are any universal phenomena, arguing, instead, that everything is plural, particular and contingent. For feminists, this critique has had most effect in challenging the notion that there is a universal female nature and/or experience of womanhood that unites women. Like the criticisms made by black feminists, this has drawn attention to the concept of difference within the women's movement. Post-structuralism/postmodernism goes further than most black feminist critics by challenging the idea that there is anything that unifies women. It is not only that women are separated by race/ethnicity, class, sexual orientation, culture and so forth; they are also divided within their various groupings (for instance, not all lesbians share the same experiences) and even within themselves as individuals. Indeed, far from being fixed and static, the category of Woman is fluid, mobile and multiple.[61] It cannot be easily pinned down.

Second, the scepticism of post-structuralism/postmodernism towards the possibility of metanarratives also challenges feminism. In endeavouring to explain the origins and maintenance of patriarchy, feminists have themselves often constructed over-arching explanations of a kind that might be termed metanarrative. For post-structuralists/postmodernists, rather than being examples of neutral, objective explanation, metanarratives always consolidate and legitimate the power of certain groups. As the objections of women of colour have revealed, in the case of feminism, it is the concerns and demands of white, middle-class women that have been taken as representative of the women's movement as a whole. These are legitimated through the accounts of oppression that have been produced where the partial experiences of some women are read as if they apply to all women. Here Nancy Chodorow's account of mothering is instructive.[62] In an attempt to develop an explanation of the emergence of gender difference, Chodorow constructs a metanarrative that treats mothering both as a single, unitary activity operating in all cultures at all times, and as *the* basis for the production of gender identity. Her claim is that as a consequence of the experience of being mothered all women develop a common relational nature while all men do not. This explanation, its critics contend, prioritises similarity over difference and thus ignores the many different culturally embedded ways in which women engage in relationships with others. If feminism is to encompass adequately the narratives of other (non-white) women, it has to give up this impulse towards metanarratives and, in their place, generate local, particular (micro)narratives.[63]

Together these two claims have implications for feminist politics. Feminism has relied on the idea of unity amongst women (based on what they have in common) to lend coherence to its political programme. The women's movement has gained some of its legitimacy from claiming to speak on behalf of all women. However, if there are no common experiences that bring women together, then what happens to feminist politics? Many feminists have rejected post-structuralism/postmodernism precisely on the grounds that it threatens the possibility of speaking for women; that it fragments and thus weakens the women's movement.[64] Others, however, have argued that it opens up new opportunities for thinking and acting politically.[65]

Conclusion

Feminism is an incredibly diverse project that draws on a wide range of existing ideologies while also making a unique contribution via the voices of women. For a relatively young movement, it has secured a number of important advances for (some) women: in the labour market; in literature, film and theatre; in politics; in relation to the politics of the body and so on. The greatest difficulty that it faces now is how to continue its momentum in the face of a political backlash that pretends that feminists have achieved all their objectives and thus are redundant, while simultaneously passing legislation that reinforces women's treatment as second class citizens in certain arenas[66] and denying the very real issue of the feminisation of poverty. These problems are exacerbated (but not caused) by the difficulties feminism faces within its own ranks over how to accommodate difference successfully. Although progress has been made in this direction, there are still marginalised women whose own particular problems, narratives and demands need to be acknowledged and addressed, not least those of women with disabilities. Feminism's emphasis on the body and on sexual politics has often excluded; and indeed hidden, the particular, plural experiences of these specific groups of women.

In a sense, however, the diverse positions occupied by feminists are evidence not of incoherence or division but of the openness of feminism. While feminists may disagree ideologically on the causes and maintenance of women's subordinate status, depending on whether they are socialists, liberals, or postmodernists, they all insist on the need to act to secure an improvement in women's lives. This is not to deny that there are also disputes within feminism over the best tactics and strategies to deploy to achieve these improvements (the pornography debate is a case in point); however, what is certain is that the varied theoretical stances adopted by feminists do not always stop them working together to secure concrete change. Rather than regard feminism as utterly fragmented it might be better to (re)think it as presenting a plural challenge to the structures and policies through which all forms of oppression (not just sexism) are perpetuated. As such, it offers multiple strategies for the radical reconstruction of society.

Notes

1. V. Randall, *Women and Politics: An International Perspective*, Macmillan, Basingstoke 1987 (2nd edn), pp.230-1.
2. A. Coote and B. Campbell, *Sweet Freedom*, Picador, London 1982, p.10.
3. On the history of the origins of second wave feminism in Britain see the following: O. Banks, *Faces of Feminism*, Martin Robertson, Oxford 1981; A. Carter, *The Politics of Women's Rights*, Longman, London 1988; A. Coote and B. Campbell, *Sweet Freedom, op.cit.;* A. Coote and P. Pattullo, *Power and Prejudice: Women and Politics*, Weidenfeld and Nicolson, London 1990; V. Randall, *Women and Politics: An International Perspective, op.cit.*; S. Rowbotham, *The Past is Before Us: Feminism in Action since the 1960s*, Penguin, Harmondsworth 1989.
4. The 1967 abortion act only provided for abortion on therapeutic grounds and needed the consent of two doctors.
5. J Lovenduski, 'Parliament, pressure groups, networks and the women's movement: the politics of abortion law reform in Britain (1967-83)' in Joni Lovenduski and Joyce Outshoorn, *The New Politics of Abortion*, Sage, London 1986, p.50.
6. A. Carter, *The Politics of Women's Rights, op.cit.*, p55; This conference also established the structure of the women's movement: that of small

autonomous groups loosely linked through national meetings but otherwise free to develop local initiatives. See: A. Coote and B. Campbell, *Sweet Freedom, op.cit.*, p.14.

7. For introductions to the ideologies of first and second wave feminism see: V. Bryson, *Feminist Political Theory: An Introduction*, Routledge, London 1992; P. Ticineto, *Feminist Thought*, Blackwell, Oxford 1995; J. Evans, *Feminist Thought Today: An Introduction to Second-Wave Feminism*, Sage, London 1995; M. Humm (ed), *Feminisms: A Reader*, Harvester Wheatsheaf, Brighton 1992; A. Jaggar, *Feminist Politics and Human Nature*, Harvester, Brighton 1983; M. Schneir (ed), *The Vintage Book of Feminism: The Essential Writings of the Contemporary Women's Movement*, Vintage, London 1994; M. Schneir (ed), *The Vintage Book of Historical Feminism*, Vintage, London 1996; R. Tong, *Feminist Thought: A Comprehensive Introduction*, Unwin Hyman, London 1989.

8. This early piece of liberal feminism bears the indelible traces of the ideas of Mill's long-time companion and later wife, Harriet Taylor, whose own work, *The Enfranchisement of Women*, appeared in 1851.

9. Arguably both are guilty of neglecting class issues concerned as they are with the plight of middle class women.

10. C. Fourier 'Theory of the Four Movements' (1808) in J. Beecher & R. Bienvenu (eds), *The Utopian Vision of Charles Fourier*, Jonathan Cape, London 1975.

11. Their most important text, published under William Thompson's name, is the *Appeal on Behalf of one Half of the Human Race, Women, against the Pretensions of the Other Half, Men, to retain them in Political, and Thence in Civil and Domestic Slavery*, Virago, London, 1983.

12. See M. Schneir, *The Vintage Book of Historical Feminism, op.cit.*, p.211.

13. S. de Beauvoir, *The Second Sex*, Penguin, Harmondsworth [1949] 1972.

14. L. Segal, 'Generations of Feminism' in *Radical Philosophy*, May/June 1997.

15. B. Friedan, *The Feminine Mystique*, Penguin, Harmondsworth [1963] 1986.

16. R. Tong, 1989, *Feminist Thought: A Comprehensive Introduction, op.cit.*, p.2.

17. S. Firestone, *The Dialectic of Sex*, The Women's Press, London [1970] 1979; A. Oakley, *Woman's Work: The Housewife, Past and Present*, Pantheon Books, New York 1974.

18. A. Rich, *Of Woman Born: Motherhood as Experience and Institution*, Virago, London 1977.

19. S. Griffin, *Woman and Nature: The Roaring Inside Her*, The Women's Press, London 1984.

20. K. Millett, *Sexual Politics*, Virago, London [1970] 1977.

21. G. Rubin, 'The Traffic in Women: Notes on the "Political Economy" of

Sex' in M.Z. Rosaldo and L. Lamphere (eds), *Woman, Culture and Society*, Stanford University Press, Stanford 1974.

22. S. Ortner, 'Is Female to Male as Nature is to Culture?' in Mary Evans (ed), *The Woman Question*, Fontana, London [1972] 1982.

23. J. Rose, *Sexuality in the Field of Vision*, Verso, London 1986; J. Mitchell, 'Women the Longest Revolution' [1966] in *Women: The Longest Revolution: Essays in Feminism, Literature and Psychoanalysis*, Virago, London 1984; J. Mitchell, *Woman's Estate*, Penguin, Harmondsworth 1974.

24. Sara Ruddick, 'Maternal Thinking', *Feminist Studies*, vol. 6: no. 1, 1980; 'Preservative Love and Military Destruction: Some Reflections on Mothering and Peace' in Joan Treblicot (ed), *Mothering: Essays in Feminist Theory*, Rowman and Allenheld, New York 1984; and *Maternal Thinking: Towards a Politics of Peace*, The Women's Press, London 1990.

25. C. Gilligan, *In a Different Voice: Psychological Theory and Women's Development*, Harvard University Press, London and Cambridge, Mass. 1982; For men this conception is an ethic of justice; for women an ethic of care.

26. H. Hartmann, 'The Unhappy Marriage of Marxism and Feminism: Towards a More Progressive Union' in Lydia Sargent (ed), *The Unhappy Marriage of Marxism and Feminism: A Debate on Class and Patriarchy*, Pluto Press, London 1981; J. Mitchell, 'Women the Longest Revolution', *op.cit.*; J. Mitchel, *Woman's Estate, op.cit.*

27. For an introduction to French feminism (here taken as the writings of Hélène Cixous, Luce Irigaray and Julia Kristeva) see: T. Moi, *Sexual/Textual Politics: Feminist Literary Theory*, Routledge, London 1985; R. Tong, *Feminist Thought: A Comprehensive Introduction, op.cit.*

28. It is inescapable because every society is presumed to have a system of gender that assigns certain traits to men and others to women.

29. J. Flax, *Thinking Fragments: Psychoanalysis, Feminism and Postmodernism in the Contemporary West*, University of California Press, Berkeley 1990, p.23.

30. E. Spelman, *Inessential Woman: Problems of Exclusion in Feminist Thought*, The Women's Press, London 1990.

31. J. Butler, *Gender Trouble: Feminism and the Subversion of Identity*, Routledge, London 1990.

32. A. Jaggar, *Feminist Politics and Human Nature, op.cit.*

33. A. Phillips, 'Introduction' in A. Phillips (ed), *Feminism and Equality*, Blackwell, Oxford 1987.

34. D. Rhode, 'The Politics of Paradigms: Gender Difference and Gender Disadvantage' in G. Bock and S. James (eds), *Beyond Equality and*

Difference: Citizenship, Feminist Politics and Female Subjectivity, Routledge, London 1992.

35. A. Phillips, *Feminism and Equality, op.cit.*, p.11.

36. Millet, *Sexual Politics, op.cit.*, p.25.

37. In M. Schneir, *The Vintage Book of Feminism: The Essential Writings of the Contemporary Women's Movement, op.cit.*, p.127 (original emphasis).

38. For example, Firestone claims that 'racism is sexism extended'.

39. Largely through the criticisms of radical feminists, liberals turned their attention to the private dimension of women's inequality.

40. The so-called domestic labour debate advocated amongst other things: wages for housework and the socialisation of childcare. Marxist feminists also attempted to apply Marx's notion of surplus value to housework. For an excellent review of this topic see: E. Kaluzynska, 'Wiping the Floor with Theory – A Survey of Writings on Housework', *Feminist Review*, no. 6, 1980.

41. H. Hartmann 'The Unhappy Marriage of Marxism and Feminism: Towards a More Progressive Union', *op.cit.*

42. J. Mitchell, 'Women the Longest Revolution', *op.cit.*; J. Mitchell, *Woman's Estate, op.cit.*; S. Rowbotham, *Women, Resistance and Revolution*, Penguin, Harmondsworth 1972; S. Rowbotham, *Women's Consciousness, Man's World*, Penguin, Harmondsworth 1973.

43. It should be noted that socialist feminists did not come to this conclusion about the interlocking nature of class and patriarchal oppressions late in the day. They had been arguing about these interconnections since the mid-1960s. It is only later, however, that they use the term 'patriarchy' to describe sexual oppression.

44. The activities covered in this section are dealt with in greater detail in the following: S. Abrar, 'Feminist Intervention and Local Domestic Violence Policy' in J. Lovenduski and P. Norris (eds), *Women in Politics*, Oxford University Press, Oxford 1996; P. Byrne, 'The Politics of the Women's Movement' in J. Lovenduski and P. Norris (eds), *Women in Politics*, Oxford University Press, Oxford 1996; A. Carter, *The Politics of Women's Rights, op.cit.*; A. Coote and B. Campbell, *Sweet Freedom, op.cit.*; J. Hanmer and M. Maynard (eds), *Women, Violence, and Social Control*, Macmillan, Basingstoke 1987; J. Holland, *Work and Women: a review of explanations for the maintenance and reproduction of sexual divisions*, (2nd edn) University of London Institute of Education, London 1981; F. Mackay, 'The Zero Tolerance Campaign: Setting the Agenda' in J. Lovenduski and P. Norris (eds), *Women in Politics*, Oxford University Press, Oxford 1996; E. Meehan, 'Implementing Equal Opportunities

Policies', *Politics*, vol. 2 1981; E. Meehan, *Women's Rights at Work: Campaigns and Policy in Britain and the United States*, Macmillan, Basingstoke 1985; V. Randall, *Women and Politics: An International Perspective, op.cit.*; S. Rowbotham, *Women, Resistance and Revolution, op.cit.*; E. Wilson, *What's To Be Done about Violence Against Women?*, Penguin, Harmondsworth 1983.

45. In a political sense, liberal feminism is more prevalent in the US than in Britain, which was dominated by socialist feminism. The Equal Pay Act was largely the result of pressure from the labour movement (including women in the Labour Party) while the Sex Discrimination Act also drew on the work of professional women's organisations, older lobby groups and the newer women's movement. They remain, nevertheless, 'liberal' pieces of legislation in their intention to secure formal parity of rights for both sexes. For this reason they have often been criticised by socialist feminists for not addressing issues such as the feminisation of poverty and women's economic dependence. See: A. Carter, *The Politics of Womens' Rights, op.cit.*; A. Jaggar, *Feminist Politics and Human Nature, op.cit.*

46. D. Cornell, *Transformations: Recollective Imagination and Sexual Difference*, Routledge, London 1993.

47. A. Jaggar, *Feminist Politics and Human Nature, op.cit.*, p.183.

48. Something similar was used recently by the Northern Ireland Women's Coalition for the elections to the Forum where potential candidates were offered training in the skills necessary to political life.

49. Such as: R. Arditti, R. Duelli Klein and S. Minden (eds), *Test-Tube Women: What Future for Motherhood?*, London 1989; G. Corea, *The Mother Machine: Reproductive Technologies from Artificial Insemination to Artificial Wombs*, The Women's Press, London 1985; R. Duelli Klein (ed), *Infertility: Women Speak Out about Their Experiences of Reproductive Medicine*, Pandora, London 1989 and Feminist International Network of Resistance to Reproductive Technologies [FINNRAGE].

50. M. Daly, *Gyn/Ecology: The Metaethics of Radical Feminism*, The Women's Press, London 1978, p.1.

51. A. Rich, 'Compulsory Heterosexuality and Lesbian Existence', in *Signs: A Journal of Women in Culture and Society*, vol. 5: no 4, 1980.

52. S. Abrar, 'Feminist Intervention and Local Domestic Violence Policy', *op.cit.*; F. Mackay, 'The Zero-Tolerance Campaign: Setting the Agenda', *op.cit.*

53. Sadly, it is still the case that the major proponents of the dominant ideologies regard feminism as, at best, a useful adjunct to their own ideology and at worst, as a diversion from real politics.

54. See: H. Safia Mirza (ed), *Black British Feminism: A Reader*, Routledge, London 1997.

55. E. Spelman, *Inessential Women: Problems of Exclusion in Feminist Thought, op.cit.*, p.122.

56. A. Lorde, *Sister Outsider: Essays and Speeches*, The Crossing Press, New York 1984, p.60.

57. A. Rich, 'Disloyal to Civilization: Feminism, Racism and Gynephobia' in *On Lies, Secrets, and Silence*, Norton, New York 1979, p.299.

58. V. Mason-John (ed), *Talking Black: Lesbians of African and Asian Descent Speak Out*, Cassell, London 1995.

59. A. Walker, *In Search of Our Mothers' Gardens*, The Women's Press, London 1983.

60. b. hooks, *Feminist Theory: From Margin to Center*, South End Press, Boston 1984, p.18.

61. R. Braidotti, *Nomadic Subjects: Embodiment and Sexual Difference in Contemporary Feminist Theory*, Columbia University Press, New York 1994; D. Haraway, 'A Cyborg Manifesto: Science, Technology, and Socialist-Feminism in the Late Twentieth Century' in *Simians, Cyborgs, and Women: The Reinvention of Nature*, Free Association Books, London 1991; K.E. Ferguson, *The Man Question: Visions of Subjectivity in Feminist Theory*, University of California Press, Berkeley 1993.

62. N. Chodorow, *The Reproduction of Mothering: Psychoanalysis and the Sociology of Gender*, University of California Press, Berkeley 1978.

63. N. Fraser and L. Nicholson, 'Social Criticism without Philosophy: An Encounter Between Feminism and Postmodernism' in L. Nicholson (ed), *Feminism/Postmodernism*, Routledge, London 1990.

64. S. Bordo, 'Feminism, Postmodernism, and Gender-Scepticism' in Linda Nicholson (ed), *Feminism/Postmodernism*, Routledge, London 1990; C. di Stefano, 'Dilemmas of Difference: Feminism, Modernity and Postmodernism' in L. Nicholson (ed), *Feminism/Postmodernism*, Routledge, London 1990.

65. J. Butler, *Gender Trouble: Feminism and the Subversion of Identity, op.cit.*; J. Butler, *Bodies That Matter: On the Discursive Limits of "Sex"*, Routledge London, 1993; D. Elam, *Feminism and Deconstruction: Ms. en Abyme*, Routledge, London, 1995; L. Nicholson (ed), *Feminism/Postmodernism*, Routledge, London 1990; E. Probyn, *Sexing the Self: Gendered Positions in Cultural Studies*, Routledge, London 1993.

66. S. Faludi, *Backlash: The Undeclared War Against Women*, Chatto and Windus, London 1992; M. French, *The War Against Women*, Hamish Hamilton, London 1992.

Green Political Thought

John Barry

Introduction: Historical Roots

Most introductions to green political theory begin with a catalogue of current environmental destruction: ozone depletion, acid rain, smog, air pollution etc. This much will be assumed for the purposes of this chapter, and the general acceptance that things are going wrong ecologically marks one of the achievements of green politics. While it is tempting to elaborate green political thought as something completely new, in truth a concern for the environment and the ecological dimensions of the 'human condition' has many historical antecedents in the history of Western[1] and non-Western thought.[2] Nevertheless, it is also fair to say that, however much the environment or 'nature' was discussed within normative thought, the subject has rarely been addressed directly in the great works of political thought: from the Greeks onward the non-human world tends to have been regarded as little more than a stage upon which the human drama unfolds.

It is with the Enlightenment that what can be called the 'problem of nature' first raises its head, and in the backlash against the increasingly negative effects of the industrial revolution one finds the early stirrings of modern green politics. On the one hand the writings of Rousseau, Wordsworth and the romantic poets offer evidence of a conscious backlash against the industrial revolution in particular and the Enlightenment in general. For these writers, the natural world has been 'disenchanted'[3]: once the realm of special values and powers, often inhabited by spirits and protected by tradition and ritual, with the advent of modernity nature is reduced to a means to serve human ends – a collection of raw materials and a waste-bin for human products. On the other hand, in the writings of Malthus[4] concerning the relationship between human population growth and food supply, one can find early indications of the green argument about ecological limits to growth.

As well as these romantic and population-based critiques of industrialism, in later political commentators such as J.S. Mill and William Morris one can also find traces of the green critique of modern industrial society. Mill for example was one of the first to outline a proto-green argument for an economic system less geared towards indiscriminate growth. In a famous passage in his *Principles of Political Economy*, entitled 'Of the Stationary State', he says:

> I cannot ... regard the stationary state of capital and wealth with the unaffected aversion so generally manifested towards it by political economists of the old school. I am inclined to believe that it would be, on the whole, a very considerable improvement in our present condition.[5]

While green politics grew primarily from a critique of the excesses of the industrial revolution, it can also be seen to have strong roots as a positive affirmation of the other revolution that characterises the Enlightenment, namely the emergence of democratic government. As will be shown below, green political theory sees itself as a part of the historical evolution of the principles of democracy and social justice.

Philosophy

Central to green political theory is a concern with the status of the non-human world and its treatment by humans. Within the wider literature there are two extreme poles of opinion on this, and between these is a spectrum along which different green positions can be plotted. At one end of this spectrum there is what can be termed an 'arrogant anthropocentrism'.[6] This position holds that the natural world is essentially meaningless and its only value lies in the instrumental value human beings accord it in using it to fulfil their ends. The philosophical origins of this are varied, the most important being the theological idea that the world has been made for our use and enjoyment.[7] Eckersley defines it as:

the belief that there is a clear and morally relevant dividing line between humankind and the rest of nature, that humankind is the only or principal source of value and meaning in the world, *and that non-human nature is there for no other purpose but to serve humankind*.[8] (emphasis added)

This arrogant anthropocentrism is, from the green perspective, part and parcel of the modern world view and a major cause of the ecological crisis.

At the other end of the continuum we find what may be termed 'extreme ecocentrism', which is most commonly associated with deep ecology. This developed as a philosophical response to the dominant, human-centred moral framework. Its proponents argued that since the root cause of the ecological crisis can be traced back to anti-environmentalism of the anthropocentric world view, the solution to the crisis is to be found in its opposite, namely a non-anthropocentric or ecocentric moral perspective. The first modern expression of this can be found in the seminal paper by Arne Naess, 'The Shallow and the Deep, Long-Range Ecology Movement'.[9] In this paper, Naess outlines one of the most well-known and developed strands of ecocentric thought, namely 'deep ecology'. Whereas both arrogant anthropocentrism and what Naess called 'shallow ecology' (whose primary concern was the effect of ecological damage on human health and well-being) view nature as possessing instrumental value, i.e. was valuable only in its capacity to serve human needs or desires, deep ecology holds that nature should be seen as having intrinsic value and should be protected for its own sake and not simply because it is of benefit to human beings. While there have been many developments within the deep ecology position since Naess's original formulation,[10] deep ecology still holds to the basic ecocentric position that anthropocentrism is part of the ecological problem and needs to be replaced with a more ecocentric or earth-centred world view.

The deep ecology position is extremely radical in its implications because it demands not simply the protection of nature but also that this protection be undertaken for the right reasons. For example, from a deep ecological point of view, not only must we preserve the Amazonian rainforests, but we must do so because the rainforests have intrinsic value and ought to be protected for their sake alone. To argue for the protection of the rainforests on the grounds that it would be prudent to do so – because the rainforests may contain important medical substances) would fall short of the deep ecology standard. From the deep ecology position any protection of nature premised on human interests is insecure, since human interests may shift at any point from protection towards development or exploitation.

However, difficulties associated with the deep ecology position, not least of which is how to translate its philosophical arguments into practical policies, and the seemingly endless disputes within green political theory between 'deep' and 'shallow' perspectives,[11] have led to recent attempts to combine the deep ecology critique of arrogant anthropocentrism with a more defensible green moral position. In essence the starting point for this new green moral framework is to argue that the mark of green moral theory is not that it must be ecocentric but rather that it displays a critical attitude towards anthropocentrism. This recent development within green theory shares the ecocentric aim of criticising the excesses and negative effects of arrogant anthropocentrism, but does not entirely reject anthropocentrism. In this view, the real target of the ecocentric critique should be the *arrogance* not the *anthropocentrism*. In other words, there may be forms of anthropocentrism which are compatible with green goals, indeed may be positively necessary if green aims and values are to be realised. One of the main problems with the ecocentric position is that it demands a complete change in the world-view and ways of thinking of those populations towards which the green message is addressed. While it may be desirable that over time a more ecocentric perspective will be required to deal with ecological problems, it may be that such a complete change in the way people think and act is unnecessary in order to achieve green goals, such as the preservation of nature and the protection of biodiversity.

Those who seek to criticise the arrogance of the dominant form of anthropocentrism and seek to base the green position on a less arrogant form of anthropocentrism, may be said to agree with Norton's 'convergence hypothesis'. For Norton, in terms of environmental policy outcomes, there is a convergence between the ecocentric position as represented by deep ecology, and a far-sighted anthropocentrism reflecting obligations to future generations. According to Norton:

> ... introducing the idea that other species have intrinsic value ... provides no operationally recognizable constraints on human behaviour that are not already implicit in the ... obligations to protect a healthy, complex, and autonomously functioning system for the benefit of future

generations of humans. Deep ecologists, who cluster around the principle that nature has independent value, should therefore not differ from
long-sighted anthropocentrists in their policy goals for the protection of
biological diversity.[12]

This convergence of concerns for future generations and concerns for
the environment is closely connected to debates around sustainable
development which will be discussed in the next section. Thus the
current debate within green moral theory is largely between those who
seek to develop a 'weak' or 'reflexive' anthropocentrism as the normative basis for green politics,[13] and those who still hold to the belief that
only an ecocentric moral basis can both sustain a green politics worthy
of the name and stand as a solution to the ecological crisis.[14]

Although much of the uniqueness of green political theory derives
from its focus on the non-human world and our relationship to that
world, it would be a mistake to see green political theory as a form of
'single issue' politics. Beyond the purely ecological questions lie
concerns about human social relations, the proper arrangement of
human society, and ideas about the 'good life'. Traditional concerns of
political theory – the scope and distribution of political authority, the
meaning of liberty, the relationship between political order and individual freedom, the interpretation of social justice and democracy also
have their place in green political theory. Where green political theory
differs from other theories, is that its moral concern extends to future
generations as well as having a global aspect, most often expressed in
terms of the relationship between the affluent (and, in green terms,
over-developed) Northern countries and the developing nations of the
South. Thus the philosophical basis of green politics can be seen to
relate to three inter-related spheres of moral concern: social-environ-
mental relations, intergenerational relations and international relations.

For reasons of space I will focus only on how green political theory
offers an alternative understanding of 'the good life'. Apart from its
focus on non-human world, green policy also differs from most other
political theories in that it offers a less materialistic view of the good
life. The reasons for this vary: some advocate it for ecological reasons
as enabling humans to 'walk lighter on the earth';[15] others see materialism as spiritually void and of no intrinsic value,[16] and it has also been
argued that the adoption of such lifestyles in the affluent countries is
essential to achieve global distributive justice.[17] However, most concep-

tions of green political thought share a common emphasis on the quality of life rather than 'quantitative' concerns such as wealth, income, or paid employment. In this respect, greens are heirs to J.S. Mill and his desire to see a 'post-industrial' stage of society in which people would concentrate on improving their minds, their relationships with each other (and we might add, with the non-human world), instead of being fixated on consuming more and more goods and services. In this way the philosophical basis of green political theory involves the re-definition of central concepts such as 'human welfare', 'development' and ultimately the whole idea of 'progress'. Older forms of development cannot be said to constitute viable or desirable forms of human progress given the various ecological and social problems humanity is presently experiencing; what is required, from the green position, is a radical re-examination of some of the central tenets of modern society, particularly the dominant view of the good life. Green debates about alternatives to the current development path will be discussed in the next section.

Politics and Policies

While green political theory has a wide range of policy goals, its overarching policy objective concerns the balance between the preservation of the environment and its development or exploitation by humans. While many green policy proposals focus on lessening the environmental costs of past and present development through such proposals as 'carbon taxes' and 'polluter pays' legislation, the ultimate aim is to prevent these environmental costs from arising in the first place, by questioning whether a particular form of 'development' should occur at all (as in recent controversies over the UK government's road-building programme).

One of the most central (and recent) policy objectives of green political theory concerns the debate about 'sustainable development'. As indicated above, the essence of sustainable development is that it integrates a concern for the environment with obligations to future human generations. In terms of its most famous definition:

> Sustainable development is development that meets the needs of the present without compromising the ability of future generations to meet their own needs. It contains within it two key concepts: – the concept of

'needs', in particular the essential needs of the world's poor, to which overriding priority should be given; and the idea of limitations imposed by the state of technology and social organisation in the environment's ability to meet present and future needs.[18]

Sustainable development is thus development within ecological constraints and limits. Another way of looking at it has been advanced by Jacobs:

> The concept of 'sustainability' is at root a simple one. It rests on the acknowledgement, long familiar in economic life, that maintaining income over time requires that the capital stock is not run down. The natural environment performs the function of capital stock for the human economy, providing essential resources and services. Economic activity is presently running down this stock. While in the short term this can generate economic wealth, in the longer term (like selling off the family silver) it reduces the capacity of the environment to provide these resources and services at all. Sustainability is thus the goal of 'living within our environmental means'. Put another way, it implies that we should not pass the costs of present activities onto future generations.[19]

On the face of it sustainable development has become, like democracy or social justice, an objective that any rational person would support. However, just like these other terms, only when one asks what sustainable development means in practice does the real debate begin. Within green political theory itself, competing definitions of sustainable development have been advanced.

In particular, radical greens have criticised prevailing notions of sustainable development on the grounds that these ideas simply perpetuate the Western-centred, capitalist-industrial model of social progress by 'greener' means:[20] rather than a shift to a 'green society', founded on different values or institutions, we simply get a pale 'greening' of the present system and the continuation of its materialistic view of the good life. For radical greens, sustainable development is rather like the social democratic compromise seen from a revolutionary socialist perspective: a 'sell out', a compromise between radical demands and the political *status quo*. Just as social democracy and the establishment of the welfare state led to what many socialists felt was simply 'capitalism with a human face', so sustainable development can be viewed as the 'greening of capitalism' and the emergence of 'green social democrocracy'.[21] As evidence of the reformist character of sustainable development, many point to its origins in the discourse of established institutions such as the United Nations and the World Bank, and reformist, pro-market economic theory such as environmental economics.[22] Radical greens argue that unless sustainable development is about a different type of development (which would have far-reaching institutional as well as individual effects), then it will not succeed in averting ecological problems; what is required is a graduated decrease in material consumption in the affluent North rather than the 'greening' of existing levels of consumption. In general, the feeling is that unless sustainable development means a shift towards a development path which makes less demands on the planet's finite resources and ecosystems, then it is not a realistic policy option for the creation of a more sustainable society.

It is at this point that the ideas of democracy and the 'quality of life' become central to debates about the notions of 'progress' and 'development'. In a recent work, Ulrich Beck has coined the term 'risk society' to denote a stage in social development when the risks or 'bads' produced as a result of society's development pattern/model begin to outweigh the goods which were the concern of the politics of 'industrial society'.[23] As Lash and Wynne point out in the introduction to Beck's book:

> The axial principle of industrial society is the distribution of goods, while that of risk society is the distribution of 'bads' or dangers.[24]

Chief among these bads are environmental risks such as those caused by global warming, declining air quality, toxins in the food-chain and ozone depletion.

What is interesting about Beck's analysis, in terms of the argument being developed here, is that he suggests an alternative model of progress and development which is compatible with green policy aims. In short, Beck argues that whereas until now 'development' was seen as the by-product of an uncontrolled process – i.e. the actions of uncoordinated individuals and groups in the form of the bureaucratic institutions of the state and the operation of the free market – the advent of the age of ecological risks suggests that development needs to be redefined. Progress must begin to be understood as *social* development, controlled by the people affected by that development, rather than as random and unregulated economic development driven by the market or state policies. In other words, progress is now seen in terms of the extension of democratic accountability to more and more areas of social life (medicine, science, education, housing, welfare policies), thereby allowing people more control over their own lives, rather than simply meaning year-on-year increases in private material consumption of goods and services or personal disposable income. Clearly, this re-definition of progress, which Beck calls 'reflexive modernisation', constitutes a new, more ecologically sustainable form of 'progress'. In this view, the policy aims of green political theory are first and foremost to alter, fundamentally and radically, the policy-making process itself, to make it more democratic and accountable to those who will be affected by policy outcomes. On this reading, green political theory makes the claim that the democratisation of society goes hand in hand with its ecologisation.[25]

In terms of more specific policy aims, all shades of green political thought are united in their opposition to the present system of intensive livestock rearing or 'factory farming'. While only some greens would go so far as to advocate mandatory vegetarianism, all would agree that there is no moral justification for the present system. Most Westerners remain ignorant of the immense suffering caused to the millions of animals 'processed' every year in order to meet the demand for cheap animal products. Within this system animals are reduced to mere objects while their needs go unmet. Greens argue that their suffering, which has been scientifically documented, cannot be justified on the grounds that this is the only way in which cheap animal products can be produced.[26] Since meat-eating is not an absolute necessity for either survival or well-being, the enjoyment humans get from consuming meat produced in this way cannot justify the suffering and pain it causes to animals. In addition to this greens typically have two other arguments against the factory farming system. The first concerns risks to human health. The recent BSE or 'mad cow' scare in the UK serves as a reminder of the risks to human health when profit-maximisation becomes the dominant concern in food production. The second argument is that meat-eating is an inefficient way to produce food since it is incredibly wasteful in terms of protein and energy consumption. As Vandana Shiva puts it:

> If you take into account all the inputs – such as natural resources, labour, capital – and include all outputs of farming systems, then industrial agriculture is found to be highly inefficient compared to organic

farming, sustainable agriculture and the poly-cultures of indigenous agriculture.[27]

A shift away from industrial agriculture centred around meat production would not only represent a more efficient form of food production, but would also create more food to be distributed throughout the world, since much of the current cereal grown globally is used to feed livestock, mostly for Western markets. Thus abolishing the factory-farming system would have three beneficial effects. Firstly, it would lead to a healthier food production system and healthier diets; secondly, it would create more food for global distribution; and thirdly, it would have a positive environmental impact: factory-farming requires a high energy input, and the amount of land currently given over to growing cereal for food animals could be decreased thus making less ecological demands on the planet's ecosystems.

Criticisms

As the newest of all political theories, green political theory has had what one might call a 'baptism of fire' in terms of the reception it has received from existing schools of political theory. Green political theory is unique in that it has been vilified from the left for being a 'petty bourgeois' ideology with conservative, anti-progressive undertones, while from the right it has been criticised as propounding an anti-technological message and seeking to return society to a pre-modern state. For the sake of brevity I will concentrate on Marxist and liberal critiques of green political theory and then outline the green responses.

Marxist Criticisms

Although green political theory is often understood (and understands itself) as 'neither left nor right but in front', it is clear that it has origins in the 'New Left' movement of the 1960s. As such one might think that greens and reds would be natural allies in the fight against capitalism. However, it is only recently, since the collapse of the Soviet Union in 1989, that one can say a genuine dialogue and attempt at *rapprochement* has begun between Marxism and green political theory. The Marxist response to the rise in ecological concerns in the early 1970s was largely negative. For many Marxists the nascent environmental movement, with its stress on ecological limits to economic growth, was simply a modern version of Malthusianism.[28] Malthus in the late eighteenth century rejected the idea that modern society could support an ever-increasing population. His argument, which anticipated aspects of the ecological 'limits to growth' position, was that food increased arithmetically (1, 2, 3, etc.) while population increased geometrically (2, 4, 6, etc.). Thus at some point a growing population would outstrip the available food source, leading to famine, social disruption and disease.[29] Marx's vehement critique of Malthus, who advocated the abolition of poor relief and the introduction of subsistence wages, on the grounds that it would discourage the working class from increasing the population, set the pattern of the later engagement between Marxists and ecologists. Green concerns with 'post-industrialism' and the necessity for a 'steady-state-economy',[30] were taken to express the anti-working class, anti-socialist character of green politics. In opposition to green arguments for a simpler lifestyle,[31] Marxists still held the domination and control of nature as a precondition for the creation of a free and equal society.[32] As such, Enzensberger, one of the earliest Marxist analysts of ecological politics, presented it as a middle-class ideology:

> The ecological movement has only come into being since the districts which the bourgeoisie inhabit and their living conditions have been exposed to those environmental burdens that industrialization brings with it.[33]

Thus, from this early Marxist response, green politics was viewed as inherently anti-progressive and reactionary, seeking to hold back the historical transition from capitalism to communism.

Some greens responded to this Marxist critique by adhering to the 'neither left nor right' position, proclaiming green politics as the politics of the 'post-industrial' age and the coming new century. Marxism represented simply another form of industrialism (like capitalism), which was the root cause of the ecological crisis. Typical of this green response was Porritt who stated that socialism and capitalism were simply two forms of the 'super-ideology' of industrialism: one was as bad as the other from an ecological point of view.[34] More coherent green responses to the Marxist critique focused on the 'productivist' obsession of Marxism and its belief that only through the creation and distribution of material abundance could a free and equal post-capitalist society emerge. The ecological impossibility of the material abundance required by the Marxist political vision was pressed home and Marxists were called upon to justify both the ecological feasibility and the desirability of material abundance.[35] At the same time, aspects of green political theory took on board the Marxist critique that unless greens addressed the problem of capitalism, and the question of the ownership and control of production, then green theory would simply be dealing with the effects of the ecological crisis as opposed to eradicating its causes. As a result of this engagement with Marxism, a novel school of 'eco-Marxist' theory has developed, in which the ecological crisis is analysed as the 'second contradiction of capitalism' (the first being the contradiction between capital and labour).[36]

By and large in the debate between Marxism and green thought, it is Marxism that has undergone the more fundamental shift. Marxists have been obliged to become less anthropocentric, less materialistic and, as a result of the problems of securing material abundance, more concerned with issues of social or distributive justice. On the other hand, greens have had to address hard issues of political economy, and face the real difficulties of political strategy: how to get from the unsustainable present to the sustainable future in the face of a global capitalist system which is against such a transition. In formulating a green critique of capitalism and strategies for resisting it, greens have learnt much from Marxists, particularly the importance of extending green political concerns beyond the interests of the middle class, making its concerns relevant to all citizens by forging a link between 'environmental' issues and those of social justice and democracy.[37]

Liberal Criticisms

Liberalism has criticised green political theory for being backward-looking, anti-technological and anti-science. Typical of the right-wing critique of green politics is that it is a modern form of Luddism, an emotional, incoherent and irrational rejection of the modern age and an attempt to turn the clock backwards. The precise time greens wish to turn the clock back to varies depending on the critic, sometimes it is feudalism, sometimes it is the stone age. An early example of the liberal reaction to green politics is Dahrendorf's view that:

> The Greens are essentially about values, an imprecise, emotional protest against the overbearing rationality of the social democratic world.[38]

This rather condescending view is also to be found in other liberal rejections of green politics, such as Allison, who takes particular umbrage to green opposition to meat-eating, blood sports and hunting, calling it:

> the revenge of the unhappy: it is premised on a hatred of life and driven by malice ... it deserves the name *evil*.[39] (emphasis in original)

Others such as Holmes,[40] see the core of green politics in its anti-science character, which is held to be based on non-scientific grounds, and its irrational rejection of the fruits of the modern age.

While much of the liberal criticism of green political theory is mistaken, it has to be admitted that certain strands of green thought are legitimate targets for liberal criticism. For example, there are certain shades of radical deep ecological thinking which do proclaim the virtues of the hunter-gatherer way of life.[41] Likewise, certain green thinkers have revealed profoundly conservative,[42] racist[43] and authoritarian[44] tendencies. It is little wonder that liberal suspicions are raised when well-known green writers such as Kirkpatrick Sale state that conflict within communities should not require recourse to formal principles of justice or political institutions external to the community. The 'natural' way to deal with disputes between an aggrieved minority and an implacable majority is for the community to divide, with the minority free to settle elsewhere. According to Sale, 'The commodious solution is not minority rights but minority settlements'.[45] Such sentiments cause justifiable concern for liberals.

Yet on the whole green political theory cannot be described as 'anti-liberal'. On the one hand, as de Geus and Doherty point out, modern green political theory does not seek 'to do away with liberal democracy [but] to change it in radical ways'.[46] On the other hand, Eckersley's view of green political theory as 'decidedly *post* – rather than *anti* – liberal'[47] is something that reflects the green endorsement of such traditional liberal values as collective self-determination via democratic government, individual autonomy and toleration. Views such as those represented by the more extreme end of radical ecology are largely aberrations, the core values of green political theory cannot be viewed as anti-liberal.

At the same time green political theory cannot be viewed as either anti-technological or anti-science. Firstly, it is more accurate to say that green politics is sceptical of technology (hence its desire to bring such technological developments as genetic engineering under democratic control), rather than anti-technology. It is in favour of appropriate, human-scale technology in line with the 'small is beautiful' philosophy of Schumacher.[48] Secondly, it is difficult to see how green political theory could be seen as anti-science when it is unique among political theories in having its roots in scientific inquiry, particularly, the sciences of ecology,[49] conservation biology and thermodynamics.[50] Indeed the charge of anti-science is difficult to square with the fact that the modern green movement can trace its origins to the publication of *Silent Spring* by Rachel Carson[51] who was herself a marine biologist. Thus while there may be aspects of green political theory which appear to be anti-technological and anti-science, on the whole these aspects are not representative of green political theory as a body of thought.

Conclusion

In conclusion it may be worthwhile to indicate future developments and challenges facing green political theory. Foremost among the challenges facing green political theory is the translation of the theory of ecological sustainability into practice. How far in the future ought we to look? What are the institutional and personal changes required by ecological sustainability? These questions will increasingly come to the fore within green political theory in the future. At the same time, the debate around ecological sustainability is likely to require green political theory to develop policy proposals which will realise sustainability or at least help bring society closer to that goal. It is likely that we will see green thought turning its attentions to issues of the economic arrangements of any 'post-industrial', 'post-full-employment' society. Finally, it is clear that global and local environmental dilemmas and risks will continue and we can be sure that green political theory will challenge 'technocratic' and technological solutions to these dilemmas, solutions which do not first and foremost see the ecological crisis as a profoundly normative rather than just a 'technical' matter. In other words, we can be sure that future developments within green political theory will set out to demonstrate that environmental dilemmas should be viewed firstly in terms of right and wrong and only secondly in terms of costs and benefits.

Notes

1. D. Wall, *Green History*, Routledge, London 1994.
2. J.J. Clark, *Nature in Question*, Earthscan, London 1993.
3. J. Barry, 'The Limits of the Shallow and the Deep: Green Politics, Philosophy and Praxis', *Environmental Politics*, 3:3 1994.
4. T. Malthus, *A Summary View of the Principle of Population*, Penguin Books, London 1970/1830.
5. J.S. Mill, *Principles of Political Economy*, Longmans, Green & Co., London 1909, p.453.
6. D. Ehrenfeld, *The Arrogance of Humanism*, Oxford University Press, Oxford 1978.
7. L. White Jr., 'The Historical Roots of Our Ecologic Crisis', *Science*, 155, 1967.
8. R. Eckersley, *Environmentalism and Political Theory: An Ecocentric Approach*, University of London Press, London 1992, p.51.
9. A. Naess, 'The Shallow and the Deep, Long-Range Ecology Movement: A Summary', *Inquiry* 16 1973.
10. See: J. Barry, 'Deep Ecology and the Undermining of Green Politics', in Jane Holder *et al* (eds), *Perspectives on the Environment*, Avebury, Aldershot 1993.
11. Barry, 1994, *op.cit.*
12. Bryan Norton, *Toward Unity Among Environmentalists*, Oxford University Press, Oxford 1991, p.227.
13. J. Barry, 'The Limits of the Shallow and the Deep: Green Politics, Philosophy and Praxis', *op.cit.*; A. de Shalit, *Why Posterity Matters: Environmental Policies and Future Generations*, Routledge, London 1995; T. Hayward, *Ecological Thought: An Introduchon*, Polity Press, Cambridge 1995.
14. A. McLaughlin, *Regarding Nature: Industrialism and Deep Ecology*, State University of New York Press, New York 1994; A. Naess, 'Deep Ecology and Lifestyle' in George Sessions (ed), *Deep Ecology for the 21st Century*, Shambala Press, Boston & London 1995.
15. A. Naess, *ibid.*; T. Trainer, *Abandon Affluence!*, Zed Books, London 1985.
16. A. Dobson, *Green Political Thought*, 2nd ed, Routledge, London 1995.
17. K. Lee, 'To De-Industrialize: Is it So Irrational?', in A. Dobson and P. Lucardie (eds), *The Politics of Nature: Explorations in Green Political Theory*, Routledge, London 1993.
18. WCED, World Commission on Environment and Development, *Our*

Common Future, Oxford University Press, London 1987, p.434.

19. M. Jacobs, *The Politics of the Real World*, Earthscan, London 1996, p.17.
20. W. Sachs (ed), *The Development Dictionary*, Zed Books, London 1992.
21. J. Barry, 'Marxism and Ecology' in A. Gamble *et al* (eds), *Marxism and Social Science*, Macmillan, London forthcoming.
22. D. Pearce *et al*, *Blueprint for a Green Economy*, Earthscan, London 1989.
23. U. Beck, *Risk Society: Towards a New Modernity*, Sage, London 1992.
24. *Ibid.* p.3.
25. B. Doherty and M. de Geus (eds), *Democracy and Green Political Thought*, Routledge, London 1996.
26. T. Benton, *Natural Relations: Ecology, Animal Rights and Social Justice*, Verso, London 1993.
27. V. Shiva, 'Mono Mania', *The Guardian*, 8 January 1997.
28. D. Meadows *et al*, *Limits to Growth*, Universe Books, New York 1972.
29. T. Malthus, *A Summary View of the Principle of Population, op.cit.*
30. H. Daly, *Steady-State Economics*, W.H.Freeman, San Francisco 1977.
31. E.F. Schumacher, *Small is Beautiful: Economics as if People Really Mattered*, Abacus, London 1973.
32. M. Markovic, *The Contemporary Marx: Essays on Humanist Communism*, Spokesman Books, Nottingham 1974.
33. H.M. Enzensberger, 'A Critique of Political Ecology', *New Left Review*, 84, 1974, p.107.
34. J. Porritt, *Seeing Green: The Politics of Ecology Explained*, Basil Blackwell, Oxford 1984.
35. J Barry, 'Marxism and Ecology', *op.cit.*
36. M. O'Connor (ed), *Is Capitalism Sustainable?*, Guildford Press, London 1995.
37. M. Jacobs, *The Politics of the Real World, op.cit.*
38. Quoted in J. Porritt, *Seeing Green: The Politics of Ecology Explained, op.cit.*, p.16.
39. L. Allison, *Ecology and Utility: The Philosophical Dilemmas of Planetary Management*, Leicester University Press, Leicester 1991, p.178.
40. S. Holmes, *The Anatomy of Anti-Liberalism*, Harvard University Press, Cambridge, Mass. 1993.
41. P. Shepard, 'A Post-Historic Primitivism', in M. Oelschlaeger (ed), *The Wilderness Condition: Essays on Environment and Civilization*, Island Press, Washington and Covelo, Ca. 1993.
42. E. Goldsmith, *The Way: 87 Principles for an Ecological World*, Rider, London 1991.
43. E. Abbey *One Life at a Time Please*, Henry Holt, New York 1988.

44. W. Ophus, *Ecology and the Politics of Scarcity*, Freeman, San Francisco 1977.
45. K. Sale, *Human Scale*, Secker & Warberg, London 1980, p.480.
46. B. Doherty and M. de Geus (eds), *Democracy and Green Political Thought, op.cit.*, p.2.
47. R. Eckersley, *Environmentalism and Political Theory: An Ecocentric Approach, op.cit.*, p.30.
48. E.F. Schumacher, *Small is Beautiful: Economics as if People Really Mattered, op.cit.*
49. J. O'Neill, *Ecology, Policy and Well-Being*, Routledge, London 1993.
50. N. Georgescu-Roogen, *The Entropy Law and the Economic Process*, Harvard University Press, Cambridge, Mass. 1971.
51. R. Carson, *Silent Spring*, Houghton Mifflin Co., Boston, 1962.

Glossary

Absolute: That which cannot be challenged or changed. Absolute values and absolute rights are those which are taken to be unquestionable and fundamental; for example, many would argue that under normal peace-time circumstances, humans have an absolute right to life. An absolute monarch is one whose power and decisions cannot be challenged or questioned.

Activist: One who works on behalf of a political organisation or cause – more usually applied to those involved at a grass-roots level.

Ancien regime: The system of absolute monarchy and rigid, privileged nobility swept away or radically curtailed by the European, liberal revolutions of the late eighteenth century and much of the nineteenth century. Often used now to refer, pejoratively, to any state system based upon entrenched privilege and antiquated customs.

Anomie: The sense of loss, confusion and despair experienced by those whose value-systems have been rendered meaningless by rapid social change. Often associated with the destruction of rural ways of life by industrialisation.

Anthropocentric: The assumption, or actions based upon the assumption, that human, as opposed to animal or ecological, interests and needs are primary. Usually applied to exploitation of the earth's resources and animal life to benefit humans. (cf. Ecocentric)

Associative democracy: A notion of democracy in which civil society associations (such as interest groups, voluntary organisations, community groups) play a major role in the decision-making and policy implementation more usually associated with the state.

Atomism: State of mind in which humans feel isolated and/or in conflict with all other humans. It has often been argued that capitalist economic systems promote atomism.

Biocentric: See Ecocentric

Biodiversity: The wide variety and quantity of plant and animal species. Argued by greens to be worthy of protection and promotion.

Capital: Technically, the resources or wealth needed to begin and maintain a business or financial project. Often used as shorthand to refer to the power of the dominant class in capitalist economies.

Civic republicanism: The belief, originating in the sixteenth century but drawing inspiration from the ancient world, that the state should be an integral part of a free, flourishing society by acting in the interests of all and being guided by the active participation of its citizens.

Civil society: A term with different meanings for different theorists but, to define it very broadly, it can be seen as associations and their activities not controlled by or originating with the state. Some, however, might only include associations which are not directly controlled by the state but are related to the state, such as trade unions and interest groups and exclude private associations such as the family. Healthy liberal democracies are generally seen as requiring flourishing civil societies – in the form of voluntary organisations, religious bodies, active families etc.; while totalitarianism is characterised by the attempt (not always successful) to place all civil society activity under the control of the state.

Collectivism: The belief that human progress and happiness is best served when all work together towards a common goal. Usually taken to refer to cooperative economic activity (as in the goal of communism). May also refer to a political strategy based upon the solidarity of many individuals, especially trade union activity. (cf. Individualism)

Contractarianism: The notion that political and social systems should be arranged as though they are based upon a rational contract agreed by all involved in those systems and thus for the mutual benefit of all those involved. A particularly influential idea in liberal thought.

Colonialism: A type of imperialism where a group originally native in (and remaining loyal to) the imperialist nation live in the vanquished nation. This group often become dominant in the economic, political, social, cultural and administrative systems of the vanquished nation. A system widely used by the European empires of the nineteenth century.

Contingent: Social or political arrangements and events are said to be contingent when it is judged that they did not have to occur as they did or indeed exist at all; i.e. they may have occurred as a result of the accidental interaction of many diverse factors. Thus such arrangements and events cannot be predicted. Postmodernists have argued that all or most social and political arrangements and events are contingent. (cf. Necessary)

Dawla Islamiyya: The Islamic republic.

Deconstruction: An approach to criticism which attempts to reveal how apparently rational works of analysis (in the arts, social sciences and humanities) rely either upon unspoken, and often unconscious, assumptions about human existence (originating with the Enlightenment), and/or rhetorical methods (such as metaphor), for their persuasive force. Jacques Derrida remains the best known practitioner of deconstruction.

Descriptive: Analysis which explains the nature or features of an object of study without any attempt to draw conclusions about how to change that object. For example, some analysts may simply describe a parliamentary system without making any recommendations on how to improve it. (cf. Prescriptive)

Dependency culture: The notion, much employed by the New Right, that many in Western society have lost the drive to support themselves and their families through proper employment as a result of the easily-obtained handouts provided by the welfare state.

Difference principle: The idea that social and economic inequalities should be arranged so that they are to the benefit of the least advantaged. Associated, most closely, with the liberal thinker John Rawls.

Discourse: In recent social and political thought this term has come to mean the assumptions and accepted values, which are often in a state of flux, underlying any social or political practice. In postmodern thought, it commonly refers to the very deeply-held understandings which emerge in commonly-accepted ideas of what counts as truth and in the ways we give meaning to our environment and behaviour.

Division of labour: The distribution of different tasks to different individuals or groups. The distribution of domestic chores and child-rearing to women and most other forms of (paid) labour to men is an example of a division of labour much criticised by feminists. Many have argued that the very elaborate and precise divisions of labour between individuals is one of the main factors that has allowed humanity to develop their productive capacity so greatly.

Ecocentric: The assumption, or actions based upon the assumption, that respect for the earth's natural environment must take precedence over, or at least be treated equally alongside, human needs. (cf. Anthropocentric)

Economic determinism: Analysis which argues or assumes that all that occurs in social, political and cultural life is the result of economic arrangements.

Economic growth: The increase in the productive capacity and wealth of a society.

The Enlightenment: A period of speedy intellectual development in Europe in the late seventeenth/early eighteenth century. Widely accepted to have been the period which replaced belief in the authority of God with the belief in the authority of human reason and thus had incalculable influence on intellectual development in the following centuries.

Epistemology: philosophical analysis of human knowledge.

Essentialism: the characteristic of some analysis to assert that all humans share a fundamental essence; for example, a tendency to greed or alternatively, co-operation. In this context it is usually used pejoratively. Essentialism can also refer to the belief that one can discover a common feature in all things or within a group of things. Plato believed, for example, that all just acts shared a common essence as do all acts which are truthful, or good, or wise. For Plato the goal of philosophy was to discover such essences.

First-wave feminism: The women's movement of the late nineteenth and early twentieth centuries which concerned itself largely, although not exclusively, with the winning of political and property rights for women, particularly the right to vote.

Forces of production: The machines, resources and labour power available for the production of goods for sale and/or use. A term usually used in Marxist analysis. (See Relations of Production)

Fordism: A method of mass industrial production, established by Henry Ford in the 1920s and imitated very widely during the twentieth century, characterised by concentration of production into one enormous factory complex, the assembly line, and a very specific division of labour on the workforce. (See Taylorism, Division of Labour)

Gama'at Islamiyya: Islamic groups/ associations. Usually applied to the illegal groups associated with radical Islamism in Egypt.

Gender: The social and cultural differences which exist between men and women. Not to be confused with the term 'sex' which refers only to biological differences.

Gradualism: The belief that social or political change must be brought about gradually; opposed to revolutionary strategy.

Hijra: Migration, specifically the migration of the Prophet Mohammed and the early community of believers from Mecca to Medina in 622 CE.

Historical materialism: A Marxist approach which understands all the great developments in history as resulting from changes in (and/or the struggle for control of) the production of the material requirements of humans (i.e. economic forces and relations). (see materialism)

Holistic: Approaches which treat the whole (human, social, cultural, environmental) as more important, or as important as, the parts which make up that whole. For example, some may argue that society cannot be understood simply by analysing individual human motivation and actions, society acts according to its own rules distinct from those governing individuals.

Homo economicus: A human primarily driven by rational assessments of how to enhance his/her wealth.

Humanism: Belief based upon the assumption, or asserting that, humans and human well-being must be at the heart of our actions and explanations. Highly influential since the Enlightenment (especially in deposing God) but has come under attack in novel ways in recent years especially from greens and postmodernists. (see Anthropocentrism, Ecocentrism, The Enlightenment, Postmodernism)

Identity: In the context of this book, the characteristics of an individual human which are most central to that person's self-image and self-understanding and which may have a fundamental bearing on their values and actions.

Identity Politics: The values and movements which have developed since the 1960s around issues of identity, in particular, gender, race and sexuality.

Imperialism: The enforced exploitation of one nation's resources by another nation for its own benefit. Imperialism usually involves some element of military, political, social or cultural domination along with the economic exploitation. The nineteenth and early twentieth centuries saw the widest systems of imperialism with European nations involved in wholesale exploitation and domination of much of the rest of the world.

Individualism: Analysis or actions based upon the assumption that the interests and needs of the individual are paramount. (cf. Collectivism)

Instrumentalism: In philosophical terms, the notion that concepts, values and ideas are neither true nor false but simply effective or ineffective in allowing us to predict future outcomes of certain situations.

Interpretivism: The belief that ethical principles are only valid if they are already employed as working principles by individuals and communities. (see Particularism, Relativism, Universalism)

Irrationalism: The belief that factors such as emotion, faith or physical desire are, or should be, more important in human behaviour and its explanation than rational calculation and analysis.

Jahiliyya: The state of ignorance in pre-Islamic Arabia. Contemporary Islamist usage implies the barbarity of modern life.

Jihad: exertion or striving, associated with the struggle to assert Islamic values and principles.

Keynesianism: The economic theory of John Maynard Keynes which asserted that economic growth and full employment could be achieved through comprehensive government investment and intervention in the economic infrastructure. Influential on government policy in the UK between 1945 and the late 1970s. (cf. Laissez-faire, Monetarism)

Khalifa: caliph; 'Successor' to the Prophet Mohammed and head of the Islamic community.

Khilafa: caliphate; the unity of Muslims under the authority of the caliph.

Labour: Technically, the process required to turn any natural object into a useful object, for example, the working on wood to produce a table or the more elaborate working on a variety of natural products to create a car. Often used as shorthand to refer to the power and personnel of the working class in capitalist economies.

Laissez-faire: An approach to economic policy which asserts that a nation's economy works most efficiently and fairly without state intervention. Sometimes also applied to other areas of policy besides economics. (cf. Keynesianism)

Leninism: A variant of Marxism, named after the leader of the Russian Revolution of October 1917 that established the USSR for seventy years, which emphasises the importance of a disciplined, hierarchical Party in leading the working-class before and after socialist revolution. Historically Leninism also stressed the importance and possibility of a union between the industrial working-class and agricultural peasantry in support of a revolution; and the role of human will – as opposed to the slow and necessary development of economic forces – in making a socialist revolution.

Libertarianism: The belief that individuals should be able to decide completely, or almost completely, how they wish to behave, free of any state or legal interference. Variants of this have influenced both the right and the left of the traditional political spectrum.

Luddism: Opposition to any technological development; usually pejorative. Taken from groups of early nineteenth-century machine breakers who were said to be led by Ned Ludd.

Materialism: Analysis based upon the belief that human behaviour and social change are determined by the material requirements of humanity such as food and shelter.

Messianic: Term applied to the belief that an end to all human suffering will occur at some time in the future following a great event such as revolution or, originally, the coming of a messiah; usually pejorative.

Meta-narrative: A grand story of human development. Postmodernists have asserted that such stories are at the heart of many modernist ideologies, e.g. the gradual march towards socialist revolution in Marxism.

Metaphysics: The philosophical study of the concepts, values and structures underlying the way we think about, analyse and understand the world.

Methodology: The practical approach one adopts to the process of carrying-out analysis. The methodologies available to an analyst are diverse ranging from formal surveying and statistical analysis (as in opinion polling or positivist approaches) to highly developed theoretical discussion (as in deconstruction, to take just one example). Debates about methodology can often be as important and heated as those about the object of analysis itself.

Mixed economy: An economy in which the state owns a significant proportion of businesses and where such 'nationalised' businesses operate side-by-side, and trade with, privately-owned businesses. The form of economic arrangement in the UK from 1945 until the Conservative programme of privatisation between 1979 and 1997.

Modernity: The historical period starting very approximately around the time of The Enlightenment until well into the twentieth century (although there is disagreement over whether such a historical definition is meaningful). Modernity is characterised, so some have argued, by a strong belief in the power of human reason, the possibility of human progress, and industrialism. A wide variety of cultural, scientific and political projects (modernism) are associated with these periods all of which are heavily influenced by the three characteristics just mentioned. Much dispute exists about whether modernity and modernism have come to an end. (see the Enlightenment, Postmodernism)

Monetarism: The economic theory which asserts that tight government control over the money supply (i.e. the amount of money circulating in the economy) is the best way to control inflation. Highly critical of Keynesianism which encouraged expansion of the money supply; influential on the New Right. (cf. Keynesianism)

Monocausal: An analysis which asserts that the subject of that analysis has only one cause. Marxism, in its more simplistic forms, was often accused of being monocausal in that it asserted class conflict as the cause of all other social, cultural and political phenomena.

Multiculturalism: The belief, and often policies based upon the belief, that different ethnic groups can and should live side-by-side and learn from one another. Criticised by the New Right for being too tolerant of immigrant communities and by ethnic communities for attempting to dilute ethnic identities into a bland mass.

Nation state: A system of government whereby a more or less centralised, sovereign administration governs a collection of cities, towns, villages and other communities within well-defined borders. The system which increasingly, in Europe, replaced strong local and regional government from, approximately, the sixteenth century onwards.

Nationalism: The political movement and ideas, prevalent since the nineteenth century, which asserts the right of individual national groups to self-determination free from external influences. (cf. Imperialism)

Necessary: In the context of social and political analysis, the term applied to arrangements or events which could not have been otherwise given the circumstances within which they arose. For example, Marxists would see class conflict as a *necessary* consequence of capitalism. (cf. Contingent)

New Left: The intellectual and political movement, originating in the 1950s, inspired by Marxist ideas but which rejected the Stalinism dominating Eastern Europe and the Western Communist Parties at that time. Influential in social, political and economic analysis but only had a brief heyday as a political movement in the late 1960s and early 1970s.

Normative: Analysis expressing judgements, or based upon judgements, about what should be considered good and what should be considered bad behaviour.

Particularism: The view that the justification for one's values can only be found within one's own culture or community, i.e. there are no universal justifications or values which apply to all cultures and communities. (cf. Universalism; see Interpretivism, Relativism)

Paternalism: Values or actions, on the part of authority (usually a government), based upon the view that the authority should act towards its subjects as a parent to a child. Thus this may mean that the authority believes it has a duty to care for its subjects but it may also mean that the state believes itself to know what is best for its subjects no matter what the subjects' own views may be.

Patriarchy: The set of social relations and values which maintains and legitimates the subordination of women.

Petit bourgeoisie: Owners of small businesses. Sometimes taken to include members of the professional classes as well.

Political culture: Those political values and practices which are commonly accepted by a community but which are not necessarily enshrined in law or written regulations (although they may be). For example, it has been argued that for a liberal democracy to flourish, a community must have a strong liberal and democratic political culture as well as liberal democratic laws, in the form of a general willingness to tolerate other points of view, respect individual rights and allow participation.

Political economy: The study of economic development as the result of interactions between the diverse interests of humans. May also refer to the aspect of the economy which is more subject to such interactions. More recently, the term has referred to the study of the overlap between politics and economics, i.e. the economic concerns of political systems and the political concerns of those involved in the economy, e.g. government budgets, international economic policy, political influences on stock markets etc.

Polity: The political system.

Positivism: The philosophy that the goal of all analysis must be merely to describe empirical reality as accurately as possible without becoming too concerned about why that reality may be the way it is or about the values that should inform it. Thus it is hostile to religious, metaphysical or overly theoretical approaches. Often used in reference to those who have attempted to employ the methods of the natural sciences in the field of the social sciences. (cf. Metaphysics)

Post-Fordism: A method of commodity production characterised by the sub-contracting of parts of the production process to a number of firms and the advanced use of new technology to make production more responsive to consumer demand. A number of analysts have argued that Fordism has been largely replaced by Post-Fordism in the last twenty years and has led to significant social, political and economic shifts, especially the decline of trade unions. (cf. Fordism)

Post-industrialism: The notion that the heavy industry, and its attendant social and political characteristics, which shaped much of the nineteenth and twentieth centuries have been replaced by the economic importance of information technology and the service sector.

Post-structuralism: Generally taken now to be synonymous with postmodernism. Possibly referring more to the philosophical and literary criticism aspects of the intellectual movement that is postmodernism and less to postmodern assertions about the nature of society.

Post-materialism: The rejection of the consumerism and individualism of Western society and the placing of a stronger emphasis upon spirituality, the quality of inter-personal relationships, personal growth and nature. Some have argued that post-materialism has become a significant force in the last thirty years.

Postmodernism: A very broad term applying to movements in nearly all fields of intellectual endeavour since the late 1960s. In social and political analysis, it can be taken to refer to approaches which reject meta-narratives, absolute truth or values, the primary importance of human reason, and the notion of a unified human subject. It can also refer to the belief that society has changed in such a way that we now live in an era of postmodernity characterised by social division and fragmentation, the importance of identity politics, the massive influence of mass communication and information technology and Post-Fordist production techniques. (cf. Modernity; see Post-Fordism, Identity politics, Post-industrialism)

Pre-modern: The long historical period prior to The Enlightenment. Generally seen as a period characterised by religious faith, rigid social hierarchy, political systems based upon aristocracy or monarchy and the dominance of agricultural production in the economy. (see Modernity, Postmodernism)

Prescriptive: Analysis which suggests ways to improve or change society or some aspect of society. (cf. Descriptive)

Private capital: The wealth possessed by individuals, free of state or collective control, and available for investment to enable further accumulation.

Productivism: The characteristic of some ideologies to emphasise or glorify the role that human productive power (especially in the form of industrialism) can play in human progress and liberation. Usually used in a pejorative sense.

Public Choice Theory: An approach which applies the economic theory of Rational Choice (i.e. that the fundamental driving-force of economics is the rational calculation by individuals of how they can enhance their material well-being) to political behaviour.

Public goods: Those practices which are deemed to be good for a society as a whole. Examples include comprehensive healthcare, national defence and widely-available education and training. Broadly accepted in post-war Europe to be the goods which should not be influenced by the interests of private individuals and thus should be regulated or provided by the state or a public authority free of market influences. This idea came under sustained and influential attack by the New Right (although national defence generally escaped such criticisms).

Productive forces: See Forces of Production

Quietism: The belief that one should play no part in politics or take no position in political divisions. Often one side of a common dispute within religious organisations.

Rationalism: The belief that the ability to reason is the unique and most valuable asset of humanity and thus should be cultivated and employed to the full, often at the expense of other irrational aspects of human behaviour. An inherent part of most social and political thought (and indeed many other fields of analysis) in the West since the Enlightenment but increasingly challenged in recent years. (cf. Irrationalism; see Postmodernism)

Reflexive: The characteristic of being able to assess and criticise one's own values and behaviour and alter them if necessary.

Reformism: Any political approach which relies on a strategy of piecemeal, legal change rather than revolutionary change. A term most commonly used on the left.

Reification: A process whereby that which is either man-made or socially constructed is made to appear 'thing-like', i.e. natural, unalterable or, even, God-given; an historical example would be the power of a medieval monarch.

Relations of production: A Marxist term referring to the way in which ownership of the means of production (i.e. the machinery, land, buildings, needed for production of goods) is arranged in any one society. Usually, prior to proletarian revolution, according to Marx, these relations are one of dominance where a minority owns the means of production, while a majority merely labours. (see Forces of Production)

Relativism: The belief that the whole diverse range of values and practices sanctioned by different communities, or sections of communities, around the world are justified. Sometimes follows from the view that since there are no universal or absolute values then whatever values and practices exist cannot be regarded as illegitimate; although those who deny universal and absolute values regularly dispute the claim that relativism necessarily follows. Often used as a pejorative term. (cf. Universalism; see Particularism, Interpretivism)

Rule of law: The social arrangement in which the law applies to all equally and is the prime guide to what is unacceptable behaviour for all individuals. Often seen as a key feature of liberalism which challenged the right of powerful individuals or groups (such as the monarch, nobility and clergy) to act outside the law and rule according to their personal whim.

Second-wave feminism: The resurgence in the women's movement from the mid-1960s onwards. This period in feminism's history has concerned itself as much with women's liberation from political, social, sexual and cultural oppression as with the winning of political rights – the main concern of first wave feminism.

Secular nationalism: The movement across the Arab world which challenged Western imperial dominance in the region whilst rejecting the traditional religious influence of Islam and adopting many Western practices especially in relation to industrialisation. An important ideological influence on Arab governments during the 1950s and 1960s in particular.

Shari'a: Islamic law.

Shi'a: The minority strand in the major religious dispute in Islam which began in the seventh century as a division over the successors to the prophet Mohammed. The Shi'a are the majority only in Iran. (see Sunni)

Social capital: The capital necessary for a successful economy over and above the short-term requirements (i.e. machinery, buildings, investment finance) of production. Thus social capital may include, schools, decent housing, training facilities etc. (see Capital)

Social construction(ism): The belief that all our values, and most importantly that which we recognise as absolute truth, are, in fact, the result of social forces rather than discovered objectively by human reason. A social construction is a value or meaning that accords with such a view.

Socialised capitalism: A society in which the market and private enterprise are still central but where some of the less desirable effects of such systems have been ameliorated through state regulation, welfare provision, and workers rights. Most commonly espoused, and implemented, by social democrats.

Statism: An emphasis on the central role of the state in achieving certain social or political goals.

Steady-state economy: The situation in which the different aspects of an economy (investment, production, wages, sales, prices etc.) grow at a constant rate and in balance with one another. Generally accepted as the basic requirement for stable economic growth. (see Economic Growth)

Sunni: The majority strand in the major religious dispute in Islam which began in the seventh century as a division over the successors to the prophet Mohammed. Sunnis are the majority throughout the Arab world.

Surplus value: The wealth produced by a society over and above that which it needs for basic survival. A central concept in Marxism since it was Marx's contention that dominant classes establish systems which allow them to use this surplus value for their own ends. In capitalism, surplus value, so he argued, takes the form of profit; hence, profit arises not from supply and demand in the market place (as in classical economics) but from appropriation by the bourgeoisie of value added to raw materials by the labour of the proletariat. (see Labour)

Taylorism: The measuring and reforming of the behaviour of factory workers and the working of the assembly line to ensure the most efficient production and highest-possible output. An important aspect of Fordism.

Technocracy: A political system within which disinterested and supposedly objective experts are in control.

Umma: The Islamic community of believers.

Universalism: The belief or assumption that values and explanations can be found which apply at all times in all places. (cf. Interpretivism, Particularism, Relativism)

Utopian socialism: A form of socialism, prevalent in the nineteenth century, which constructed elaborate visions of a perfect, egalitarian and ethical society (on paper and sometimes in practice) and urged authorities and/or the workers to help build these visions. Much criticised by Marxists. Also known as 'true socialism'.

Utopianism: A characteristic of certain ideologies which asserts or implies that the perfect human society can be created.

Index

Contributors

John Barry is Lecturer in Politics at the University of Keele. He is the author of *Rethinking Green Politics: Nature, Virtue and Progress*, due for publication in 1999.

Martin Durham is Senior Lecturer in Politics at the University of Wolverhampton. He is currently writing a book on the Christian Right and American conservatism.

Matthew Festenstein is Lecturer in Politics at the University of Hull. He is the author of *Pragmatism and Political Theory*.

Tony Fitzpatrick is Lecturer in Social Policy at the University of Luton. He is the author of *Freedom and Security* due for publication in 1999.

Elizabeth Frazer is a College and University Fellow at New College, Oxford University. She is currently completing a book on politics and community.

Michael Harris is Lecturer in Politics at the University of Middlesex. His Ph.D dealt with citizenship and the New Right.

David Howarth is Lecturer in Political Theory at Staffordshire University. He is currently writing a book entitled *Discourse*.

Adam Lent is Lecturer in Politics at the University of Sheffield. He is co-editor (with Tim Jordan) of *Storming the Millennium: The New Politics of Change* due for publication in 1998.

Moya Lloyd is Lecturer in Politics at Queens University, Belfast. She is co-editor (with Andrew Thacker) of *The Impact of Michel Foucault on the Humanities and Social Sciences*.

Phil Marfleet is Lecturer in Development Studies at the University of East London. He is co-editor (with Ray Kielz) of *The Third World in the Global Era* to be published in 1998.

Simon Thompson is Senior Lecturer in politics at the University of the West of England. He is co-editor (with Matthew Festenstein) of *Richard Rorty and Political Theory* to be published in 1998.